PAPER MILL
PLAYHOUSE
The Life of a Theatre

by *Regina Benedict Reynolds*
with the staff of the Paper Mill Playhouse

DAVID M. BALDWIN, PUBLISHER

PUBLISHER
David M. Baldwin
113–117 Cedar Street
New York, New York 10006

Editor/Project Manager: William L. Broecker
Designer/Production Manager: Laura Smyth, smythtype

International Standard Book Number ISBN 0-9673792-0-2
Library of Congress Catalog Card Number LC: 99-73653

Table of Contents

It always begins with an empty stage. A black box in which nothing exists except memories and dreams. Then something magical happens. It becomes filled with the words of the playwright; the songs of the lyricist and composer; the vision of each director; the infinite variety of the choreographer's steps; the grand palaces and hovels and rivers and skies of the scenic designer; the sunsets and stars and rainbows and storms of the lighting designer; the petticoats and shimmering gowns and uniforms and haberdashery that the costume designer so carefully fits to the unique look of each performer. Yes, the performers, the actors and actresses for whom we all are there. Those wonderful spirits who inhabit these environments, live these words, touch our hearts, make us laugh, help us to see worlds we have never experienced. For over sixty years, thousands of artists have been filling the empty stage of the Paper Mill Playhouse. Without them the empty stage is just that — empty. With them, it transforms each time the curtain rises into something unique, glorious, life-affirming. This is their story.

THE KINGDOM
OF GOD

1938

An abandoned paper mill
is bought by a troupe of thespians
who envision an artistic haven
for their friends and colleagues.
They transform this building
into their theatre and begin a journey
that has never ended. A journey filled
with triumphs, disasters, obstacles, and
challenges. From the first production
in 1938 of Martinez Sierra's
The Kingdom of God, countless artists
have created and millions have enjoyed
the diverse entertainment, inspiration,
and innovation that is
the Paper Mill Playhouse.

FOLLIES

1998

Dedicated to the patrons and contributors whose financial support
has helped make the Paper Mill Playhouse a reality;

to the more than 50,000 actors, directors, designers, musicians, stagehands and
administrators who have helped create a legacy of outstanding productions;

and especially to the warm, enthusiastic, loyal audiences
without whom Theatre could not happen.

The Old Mills of Millburn

The old Diamond Paper Mill on Brookside Drive, Millburn, New Jersey,
late nineteenth century.

PAPER WAS MANUFACTURED HERE BY 1795. STANDING ON THE SITE OF A FORGE AND SAWMILL IN COLONIAL TIMES, THIS WAS ONE OF THE FIRST MILLS TO USE THE POWER OF THE WEST BRANCH OF THE RAHWAY RIVER. DESPITE FIRE AND CHANGING TIMES IT CONTINUED AS A MILL UNTIL 1926 AND IN 1934 THE PAPER MILL PLAYHOUSE WAS FOUNDED AND THE BUILDING REMODELED.

IN THE EARLY SEVENTEENTH CENTURY, in a bucolic setting where the Paper Mill Playhouse now stands, members of the Minnisink tribe wandered and sometimes made camp. The long-established trails from their villages along the Delaware to the ocean crossed the Passaic River and passed through present-day Millburn. The area, then controlled primarily by the Dutch West India Company, was surrendered to the English in 1664. Charles II of England granted vast acreage to his brother James, Duke of York—land that included all of what became New Jersey. The native tribesmen entered into negotiated settlements of land and soon new settlers from other early colonies and from England were encouraged to come to the area, where they could enjoy religious freedom and ownership of land that was rich with streams, good soil, and wildlife. By 1764, there were forty landowners in the region.

In 1709, Nicholas and Thomas Parsil had received a Queen Anne grant to land described as extending from the "foot of Squaw Hill to the Button Ball tree to the White Oak." There they built a house by a running brook, part of the Rahway River. The Parsils flourished on this land and soon were building small hotels on the roads nearby. Near the site of the Parsils' original house, on June 23, 1780, General George Washington watched his troops battle the British, who were attempting to reach Morristown and Washington's supplies. The encounter is known as the Battle of Springfield; the weary Continental Army lost. Springfield had been part of Elizabeth, and the village behind it was called by a variety of names over the years—Rum Brook, Riverhead, Vauxhall, Milltown, Millville, and finally, in 1857, Millburn. The names Rum Brook and Rum Creek also applied to the section of the Rahway River running by the Parsil property because of the mash runoff from homemade applejack made just upstream. It is said that the name Millburn was formed to refer to both the many mills in the area and the brook—"burn" in Scottish. The mills had been built throughout the eighteenth century and served many purposes. There were lumber mills, grist mills, and "cyder" mills and, later, mills that manufactured cloth.

In 1790, one Samuel Campbell, originally from Edinburgh, took possession of over 120 acres earlier granted to him by George III and on it he built a mill to produce paper, the Thistle Mill. His first contract was with the new United States Treasury to supply paper for the printing of banknotes. (It is said he had married well to a member of a family influential with the new government of George Washington.) The paper was watermarked with a thistle, the symbol of Campbell's native country. The Campbell family operated Thistle Mill until the late 1860s, when a fire destroyed it.

Samuel Campbell also bought the site on which now stands the Paper Mill Playhouse. Records are a bit confusing, but a mill was eventually built (or rebuilt) on that site—possibly with Campbell as an investor—by Abraham and Jonathan Parkhurst, descendants of one of the first settlers. The Parkhursts operated the mill for thirty-five years.

Samuel Campbell, builder and owner of the Thistle Mill, also owned the site on which the Paper Mill Playhouse now stands.

Mrs. Samuel Campbell, wife of the mill owner. They were prominent landowners in the community.

The mill was then purchased by Israel Condit. In addition to being a legislator, philanthropist, and mill owner, Israel Condit helped to organize the Morris and Essex Railroad. The coming of the railroad, in 1837, gave easy access to towns like Millburn from Newark and the adjoining communities and, eventually, the New York metropolis. With this impetus, the population and local business increased rapidly. The mill was eventually purchased by the Diamond Mills Paper Company and continued successfully until 1928. New methods of production, the First World War, and the area's changing character all contributed to its demise. When it finally closed its doors, its 20,000 square feet went on the market for $30,000 but there were no takers—until a band of players came upon it.

Israel Condit, an owner of the mill that would eventually become the Paper Mill Playhouse. He was also a legislator and did much to bring the railroad to the Millburn area.

The old Diamond Paper Mill and employees, circa 1900.

During its years of operation, the Diamond Paper Mill produced binder board, wallpaper, paper for newspapers and books, and tissue paper, including, it is said, toilet tissue for Queen Victoria.

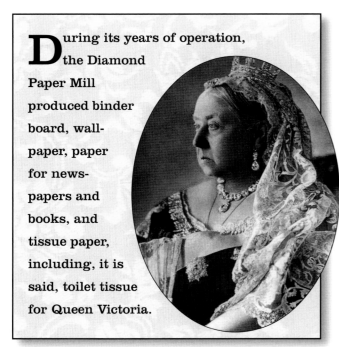

Can You Use This Factory?

FOR SALE OR LEASE-- POND AND VALUABLE WATER RIGHTS ARE INCLUDED

OVER 20,000 SQ. FT.

Most of Which is

GROUND FLOOR SPACE

Conveniently Located in the New Jersey Commuting Area Only 17 Miles from Manhattan

MILLBURN, NEW JERSEY lies just beyond the Oranges on the line of the Lackawanna Railroad. 30 trains each way daily and bus service to Newark and all points within a wide radius. The Lackawanna's new electric trains will be in operation by the time you move in. Main trucking highways in all directions. Plenty of good labor available.

THE WATER RIGHTS ALONE ARE WORTH THE PRICE AT WHICH YOU CAN BUY THIS FACTORY. There is no pollution of the water possible above this plant. The west branch of the Rahway River flows through the Essex County Park Reservation and is drawn on by the City of Orange for drinking purposes. The pond and water rights of this mill date back a hundred years or more. The water enters above second floor level.

LESS Than $30,000 Will Buy This Plant

But You Must Act Now!

This is your opportunity. Own your own plant and reduce your overhead.

I stand ready to give you personal service—Let me hear from you.

GEO. WRIGHT CAMPBELL
"Factories That Fit"

103 PARK AVENUE   NEW YORK CITY
Telephone, Lexington 0345

This advertisement, offering potential buyers all the land and buildings of the Diamond Paper Mill, caught the attention of Antoinette Scudder and Frank Carrington.

A Theatre Is Born

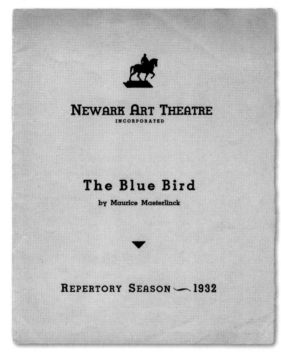

NEWARK ART THEATRE
INCORPORATED

The Blue Bird
by Maurice Maeterlinck

▼

REPERTORY SEASON — 1932

The theatre is not a luxury or a rich man's diversion; it has always been a necessity to civilization, a far-reaching and enlightening influence.

—Frank Carrington

THE NEWARK ART THEATRE CAME into being in the 1920s when members of the Newark Art Club, impressed by the theatrical talent and enthusiasm of several of its members, suggested they organize a resident professional theatre. The group was headed by Frank Carrington, a young actor and director who had teamed up with Antoinette Scudder, an art-minded New Jersey socialite who had established herself as a poet and playwright. Miss Scudder had met Carrington when he appeared in the principal role in her play *Prince Pentaur* at a small theatre at Fifth Avenue and 12th Street in New York. After the New York production, the play was presented in Newark to considerable success and was followed by a number of other small productions.

From 1928 to 1930, the group presented classic programs including *The Blue Bird, Androcles and the Lion, Heartbreak House, Quality Street*, and *A Romantic Young Lady*, the last by Martinez Sierra, to whose work they would later return to open their new theatre. Their productions were presented in school auditoriums with few if any technical facilities. Perhaps this

was all to the good as their success, in spite of the lack of proper theatres in which to perform, led them to consider finding a true home of their own.

In 1934, after extensive searching, they came upon an old mill, the now derelict Parkhurst/Condit/Diamond paper mill. The setting was perfect—by a brook, in an attractive, well-located,

Right: Frank Carrington and Antoinette Scudder, founders of the Paper Mill Playhouse, worked together in planning the theatre's early productions.

The Newark Art Theatre presented many striking productions in a great variety of performance spaces. Above, a scene from *The Blue Bird*.

community with good public transportation. The building left much to be desired but had the promise of tremendous charm and the space to erect a good-sized auditorium. Miss Scudder purchased the mill, and in 1934 an organization named Paper Mill Playhouse, Inc., was incorporated "to create a greater interest in art, music, drama, history, literature, education, and the theatre." She enlisted the help of her cousin, Henry D. Scudder, an architect, and plans were begun to transform the mill into a theatre. It was to take four years and considerable money ($1.5 million), supplied by Miss Scudder, to bring the proj-

ect to fruition. During those years, the group continued to present a variety of shows in the same, often inadequate spaces they had been using.

When the building was finished, it boasted a playhouse as fully equipped as any on Broadway, complete with good dressing rooms and office space. The acoustics had been planned by Harold Burris-Meyer of the Stevens Institute of Technology, a renowned expert on theatre sound who commented in his book *Scenery for the Theatre* that the Paper Mill Playhouse was one of only a few theatres in America that was constructed "correctly."

... to create a greater interest in art, music, drama, history, literature, education, and the theatre.

The theatre lobby was made cozy with antiques and a large fireplace. Stairs led from the lobby to an art gallery above.

Antoinette Scudder's interest in art called for the building of a gallery above the lobby where rotating exhibits, initially of her own paintings and personal art collection and later the work of both local and national artists, were shown. An old wishing well added to the attractiveness of the theatre's outside area.

For some time before the formal opening of the Playhouse, the group had been presentings concerts, dance recitals, dramatic sketches, lectures, and art exhibitions. Special evenings included, in cooperation with the Metropolitan Opera Guild, the pianists Olga Samaroff Stokowski and Joseph Battista, and a lecture series with Eunice Harriet Avery, a "distinguished interpreter of world affairs." There were Arthur Mahoney and Thalia Mara, "classical ballet, Spanish and Modern Negro dances"; the New English Singers, "the most perfect small choir in existence"; Gaspar Cassado, "sensational young Spanish cellist"; Dorothy Crawford presenting "a program of original character sketches," and Angna Enters in "a new group of inimitable dramatic episodes in dance form." Cornelia Otis Skinner did her one-woman show at the Paper Mill. There were two photography courses by Thomas O. Sheckell, president of the Pictorial Photographers of America. The art gallery presented an exhibit of work of Cape Cod artists, New Jersey artists (including Antoinette Scudder), and paintings by Gainsborough, Reynolds, and "other masters of the English School" from the Harold W. Hack collection. For children there were puppet shows on Saturday afternoons: *Dick Whittington*, *Winnie the Pooh*, *The Pied Piper of Hamelin*, and *Toby Tyler or Ten Weeks with the Circus*. These were performed on a platform stage built over the orchestra pit in the auditorium. The Paper Mill Playhouse was also made available to various political and social clubs for meetings and "teas," among them the Independent Women's Republican Club, the Women's State Republican Club, the Clee for Governor Club (Senator Lester H. Clee), and any other groups that would introduce their members to the new theatre and afford Paper Mill a little publicity.

as. Miss Vesta Tilley

Cissie doing one of her famous impersonation

Cecilia "Cissie" Loftus was one of the many performers of specialty material who appeared at the Paper Mill Playhouse in its early days. She was a popular star in British music halls and American vaudeville.

Antoinette Quinby Scudder

Antoinette Scudder, co-founder of the Paper Mill Playhouse.

A poet and artist, Antoinette Scudder, in partnership with Frank Carrington, became founder of the Paper Mill Playhouse. As the daughter of Wallace M. Scudder, founder of the *Newark Evening News*, and Ida Quinby Scudder (whose father, James M. Quinby, was three times mayor of Newark and a member of Congress), she had early in her life become a wealthy patron of the arts and it was she who bought the old paper mill, paid for its remodeling into the Paper Mill Playhouse, and continued to subsidize it for many years. She seemed happy to do so and once told a reporter, "I've been completely stagestruck since childhood."

Antoinette Scudder studied at Columbia University, the Art Students' League of New York, the Cape Cod School of Art, and with many of the outstanding artists of the day. She was well known for her landscapes, many of the New England coast and countryside, and for her flower studies. Her oils and watercolors were exhibited widely, winning many prizes. She was also a writer of merit, with thirty plays and several volumes of verse to her credit. One of her plays, *The Second Generation,* won first prize in 1930 from the Women's Arts Club and was produced by various groups in Newark, New Jersey. In 1932, she won second prize in the annual play contest of the National League of American Pen Women with her one-act play *Rescue,* which later was presented at the Paper Mill Playhouse. Her dramatization of Hans Christian Andersen's *Snow Queen* was broadcast over WOR radio in the winter of 1938–1939.

Antoinette Scudder died in her sleep at her Newark home on January 26, 1958, at the age of 72. She had brought the dream of a theatre from the meager beginnings of amateur enthusiasts to one of the most renowned playhouses ever to exist.

Publications by Antoinette Scudder include:
- *Indian Summer* (1925)
- *The Soul of Ilaria* (1926)
- *Provincetown Sonata* (1926)
- *Huckleberries* (1928)
- *The Maple's Bride and Other One-Act Plays* (1930)
- *Out of Peony and Blade* (1931)
- *East End, West End* (1934)
- *The Cherry Tart and Other Plays* (1938)
- *Italics for Life* (1947)
- *The World in a Match Box* (1949)

A scene from *The Poppet* by Antoinette Scudder, scenery by Frank Carrington, produced by the Newark Art Theatre.

Frank Carrington

Frank Carrington, son of an army man, was born on Angel Island, California, a former army base. At the age of six he wrote a five-act play, and by twelve he was doing various small jobs at the Pasadena Playhouse. His first stage role was at age thirteen. When his family moved to New Jersey, he became active in local theatre. He lived on Park Road in Short Hills, from where he could hear the old whistle at the Diamond Paper Mill and he often passed the mill, thinking it would make a good theatre. At that time, he was working in a law office and studying theatre at night. Although discouraged by his father, Carrington pursued a career in acting and directing. He was one of the founders of the Cherry Lane Theatre in New York, and was very active in the New York theatre scene, becoming a friend of many of the theatre greats of the time.

Those friendships allowed him later to call on many famous personalities to appear at the Paper Mill Playhouse. In 1924, he was asked to join Eva Le Gallienne in her 14th Street Civic Repertory Theatre but chose instead to appear in Antoinette Scudder's play *Prince Pentaur,* a decision that led to their long relationship as founders of the Paper Mill Playhouse. Although described as "patrician" and called "Mr. Carrington" by everyone connected to Paper Mill, he was always interested in and thoughtful of his staff and the performers who appeared there. In turn, he received devotion and complete loyalty from all of them. Frank Carrington died in 1975 after a long struggle with cancer. His exact age is uncertain as he refused to give his birth-date, joking that the records had been "conveniently lost" in the San Francisco earthquake of 1906.

Frank Carrington, co-founder of the Paper Mill Playhouse.

Frank Carrington filled many roles at the Newark Art Theatre—director, scene designer, actor. Here he appears (second from left) as Don Antonio in Martinez Sierra's *The Two Shepherds*.

Bert Lahr and Beatrice Lillie in *The Show Is On,* 1936.

Broadway in the '30s

The Paper Mill Playhouse opened its doors in 1938, hardly an auspicious time to start a new theatre. The number of theatres in New York had been reduced by half in the early 1930s. The minimum Broadway wage for chorus girls and boys was thirty-five dollars a week and, reportedly, 5,000 Broadway actors were out of work. Even the Shuberts had gone into bankruptcy. Many of the strongest personalities in all branches of the theatre had died: Florenz Ziegfeld in 1932, Will Rogers in 1936, George Gershwin in 1937.

With all of that, it was an exciting decade for the theatre. The Theatre Guild was very active. In 1935, it presented the then-daring *Porgy and Bess* by George Gershwin. An offshoot of the Guild, the Group Theatre, produced Clifford Odets' *Awake and Sing, Waiting for Lefty,* and *Golden Boy,* and Sidney Kingsley's *Men in White.* Eva Le Gallienne's Civic Repertory Theatre was busy on West 14th Street and the WPA Theatre Project and Orson Welles' Mercury Theatre mounted numerous shows.

Many of the most respected and beloved performers appeared in a variety of productions. Katherine Cornell did *The Barretts of Wimpole Street* (1931), *Romeo and Juliet* (1934), and *St. Joan* (1935); Helen Hayes did both *Mary of Scotland* (1933) and *Victoria Regina* (1935); Walter Houston played the lead in Sinclair Lewis's *Dodsworth,* and Fred Astaire (without his sister Adele) was in *Gay Divorce* (1932). Beatrice Lillie and Bobby Clark did sketches in *Walk a Little Faster* (also 1932).

1933 brought *As Thousands Cheer,* with sketches by Moss Hart and songs by Irving Berlin. It starred Clifton Webb,

Ray Bolger and Tamara Geva danced George Balanchine's "Slaughter on Tenth Avenue" in *On Your Toes,* 1936.

Leave It to Me, with music by Cole Porter, included "My Heart Belongs to Daddy," a number that made another newcomer a star, Mary Martin, who sang it wrapped in furs that she slowly discarded.

These people were part of Broadway in the 1930s...

GEORGE ABBOTT (Director, *The Boys from Syracuse,*1938)
BILLIE BURKE (presented *Ziegfeld Follies of '36*)
EDDIE BRACKEN (*Too Many Girls,*1939)
KITTY CARLISLE (*Champagne, Sec,*1933; *The Great Waltz,* 1936)
IMOGENE COCA (*Garrick Gaieties,*1930; *Ziegfeld Follies,* 1931; *New Faces,* 1934; *Fools Rush In,* 1934; *New Faces of 1936,* 1936; *Who's Who,* 1938)
HELEN HAYES (*Mary of Scotland,* 1933; *Victoria Regina,* 1935)
ALLAN JONES (*Bitter Sweet,* 1934; *Music Hath Charms,* 1934)
BERT LAHR (*Flying High,* 1930; *Hot-Cha,* 1932; *George White's Music Hall Varieties,* 1932; *Life Begins at 8:40,* 1934; *George White's Scandals of 1936, The Show Is On,* 1936)
BEATRICE LILLIE (*The Third Little Show,* 1931; *Belmont Varieties,* 1932; *Walk a Little Faster,* 1932; *At Home Abroad,* 1935; *The Show Is On,* 1936; *Set to Music,* 1939)
ANN MILLER (*George White's Scandals of 1936*)
GINGER ROGERS (*Girl Crazy,* 1930)

...and later were part of the history of Paper Mill Playhouse.

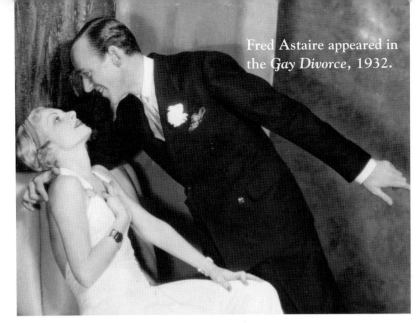

Fred Astaire appeared in the *Gay Divorce*, 1932.

Helen Hayes in *Victoria Regina*, 1935. After its Broadway run, she toured the show, traveling 10,000 miles to forty-seven cities in twenty-five states and two Canadian provinces, and grossing $1,200,000.

Helen Broderick, Ethel Waters, and Marilyn Miller in her last appearance. *The Threepenny Opera* lasted only a week and a half but introduced the work of Kurt Weill and Bertolt Brecht to theatre audiences.

The year 1934 saw both innovation—in Gertrude Stein's *Four Saints in Three Acts*—and outstanding musicals of more conventional style. Bert Lahr and Ray Bolger helped make a success of *Life Begins at 8:40*. *Anything Goes* made a star of Ethel Merman. In 1935, Billy Rose presented *Jumbo* at the Hippodrome starring Jimmy Durante. Willie and Eugene Howard, Bert Lahr, and Rudy Vallee were in *George White's Scandals of 1936* (with a very young Ann Miller in the chorus). Fanny Brice, Bob Hope, Gertrude Niesen, Eve Arden, Judy Canova, and Josephine Baker were in that year's *Ziegfeld Follies* (now produced by the Shuberts but "presented" by Ziegfeld's widow, Billie Burke). The really big hit of 1936 was George Abbott's *On Your Toes*, for which George Balanchine created a landmark ballet, "Slaughter on Tenth Avenue." The following spring, *Babes in Arms* introduced fresh young talent—Alfred Drake, Ray Heatherton, Dan Dailey, and Mitzi Green among others—in a lively show with choreography by George Balanchine and music by

Rodgers and Hart that included such now-standard songs as "The Lady Is a Tramp," "My Funny Valentine," "Where or When," and "I Wish I Were in Love Again." It was a tremendous success.

Many other plays and musicals that have become classics of American theatre were first produced in the 1930s: *The Time of Your Life*, *Life With Father*, *Tobacco Road*, Eugene O'Neill's *Ah, Wilderness!*, and Jerome Kern's *Roberta*. In 1938 alone, the year the Paper Mill Playhouse began, there was *I Married an Angel*, music and lyrics by Rodgers and Hart; *Hellzapoppin'*, with Olson and Johnson; *Knickerbocker Holiday*, starring Walter Houston singing "September Song," music by Kurt Weill, lyrics and libretto by Maxwell Anderson; and George Abbott's *The Boys from Syracuse*, music by Richard Rodgers and Lorenz Hart. Thornton Wilder's *Our Town* won the Pulitzer Prize for drama.

Brian Aherne and Katherine Cornell (below, left) as they appeared in *The Barretts of Wimpole Street*, 1931. The new Paper Mill Playhouse would reopen in 1982 with the musical version, *Robert and Elizabeth* starring (below, right) Marc Jacoby and Leigh Beery.

The First Two Years

The first production at the Paper Mill Playhouse opened on November 14, 1938—a play by Martinez Sierra titled *The Kingdom of God* (which had also opened the Ethel Barrymore Theatre on Broadway ten years before, with Ethel Barrymore herself in the leading role). For the first two years, Paper Mill presented only plays, no operettas or musical plays. Among the productions were *Androcles and the Lion*, *Tonight at 8:30*, *Man in Possession*, *Flight into China*, *Men in White*, *Pursuit of Happiness*, *Jeannie*, and *I Killed the Count*. Eva Le Gallienne and Rex O'Malley appeared in *Private Lives*. *Papa Is All*, which starred Jessie Royce Landis, went on to Broadway as a Theatre Guild production, under the direction of Frank Carrington and Agnes Morgan, who had joined the Playhouse as co-director.

Frank Carrington had a great sense of promotion from the very beginning. The first program for the Playhouse shows, as members of the advisory council, some of the grand leading ladies of the theatre: Laurette Taylor, Eva Le Gallienne, Cornelia Otis Skinner, Jane Cowl, and Blanche Yurka. They had been "guests of honor" at various Paper Mill Playhouse events and Carrington had charmed them into further support of his project. Antoinette Scudder brought along the social set and, as she was the daughter of Wallace Scudder, who was the owner of the *Newark Evening News*, it was not difficult to attract a good deal of publicity in the press.

Carrington established a theatre school that offered instruction in all aspects of the theatre to youngsters who had not only an interest but at least a

Eva Le Gallienne and Rex O'Malley in Noel Coward's *Private Lives*.

Flight into China, with (left to right) June Walker, Toni Selwart, and José Ferrer and staged by Lee Strasburg, was an early production at the Paper Mill Playhouse.

Paper Mill Playhouse in its first years.

modicum of talent in the theatre arts. In 1939, he put on the First New Jersey Theatre Festival, and a year later he announced that the Paper Mill Playhouse would become a permanent repertory theatre experimenting with producing shows year-round.

Carrington attracted great attention by announcing he was bringing in stars, who had agreed to salary cuts, to appear in productions that would benefit British War Relief. This led to a case brought before Actors Equity by Cheryl Crawford, who ran the Maplewood Theatre. She claimed this was an unfair practice that would endanger the livelihood of other theatres which were already competing for Broadway audiences. But Equity could find no fault with the scheme and Carrington went ahead. This undertaking was called the Paper Mill Playhouse Festival. For this Carrington coaxed Irene Castle out of retirement to appear with Rex O'Malley in *Shadow Play*, one of the sketches in Noel Coward's *Tonight at 8:30*. He also managed to line up a sponsor list for this festival that included Eleanor Roosevelt, George Abbott, Tallulah Bankhead, George M. Cohan, Joan Crawford, Ann Harding, Sinclair Lewis, Billy Rose, Clifton Webb, and Margaret Webster. The project was a hit. In August, he wrote exuberantly to Antoinette Scudder:

> *Dear Antoinette,*
>
> *Apparently we are a success! We seem to have gone over the top. Crowds, crowds, crowds—endlessly. Practically every performance a sell-out—the great rank and file of the middle-class theatre-going public. I've so wanted to tell you all about it but we are all working like fools from early morning till midnight every day. At every performance there is a line at the box office reaching to the front gates—there have been three or four of us in the box office trying to get the crowds in by curtain time…. I'm simply thrilled having the chance to prove that there is a tremendous potential audience here—it gives me back a great deal of belief in myself and makes me feel that we have not been two such babes-in-the-woods after all. Many of the well-known managers have been out here this week—they have all said the same thing voluntarily, "This is a potential gold mine." We have had the most marvelous publicity from coast to coast and if nothing else is accomplished, from our own point of view, we are at least on the map in a big way and definitely in the public eye.*
>
> *Frank Carrington*

Costume design, by Anne Andrews, for Red Joe in the Newark Art Theatre production of *Wappin Wharf*. The character of Red Joe was played by Frank Carrington.

Set design by Anne Andrews for *The Snow Queen*, adapted by Antoinette Scudder and produced at the Paper Mill Playhouse in 1940.

Costume designs by Anne Andrews for the Paper Mill Playhouse production of *Rescue* by Antoinette Scudder.

Costume designs by Anne
Andrews for *The Snow Queen*.
Clockwise from above:
Costumes for The Raven,
Rose, Kay, and Gerda.

The Early Operettas

From 1940 to the early 1950s, the Paper Mill Playhouse became known for its productions of operettas. Audiences returned year after year to see these beloved shows and the most popular ones were repeated often. Gilbert and Sullivan were always welcome, as was anything from the pen of Sigmund Romberg, Franz Lehar, or Rudolph Friml. Audiences also flocked to see George Gershwin's *Rosalie*, Jerome Kern's *Sally*, and Noel Coward's *Bitter Sweet*. Paper Mill was very much a repertory company in those years and the shows featured the same performers in a variety of roles. Audiences were faithful to their favorites, among them Dorothy Sandlin, Donald Gage, and Clarence Nordstrom.

The Chocolate Soldier, 1948

Dorothy Sandlin in **The Chocolate Soldier, 1942**

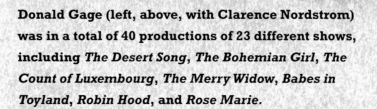

The Mikado, 1946

Donald Gage (left, above, with Clarence Nordstrom) was in a total of 40 productions of 23 different shows, including *The Desert Song*, *The Bohemian Girl*, *The Count of Luxembourg*, *The Merry Widow*, *Babes in Toyland*, *Robin Hood*, and *Rose Marie*.

Clarence Nordstrom played dozens of character parts in the operettas, including the role of Lutz in *The Student Prince* for more than 1,500 performances over a span of seven seasons. All told, he was in 30 productions of 22 different shows.

The Merry Widow, 1942

Dorothy Kirsten (below, with Walter Cassel, left, and Ralph Riggs, center) appeared in *The Merry Widow*, then went on to be a star of the Metropolitan Opera.

Mademoiselle Modiste, 1942

Dorothy Sandlin (right, with Donald Gage) would appear in 22 productions at the Playhouse including *M'lle Modiste, The Chocolate Soldier, Sweethearts, The Vagabond King, The Desert Song, Maytime,* and *Bitter Sweet.*

There have been eight productions of *The Merry Widow* at Paper Mill. Above, Dorothy Sandlin in the 1967 production with Richard Fredericks (left) and Edward Everett Horton (right).

The Desert Song, 1942

The Desert Song has the all-time record for most productions—nine from 1942 through 1984.

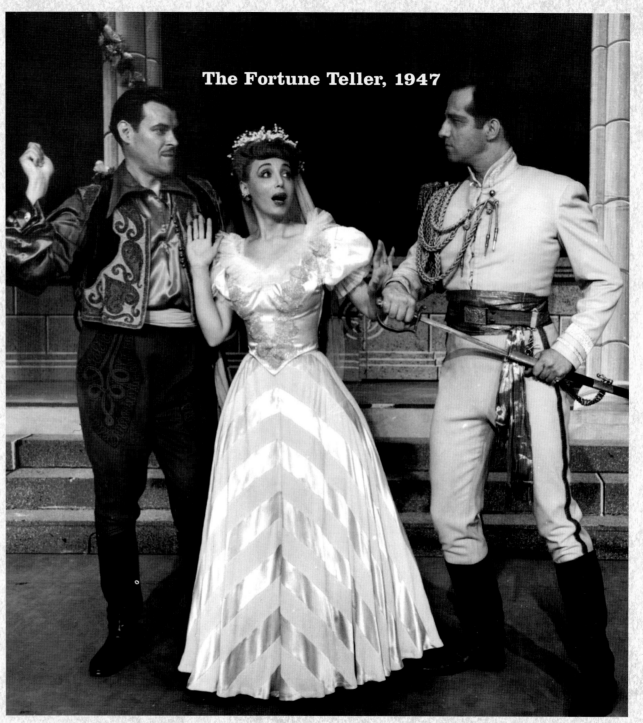

The Fortune Teller, 1947

Rosemary Brancato starred in twelve productions, including *Naughty Marietta, Rose Marie, The Count of Luxembourg, Song of Norway,* and *The New Moon.*

The Love Wagon, 1947

The Paper Miller

The operettas at Paper Mill were so popular that, during the war years, the railroad ran "The Paper Miller" so that both local and distant audiences, restricted in their use of automobiles because of gas rationing, could continue attending performances. The railroad reportedly checked the time the curtain came down for each show and scheduled a stop to pick up audience members leaving the theatre.

Babes in Toyland, 1942

The Student Prince, 1944

The Student Prince will tie *Desert Song*'s record when its ninth production is mounted in the year 2000.

Cavalcade of Stars

My sweetest memory of the Paper Mill was every performance at "half hour" call before curtain time. Mr. Carrington…would appear at each dressing room door and bid us individually a "wonderful performance, a happy day— and I so appreciate your being at the Paper Mill."
—Betsy Palmer

Betsy Palmer in *Maggie*, 1962.

DURING THE 1940s, PAPER MILL STAGED tried-and-true operettas and plays, certain in the knowledge that they would always draw an appreciative audience; but Frank Carrington wanted to take a chance on musicals. The theatre had been improved, allowing a larger (and more comfortable) audience, and he wanted to present more lavish productions. Although the operettas continued, popular shows were added each season, among them *Show Boat*, *Brigadoon*, *Annie Get Your Gun*, *Up in Central Park*, *Song of Norway*, and *Finian's Rainbow*, and in the next few years, *Kiss Me Kate*, *Where's Charley?*, *Carousel*, *High Button Shoes*, *Call Me Madam*, *Paint Your Wagon*, and *Oklahoma*.

By the mid-1950s, Paper Mill had a well-established reputation for outstanding presentations. Even with an always limited budget, the quality of the direction and the productions made it easy to attract stars to appear there. Billie Burke played in the 1955 production of *Mother Was a Bachelor*, and that same year the early darlings of the silver screen Dorothy and Lillian Gish were seen at Paper Mill in *The Chalk Garden*. Celeste Holm had appeared on Broadway and toured in the Theatre Guild produc-

tion of *Papa Is All*, which had originated at the Paper Mill Playhouse in 1939, directed by Frank Carrington and Agnes Morgan. At Paper Mill she appeared in *Royal Enclosure* (1958), *Invitation to a*

The delightful Billie Burke appeared at the Paper Mill Playhouse in *Mother Was a Bachelor*, 1955.

March (1961), and later, *Light Up the Sky* (1975). Shelley Winters appeared in *Two for the Seesaw* (1958), *The Country Girl* (1961), *A View from the Bridge* (1961), and in the years to come, *Days of Dancing* (1964) and *The Effect of Gamma Rays on Man-in-the-Moon Marigolds* (1973). In 1962, Betsy Palmer appeared in *Maggie* and *South Pacific*, the first of ten productions she would be seen in at Paper Mill.

In 1956, a cooperative effort between Carrington and Scudder and John H. Bosshart, president of the New Jersey Symphony, produced a series of concerts resulting in New Jersey's First Summer Music Festival. Those festivals began the continuing tradition of special music programs at Paper Mill presented over the summer months and eventually year-round.

Myrna Loy appeared in
There Must Be a Pony, 1962.

Popular silent screen stars Dorothy and Lillian Gish appeared together in *The Chalk Garden,* 1955.

Shelley Winters in *The Country Girl* with Joseph Anthony, 1961.

Agnes Morgan
co-director

Agnes Morgan was co-director at the Paper Mill Playhouse for twenty-eight years until her retirement to California in 1968. Frank Carrington had known and worked with her in New York, where she had been a director for the Neighborhood Play-house. While working there, she had written the book and lyrics for the *Grand Street Follies,* which opened in 1923 at the Grand Street Theatre and became an annual production for ten consecutive years, playing at various theatres in New York including the Bronx Opera House, the Little Theatre, the Shubert Riviera, and the Booth Theatre, and at the Walnut Street and Shubert-Lafayette theatres in Philadelphia. She was a producer for the Shuberts, the Theatre Guild, and many stock companies throughout the country. With Frank Carrington she directed *Papa Is All,* which was a tremendous success at the Paper Mill Playhouse and went on to Broadway as a Theatre Guild production with the two of them as directors. She is credited with having contributed greatly to Paper Mill's advancement as a major regional theatre.

It must have been 1940 when I first appeared at the Paper Mill Playhouse.... On our drive out to the theatre, there was construction on Route 22 and we were stuck for forty-five minutes. My heart was racing as I tore into the theatre. Frank Carrington had made a lovely speech telling the audience how reliable I was and that he was sure I'd be there soon. As I ran backstage, Frank was holding out my gorgeous gold dress in which I was to make an entrance. He quickly turned his back while I stripped and stepped into it, he neatly zipped it up, and on with the show! Had I put makeup on in the car? I don't remember. Frank told this story many times! When appearing once more at the Paper Mill, Route 22 was at it again—reconstructing just before show time. I think the workmen liked to do it. It gave them a feeling of power! Does this still happen or has Angelo spoken to the Department of Highways and explained the situation?—CELESTE HOLM

Invitation to a March, 1961, starring Celeste Holm and Wesley Addy.

THE 1940s AND 1950s had seen both highs and lows at the Playhouse, but for the most part all had gone well. Then, in January 1958, the organization suffered a severe blow. Co-founder Antoinette Scudder, who had encouraged everyone for all those years, who had never lost faith, who had contributed so much, died. She had found a life of both excitement and peace at Paper Mill Playhouse. She had held her own interests, writing and painting, but had also made the Playhouse her home and a central reason for her very existence. She would be greatly missed.

Antoinette Scudder at work in her studio.

Without Antoinette, Frank Carrington faced a difficult time. She had not only provided the financial backing for Paper Mill but had served as a sounding board for Frank's ideas and contributed her personal efforts to see them realized.

Carrington had tried working with various associates during Scudder's time. In 1957 he brought in Laurence Feldman and Henry Weinstein,

who had founded several stock theatres. Feldman and Weinstein were a very successful team, packaging many productions, which now would also play at Paper Mill.

In 1959, while working with Paper Mill, Feldman was in a near-fatal car crash, after which he stated "Now that I know death has wings and wants me...I'm taking everything I can lay my hands on." And take he did. Before becoming a producer, he had practiced law, specializing in negligence cases. By 1963, he was suspended from law practice because of various questionable pursuits. He became quite a dandy, wearing chesterfield coats, homburg hats, and carrying a black-and-silver cane. He maintained a posh five-room, three-bath penthouse in a fashionable part of Manhattan, and his little black telephone book was filled with hundreds of names of beautiful women and "business associates." It was reported that he was known by every bookie in Times Square.

On the night of March 9, 1967, the forty-year-old bachelor-playboy rode home in a taxi with his secretary and later had dinner with a "mystery woman" with whom he returned to his apartment. A "Miss Florida" later came forward to say she was the woman and that she had left his apartment at 2:15 a.m. The following day, when Feldman failed to show up at his office, his secretary and the building superintendent found him dead in his apartment—viciously murdered. Over the next few years, police

Above, left: Arlene Francis appeared in *Amphitryon '38*, 1960, and *Old Acquaintance*, 1962, both directed by Martin Gabel, and *Kind Sir*, 1964.

Above: Gloria Swanson in *Between Seasons*, 1961.

Right: Claudette Colbert and Cyril Ritchard appeared in *The Irregular Verb to Love*, 1963, one of several plays that moved from Paper Mill to Broadway.

followed a trail of jewelry left at pawn shops and eventually indicted two cat burglars for the crime. One pleaded guilty to manslaughter and was imprisoned from 1972 until his release in 1981. The other was judged incompetent to stand trial and was remanded to a mental hospital.

With Paper Mill's relationship with Feldman and Weinstein ended, Frank Carrington again found himself alone. The theatre was losing money. He needed someone who could encourage him and help lead the theatre to

a strong future. He brought in Orrin Christy as associate producer and a young Angelo Del Rossi as casting director. Christy had connections with a Broadway agent through whom Paper Mill made a number of arrangements for star appearances in their productions. But Christy remained at Paper Mill for only two years and Carrington continued to seek someone who could be both his production partner and a creative contributor to the Playhouse. He found that person in Angelo Del Rossi.

Clockwise from above: Genevieve in *Irma La Douce*, 1963; Frank Carrington with Imogene Coca; Eileen Brennan as *Little Mary Sunshine*, 1962, with a young John McMartin on his knee to the left.

Tallulah Bankhead, far right, and Estelle Winwood, second from right, appeared together in *Here Today*, 1962, along with Richard Kendrick and Jill Kraft (center).

Left: Tom Bosley (on telephone) in *Fiorello*, 1962, posing with Township of Millburn committee members. Below: Bert Parks and Virginia Mayo in *Good News*, 1977. Bottom left: Dick Smart and Jacqueline James in *Call Me Madam*, 1953. Bottom right: Tom Posten and Chita Rivera in *Bye Bye Birdie*, 1962.

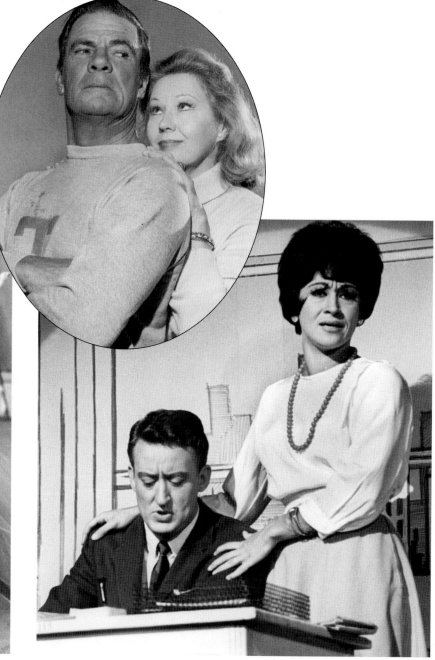

Betsy Palmer

There are numerous performers who have appeared at the Paper Mill Playhouse so often that they have become members of the theatre's family. Betsy Palmer is among them. First appearing at the Paper Mill in 1962 in *Maggie* and as Nellie Forbush in *South Pacific*—a role she repeated in the 1974 production—she went on to play Anna in *The King and I* in 1963, and starred in *Peter Pan* in 1966. In 1971 she starred in *Hello, Dolly!* She was also seen at Paper Mill in *Affairs of State* (1965), *LUV* (1967), *The Prime of Miss Jean Brodie* (1969), *Mary, Mary* (1973), *Life with Father* (1975), and *Same Time Next Year* (1978). Ms. Palmer has often lent her support to Paper Mill for fund-raising events and in presenting the theatre's cause in requests for arts grants.

With William Chapman in *South Pacific* (inset) and *The King and I* (above), and in *Peter Pan* (left).

Basil Rathbone appeared in several productions at the Paper Mill Playhouse. Above (seated, right) in *Separate Tables* with Geraldine Page (seated, left), 1958, and at left in *Witness for the Prosecution* with Anne Meacham, 1957.

Right: Hans Conreid and Cornelia Otis Skinner in *The Pleasure of His Company*, 1961.

Clockwise from left: Tresa Hughes and Gertrude Berg in *Dear Me, the Sky Is Falling*, 1964; Molly Picon in A *Majority of One*, 1961, visited backstage by Pat Carroll; Dane Clark and Teresa Wright in *Tchin, Tchin*, 1963.

On Their Way to Stardom

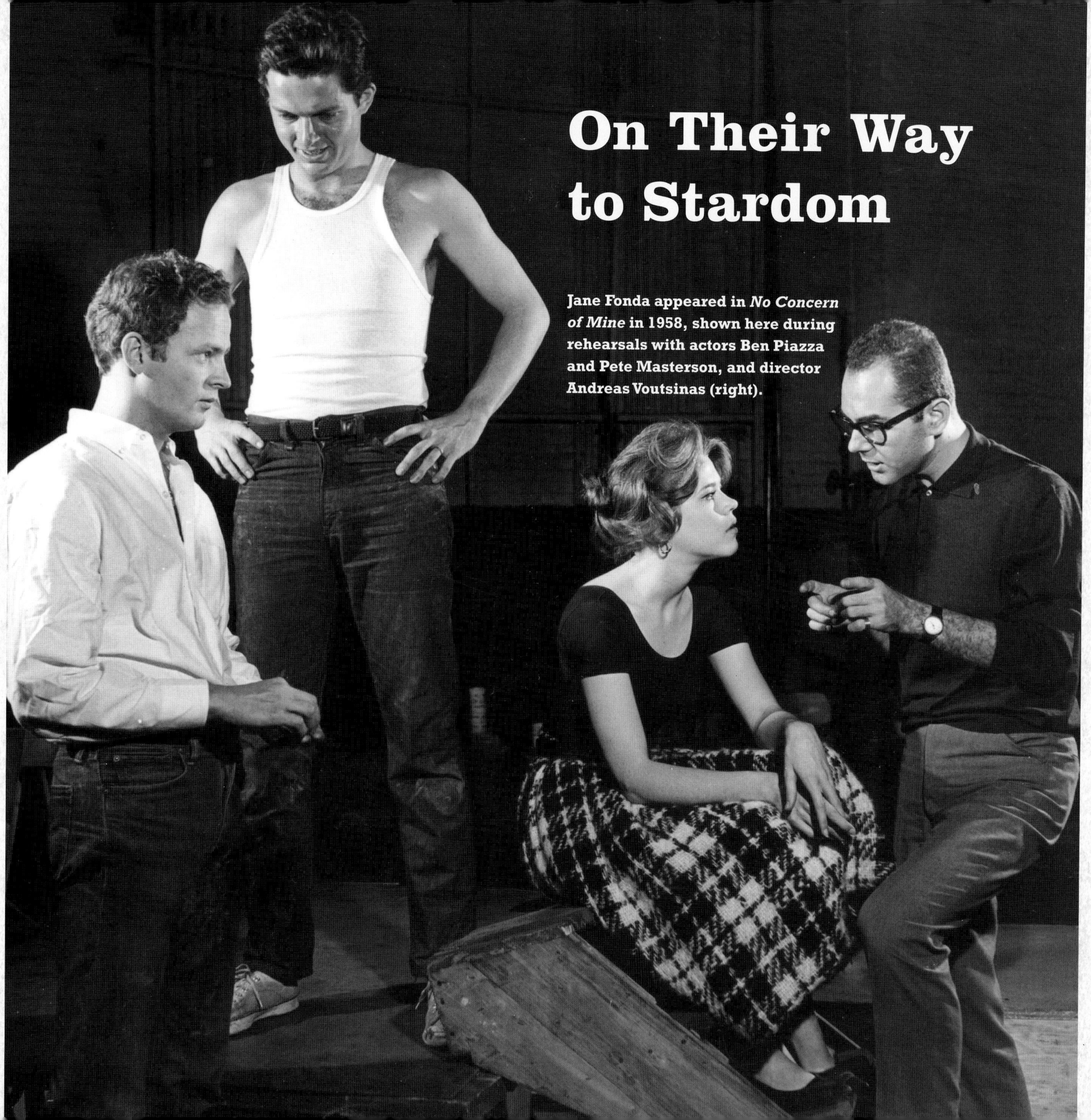

Jane Fonda appeared in *No Concern of Mine* in 1958, shown here during rehearsals with actors Ben Piazza and Pete Masterson, and director Andreas Voutsinas (right).

Many outstanding performers can claim to have had their start at the Paper Mill Playhouse. A very young Jane Fonda was seen there in 1958 in *No Concern of Mine*. Marjorie Bell, a dancer who appeared in *Sally* at Paper Mill in 1944, married Gower Champion and became his partner in one of the best-known dance teams in show business. In 1961, Patrick Swayze could be seen in *The Music Man*. Both Carol Channing and Gene Wilder appeared in *The Millionairess* in 1963, and from that performance Channing was chosen by producer David Merrick and director/choreographer Gower Champion for the lead in *Hello, Dolly!*, a part with which she has been associated for all the years since. An up-and-coming Liza Minnelli was seen in *Carnival* in 1964, Sandy Duncan appeared in *The Boy Friend* and in *Peter Pan,* as Wendy, in 1966, and Bernadette Peters was in *Dames at Sea* in 1973.

Liza Minnelli in *Carnival*
with David Daniels, 1964.

A very young Patrick Swayze, third from right, back row, in *The Music Man*, 1961, with other members of the chorus. This was his first professional acting job, for which he became a member of Actors Equity.

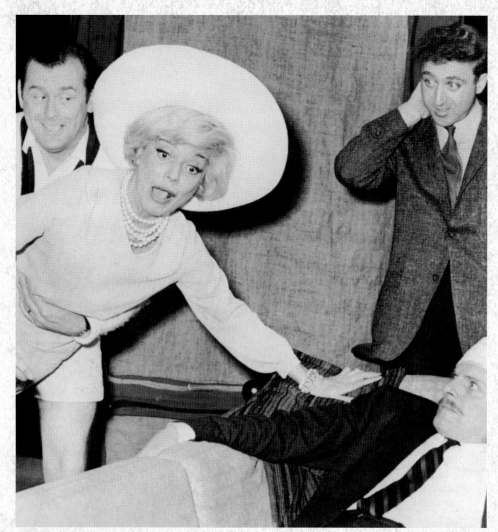

Carol Channing and Gene Wilder in *The Millionairess*, (1963), with John McMartin (on couch) and Eugene Roche giving Miss Channing a boost!

Bernadette Peters in *Dames at Sea*, 1973.

I was appearing at the Playhouse
in *The Millionairess* by George Bernard Shaw.
Yes! I was a classical actress! I really was.
Well—David Merrick came to see me in that
production and was so impressed that he
offered me the lead in a new musical
he was about to produce on Broadway called *Hello, Dolly!*
Well—the rest is history. Thank you Paper Mill!

CAROL CHANNING

Donna McKechnie was featured in *Redhead* in 1960 (below), before she went on to acclaim in Broadway's *Promises, Promises* and *Company*, and to win a Best Actress Tony Award for *A Chorus Line*. She returned to Paper Mill for *Follies* in 1998.

Sandy Duncan, at left above, appeared in *The Boy Friend*, 1966, with Chele Abel, Jacqueline Ullendorf, and Isabell Farrell. She went on to play the same role in the Broadway revival of the show, which took her to stardom.

Angelo Del Rossi, Producer

When Jack asked who I had in mind to play Pseudolus, I said Dom DeLuise. He said, "Who's that?" It wasn't long before they became fast friends and Dom, along with the incomparable Gilford, was outstanding. It was during the run of Forum that Dom was seen by a TV producer and thus started his first television series.

—Angelo Del Rossi

The life of the arts, far from being an intrusion, a distraction, in the life of the nation, is very close to the center of a nation's purpose and is a test of the quality of a nation's civilization.
—President John F. Kennedy

AMONG FRANK CARRINGTON'S greatest legacies to the Paper Mill Playhouse was the discovery of Angelo Del Rossi, a reserved young man in whom he recognized a special talent for integrating all the aspects of a successful theatre. Always comfortable with others taking bows for his accomplishments, in the years ahead he would provide the opportunity for many performers to find success.

In his new role, Del Rossi moved the Paper Mill Playhouse into new fields of production with shows that would attract new audiences as well as maintain the interests of the well-established audiences that had always been faithful to the Playhouse. Over a period of time, he hired new staff members to cover the business of the theatre and talented creative people to produce the outstanding shows for which the Playhouse has become known.

Del Rossi found particular interest in the regional theatre movement which was just beginning and wanted to be part of it. Organizations known as the Council of Stock Theatres and the League of Resident Theatres were established, creating the beginnings of the regional theatre movement across the United States. It was during this time that Paper Mill concentrated on plays more than musicals. There were many more theatres with which to

exchange plays rather than the large musicals and this was a time when the East Coast was alive with theatre. It was also the time of "packages," a term used for productions of plays (and sometimes musicals) that would travel with the same cast from theatre to theatre. Paper Mill had a relationship with the Mineola Playhouse on Long Island and sent most of its musicals there, while some of the plays went to other theatres on the circuit. The Paper Mill Playhouse, the Ogonquit Playhouse, the Westport County Playhouse, the Cape Playhouse, and other regional theatres worked together for many years under this program. In one such year, 1965, Paper Mill produced eleven plays and five musicals.

Many Hollywood stars who were looking to do theatre appeared at Paper Mill, including Van Heflin, June Allyson, Dana Andrews, George Hamilton, Bert Lahr, Martha Raye, and Joan Fontaine. Dom DeLuise starred in *A Funny Thing Happened on the Way to the Forum*, directed by Jack Gilford. Recreating their original roles, Sam Levene and Vivian Blaine teamed up for the twenty-fifth anniversary production of *Guys and Dolls*. That was followed by Barbara Cook starring in *The Boy Friend* with Sandy Duncan playing Maisey. A year or two later, Sandy did the same part in a Broadway revival and was tapped for her first TV series.

Mrs. Lyndon Johnson (left) with Helen Hayes, who narrated the White House performance shown here.

George Grizzard and Maureen Stapleton.

Pat Hingle and Piper Laurie.

Paper Mill's production of *The Glass Menagerie,* starring Maureen Stapleton, George Grizzard, Piper Laurie, and Pat Hingle, moved from the Playhouse to Broadway and then was honored with an invitation to the White House Festival of the Arts to give a special performance for President and Mrs. Lyndon Johnson.

The White House Festival of the Arts
June 14, 1965

Prose and Poetry
Music
Drama
The Motion Picture
Dance
Jazz
Painting
Photography
Sculpture

Angelo Del Rossi

Angelo Del Rossi left Rutgers University after one year, and at the end of a three-year stint in the Navy's communications division (with never a ship assignment but duty in Chicago, San Diego, Washington D.C., and a year and a day in Adak, Alaska), he turned down the offered commission and went home to Camden, New Jersey. Recalling happy times he'd had in a high school musical directed by Ruth White (who was a star on Broadway and played James Dean's mother in *Rebel Without a Cause*), he thought of her suggestion that he consider an acting career.

Thus began Angelo Del Rossi's pursuit of a life in the theatre. He joined the Bessie V. Hicks School of Theatre in Philadelphia, then auditioned for and was accepted to a two-year intensive theatre training program at the Neighborhood Playhouse in New York City. He studied acting with Sanford Meisner and his assistant, Sidney Pollock (who later directed *Out of Africa, Tootsie,* and many other films), modern dance with Martha Graham, ballet with Pearl Lang, music with Louis Horst, and speech with Robert Neff Williams. Among his fellow student actors were Robert Duval, Suzanne Pleshette, Wayne Rogers, and William Esper, now department chairperson, master teacher, and director of Graduate Programs in Acting at Rutgers. Two summers of stock at the Mill Playhouse in Hammonton, New Jersey, were followed by his first Broadway show, Colette's *Cherie,* adapted by Anita Loos and directed by Robert Lewis. It starred Kim Stanley and Horst Buchholtz.

I played Prince Guido. My agent sent me a telegram opening night which said, "Someday you'll be King!" His prediction did not come true and the play closed within a few months. I did other plays off-Broadway, some television, and a film with another young actor, Rue McClanahan.

But the lure of being a performer began to wane and Del Rossi realized he was more interested in other aspects of the theatre. When he was offered the position of casting director at the Paper Mill Playhouse, he accepted on the condition he not receive a salary and would therefore not feel an obligation to continue if he found the job was not for him.

I began my new venture on the other side of the footlights and in a short time learned I was like a sponge to water. It was a very productive time for Paper Mill. Frank Carrington had been joined by Orrin Christy as associate producer. Christy had many good theatre friends, including super agent Milton Goldman, who helped enormously in attracting actors to appear at the Playhouse. When Christy left Paper Mill to pursue other ventures, I advanced to associate producer and continued in that position until Frank's death in 1975, when I then became executive producer.

It was to be a momentous step for Del Rossi and for the Paper Mill Playhouse, for it is through his imagination, diligence, and forethought that Paper Mill Playhouse arrived at its position of honor among the regional theatres of today. He is credited as the force behind the rebuilding of the Playhouse. His strength in the face of fire, destruction, and rehabilitation, his ability to balance the needs of the theatre with the needs of the community, his determination in the difficult role of fundraiser, and his generosity of intellect and spirit in allowing the creative people around him the freedom to apply their talents to the exemplary work that can be seen there are his true gifts to Paper Mill. If you are looking for his monument, look to the Paper Mill Playhouse.

Angelo Del Rossi with (from left) Ann Miller, Ginger Rogers, and Virginia Mayo.

Above: Beatrice Lillie in *High Spirits*, 1965.
Left: Joan Fontaine (right) in *Susan and God*, 1960, with Lily Lodge and William Taylor.

Far left: Tony Perkins (center) with Lynn Benish and Remak Ramsey in *Star Spangled Girl*, 1967.
Left: Shirley Booth (center) in *The Vinegar Tree*, 1971 with Staats Cotsworth and Joan Wetmore.

Above: Nancy Carroll and Bert Lahr in _Never Too Late_, 1965. Right: Julie Harris in _The Belle of Amherst_, 1977. Below: June Allyson in _Janus_, 1965.

Del Rossi recalls: _Starting off the 1966 season, we had the good fortune to have Dorothy Collins star in_ Do I Hear a Waltz? _She asked who I had in mind to play opposite her. I said, "Ron Holgate." She said, "Who's that?" Well, they met, they did the show, they married and had two children._

That year, the Playhouse also had the heartthrobs Tommy Sands and Fabian, along with Nancy Walker, Tom Bosley, Chester Morris, Betsy Palmer, Maureen O'Sullivan, Rita Moreno, Janis Paige, Kevin McCarthy, Dina Merrill, Linda Lavin, and John Gavin (later to be appointed U.S. ambassador to Mexico) in his musical debut in _The Fantasticks_, and Paper Mill brought back two operettas, _Blossom Time_, with Allan Jones, and _The Student Prince_. Heading the 1968 season were Tony Perkins, Thelma Ritter, Tab Hunter, Orson Bean, Menasha Skulnick, Paul Ford, and Sam Levene (now a Paper Mill regular), and the sixties ended with an outstanding production of _Lamp at Midnight_ with Morris Carnovsky, directed by Sir Tyrone Guthrie. From 1960 to 1969 Paper Mill had presented 145 productions.

There were many things during those years that I will never forget. Julie Harris, that incandescent actress, would iron her costumes in her dressing room. When I asked if wardrobe could help, she answered, "Oh, no. It gets me in the mood. It prepares me for what's to come."

And Geraldine Page, as I sat in the audience prior to a run-through of The Little Foxes, _walked on stage alone in a beautiful black gown, sat down, and tore open a small seam in her dress. What was going on? The rehearsal started and, in the scene with the black dress, I noticed her trying to hide the tear from her guests, annoyed that the dress wasn't perfect. The distraction gave her already brilliant characterization yet another dimension. I begged her to do Amanda in_ The Glass Menagerie _but she refused. She had been an usher at the theatre where Laurette Taylor starred in that role and she said she could never erase Taylor's performance from her mind. However, years later when I asked again, she relented and said she would play the part for us. Alas, with her untimely death, that was not to happen._

Janus, with June Allyson, is noteworthy because Miss Allyson did only one performance and became ill. Imogene Coca, who had played the part years earlier, was called. "I'll be there!," she said. She was quickly flown in and opened with just a few hours of rehearsal. She did a letter-perfect performance.

There were many extraordinary performers and performances by a Who's Who of the Theatre. As already mentioned, Geraldine Page, Sandy Dennis, and Rip Torn in The Little Foxes, _and Shelley Winters in a variety of plays. John Carradine as Fagin in_ Oliver _would arrive at the theatre at 5 P.M. to begin his makeup. The most beloved actor, the one by whom I was awestruck was Bert Lahr. I would intrude myself into his dressing room just to be with him and try to get him into conversation. It was not an easy task, but I did succeed. I once told him that, because of him, the run was sold out. He was astonished by that news. "You mean they're coming_ to see me?" "Yes!" "An agent told me no one was interested in me anymore." He was a dear sweet man.

More stars flocked to Paper Mill. Janet Blair, Dody Goodman, and Vivian Vance appeared at the Playhouse. The theatre presented *The Tender Trap* with William Shatner, followed by Louis Nye and Maureen O'Sullivan in *Charley's Aunt*. Tammy

Grimes, Eddie Bracken, Barbara Baxley, Shirley Booth, and Edward Mulhare started the 1971 season, followed by Hugh O'Brien and Bonnie Franklin. Jerome Hines starred in *Man of La Mancha*. Douglas Fairbanks, Jr., Barbara Rush, Gloria Swanson, Bernadette Peters, Sada Thompson, and Shelley Winters all followed one another into 1973. Mickey

Above: John Carradine as Fagin in *Oliver*, 1976. Left: Geraldine Page and Rip Torn in *The Little Foxes*, 1978.

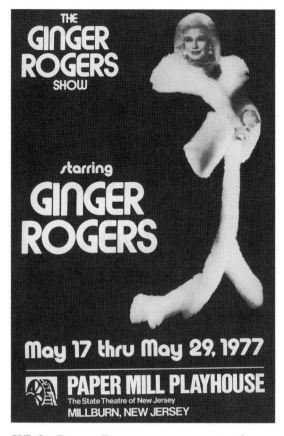

THE GINGER ROGERS SHOW

starring GINGER ROGERS

May 17 thru May 29, 1977

PAPER MILL PLAYHOUSE
The State Theatre of New Jersey
MILLBURN, NEW JERSEY

While Ginger Rogers was appearing here, her mother passed away. I was asked to give her the sad news. I did and said I'd cancel the show so she could go home, but she said no, that the show would go on—and it did.
—Angelo Del Rossi

Robert Anthony, Fawne Harriman, and Douglas Fairbanks, Jr., in *The Pleasure of His Company*, 1972.

Rooney, who had played Puck in the 1935 film of *A Midsummer Night's Dream*, starred as Bottom in the Paper Mill production. Returning to the stage after a serious accident, Ann Miller starred in *Anything Goes* and later returned to do *Panama Hattie*. Phyllis Newman did *Annie Get Your Gun* and Kitty Carlisle appeared in *You Never Know*. Tab Hunter and Thelma Ritter did 6 *Rms. Riv Vu*. David McCallum appeared in *The Mouse Trap*, and the beautiful Eva Marie Saint starred in *The Fatal Weakness*. Sandy Dennis and Jean Marsh were seen in Noel Coward's *Fallen Angels* and Dolores Gray caused a sensation performing Rose in *Gypsy*. John Raitt starred in *Shenandoah* and Tony Roberts, Stiller and Meara, Walter Abel, Kay Medford, Celeste Holm, Arlene Dahl, Nancy Dussault, and Pat Carroll all graced the Paper Mill stage. *Fiorello* was the last musical produced in the old theatre prior to a fire in 1980.

Jerome Hines in *Man of La Mancha*.

For *Panama Hattie*, Angelo Del Rossi got me a prize sheep dog called Rosie to work with on stage. In rehearsal, Rosie was fine, but when the audience arrived Rosie wanted to get into my lap. When I stood up she would lick my face and knock me flat! The audience loved it.

ANN MILLER

Ann Miller appeared in *Panama Hattie*, 1976 (left), with Terence Monk, Olivia Barash, and Rosie, and in *Anything Goes*, 1974 (below). She would bring audiences to their feet in 1998 in *Follies*.

In 1972, Frank's Carrington's health began to give way, and by late 1973 he was seldom in his office. Angelo Del Rossi took on Carrington's duties in addition to his own. He visited Carrington, who lived on the Playhouse grounds, regularly to discuss what was being planned.

By Carrington's death in 1975, Del Rossi had long been acting as Playhouse producer. The transition to executive producer was natural, and Del Rossi dedicated himself to continuing the legacy of great Paper Mill Playhouse productions established by Carrington over four decades.

John Gavin in the title role of *Mr. Roberts*, 1968.

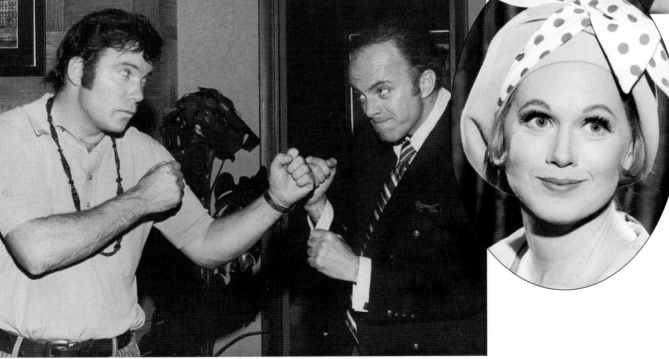

Clockwise from top left:
Monica Moran, Thelma Ritter, and Tab
Hunter in *Barefoot in the Park*, 1968.
Walter McGinn, Maureen O'Sullivan,
and Chester Morris in *The Subject
Was Roses*, 1966. Barbara Cook in
The Boy Friend, 1966. William
Shatner (left), who appeared in
There's a Girl in My Soup, 1969;
The Tender Trap, 1970; and *Period
of Adjustment*, 1971.

Above: Ann Meara and Jerry Stiller in *LUV*, 1976. Below: Martha Raye and Donald Maryr in *Everybody Loves Opal*, 1965.

Viviane Blaine, Sam Levene and Kay Medford in *Light Up the Sky*, 1975.

Kitty Carlisle on the set of *You Never Know*, 1976, designed by Billy Puzo.

State Theatre of New Jersey

In 1971, a committee appointed by Millburn mayor Ralph Batch passed a resolution that praised Frank Carrington and the late Antoinette Scudder for "their foresight, dedication and perseverance, which culminated in this fine cultural center," and praised the Paper Mill Playhouse for having "gained national recognition in public and theatrical circles…not only providing a location for a cultural center but also preserving for the public benefit an historical site." The resolution was forwarded to Governor William Cahill, and on June 20, 1972, he proclaimed that the Paper Mill Playhouse was the State Theatre of New Jersey.

Governor Cahill (seated) at a Paper Mill reception with (from left) Millburn Mayor Ralph Gero, Mary Tennant, Richard Scudder, John White, and Frank Carrington.

Fire: The End of an Era

It's the death almost of an individual. It has a kind of human feeling about it. It's not just a building that's going down, it's years and years of culture and history.
—Reverend Joseph Herring
Chaplain, Millburn Fire Department

January 14, 1980

In the offices of the Paper Mill Playhouse, the staff was busy making preparations for the upcoming production of *The Winslow Boy*. Upstairs in the gallery, a meeting of the Women's Guild was just breaking up. Most of the construction workers, there to build the new additions to the Playhouse, were taking their lunch break.

At 12:15 p.m., two electricians returning to work discovered a fire growing rapidly in the backstage area of the theatre. Construction foreman Gary Mustachio and several other workers tried to put out the blaze with fire extinguishers, but the flames quickly reached ten to eleven feet. Mustachio ran outside for a hose and dragged it back into the theatre spraying full force. But the water only intensified the smoke, and the hose, used to supply water to a cement mixer, burst. Enveloped in smoke, Mustachio momentarily thought he was trapped, but then spotted the two big yellow doors that led out of the theatre. As he ran outside, he knew they needed professional help. At 12:24 p.m., the Millburn fire department received a desperate call.

Upstairs in the adjoining building that housed the theatre's offices, public relations director Albertina Reilly was told of the problem. By then the fire had reached the old timbers and was crossing the ceiling of the auditorium and into the roof area, which soon collapsed into the auditorium. Afraid of panic, Mrs. Reilly quietly and without explanation asked the ladies of the Women's Guild to put down their tea and sandwiches and evacuate the building. Edith Skiorski, subscription manager, grabbed cash boxes and Playhouse records and made repeated trips rushing documents out of the building until she too was forced to evacuate.

The three-alarm fire brought fire companies from Summit, Springfield, Livingston, Maplewood, West Orange, South Orange, and Union to join the Millburn Fire Department. Engine No. 1 was headed by Ray Lenhart, later to become assistant director of the gallery at the theatre. When they arrived, the area under the stage was completely engulfed with flames. The fire was so strong that suction prevented opening the doors. Firemen on aerial ladders trained their hoses on the central section of the theatre, hoping to contain the fire there, but new areas continued to break out in flames.

The fire spread rapidly, engulfing the theatre. One of the first areas to go was the back of the stage where canvas-covered scenery was stacked. An asbestos curtain lowered between the stage and audience area failed to block the intense blaze. "Crackling flames feeding on the interior of the 1,000-seat theatre and its frame roof converted the building into an inferno…the flames raged through the cockloft over the theatre then leapt at least 30 feet above the top of the building," reported *The Item*, a local newspaper. Black smoke billowing from the roof could be seen and smelled in neighboring towns. Most of the historic building, except for a three-story addition on the north side, was gutted by the fire.

Firefighters from neighboring towns joined local forces to try to save the landmark building.

Some hoses had to stretch hundreds of yards in the desperate effort to rescue Paper Mill.

In the parking lot, a young volunteer fireman offered to move Albertina Reilly's car away from the fire trucks. "I gave him the keys. I thought he was so kind to be of help," she said.

Fire engines and a ladder truck remained at the site until the early hours of the next morning, and bits of flame could still be seen flickering along the roof edge seven hours after the fire began, even after the roof had buckled. Volunteers from the Red Cross remained to dispense sandwiches and coffee to the exhausted firefighters. Five firemen were treated for medical problems, but fortunately they had suffered only minor injuries.

Angelo Del Rossi was in New York at a rehearsal of *The Winslow Boy*, which would first play at the Royal Poinciana Playhouse in Florida. He recalled: *When I left rehearsal, I called the theatre. All the lines were busy. I kept trying and trying and finally called our bank to see if their phones were operating properly. The woman who answered screamed, "Oh, Mr. Del Rossi, the Paper Mill is burning." I don't think I hung up the phone and was soon in my car heading for Millburn. I turned on the radio and heard the announcer say that the famed Paper Mill Playhouse had burned to the ground. I really don't remember the rest of the trip, but just as I got to the theatre, the roof collapsed into the auditorium. There were fire trucks and water and smoke and what appeared to be hundreds of people. CBS put a microphone to my face and asked "What are you going to do now?" I know I didn't hesitate a second before I said, "We are going to rebuild." I've thought about that statement many times and I wonder where it came from. We had paid off our mortgage a few years earlier and on January 11th we had made the last payment on the new building attached to the theatre which was to house rehearsal space and the scene shop. It too was damaged.*

There was much speculation on the cause of the fire—workers' electric lights near combustibles, electrical work itself, work being done on the removal of a wall in the rear of the theatre. The fire

To the eternal dismay of actors, the dressing rooms didn't burn.

ANGELO DEL ROSSI

chief felt that if they had only been called immediately the firemen could have controlled it. In April, a volunteer fireman who had been working as an electrician on the new addition to the Playhouse was indicted by the Essex County Grand Jury for setting the fire, the same young man who had been so helpful to Albertina Reilly.

The police and fire department had apparently suspected arson from the beginning, but had kept the staff in the dark, for all were suspects. Concurrent with the construction activity and fire at the Paper Mill, there had been two suspicious fires at the mall in neighboring Short Hills, New Jersey. The names of all those who were working there were taken and one name came up three times—the same young man who had been working at Paper Mill. When the indictment was announced, executive producer Angelo Del Rossi was at lunch in a New York restaurant, where CBS tracked him down by telephone to ask for a statement. He thought it must be a crank call and checked back with CBS. He was stunned to hear that it was arson. When the arsonist came up for parole (he had been given one year in prison and a $1,000 fine), Del Rossi was asked if he had any objections. Bringing the theatre staff together to discuss the matter produced agreement that parole was acceptable, but with the suggestion that the man should spend three months in the burn unit at a local hospital seeing what terrible injuries he could have inflicted on people.

The theatre, beloved by those who had worked so hard to make the magic within its walls, was gone. In newspapers and on radio and television, the loss of the Paper Mill Playhouse was noted with true sadness. In London, the British Broadcasting Corporation said it was "the loss of one of the finest regional theatres in the United States."

In my deep sense of loss that day I never dreamed that a beautiful restored and vibrant playhouse would arise from the ashes.

MAUREEN OGDEN
Former mayor of Millburn and
New Jersey State Assemblywoman

Rebuilding

Out of disaster and ashes has risen a greater playhouse of which we can be justly proud.
—Floyd Bragg
Chairman of the Board of Trustees 1981–1983

The day after the fire, making sure no embers rekindle the flames.

IT HAS BEEN SAID THAT THEATRE architecture progressed only because all theatres eventually burned to the ground. The very nature of a theatre's structure and contents—the stagehouse literally forming a chimney; canvas; oil paints and turpentine—invited fire, but without those destructive events we might today be watching productions in ancient wooden structures not unlike those of Elizabethan times. The tragedy of the Paper Mill fire proved to be a blessing, presenting the opportunity to build a new facility with state-of-the-art equipment and comfort. The old theatre had run its course and had been badly in need of updating. It would not have been easy to upgrade within the old framework.

After the immediate shock of the loss, Angelo Del Rossi was determined to rebuild. Many did not agree. In fact, some members of the Paper Mill board of directors resigned when he expressed his intention, but there were those who felt as he did and put forth their best talents to make plans, seek money, and raise their phoenix from the ashes.

Del Rossi began the business of trying to figure out what to do first: *It was a tumultuous time: meeting after meeting, discussions with everyone from lawyers and insurance companies to policemen and firemen, all doing their jobs and all trying to determine the cause of the fire. The play we were scheduled to present at the time was currently running in Florida and the production would soon make its way north. At one of these many meetings during the week following the fire, a friend from Florida called to say he had just heard about our disaster. He told me that he had just seen the play that would have been on its way to us, and said that if that play were coming to his theatre, he'd burn it down too. All the tension that had built up in me over the last week was suddenly released in this burst of laughter that shook my whole body. Everyone at the meeting thought that I had "lost it"—and I had.*

There was $1 million paid by insurance covering the fire, but that would hardly be enough to build a new and improved theatre. The cost of rebuilding was estimated at $4.5 million; it totaled $7 million. Assemblywoman Jane Burgio and Assemblyman Walter Kavanaugh arranged for a start-up funding drive by convincing the New Jersey State Council on the Arts to come forward with a grant of $350,000. The National Endowment for the Arts provided a design grant of $20,000, and the New

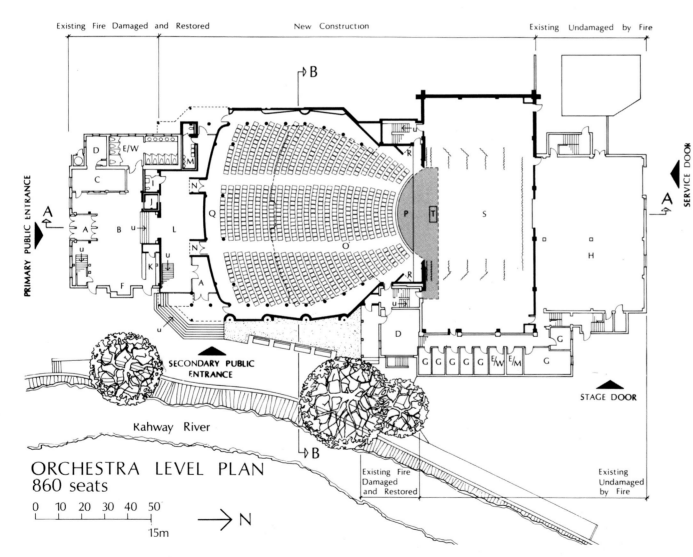

ORCHESTRA LEVEL PLAN
860 seats

Architect Ashok Bhavnani's blueprint for the new theatre incorporated what could be salvaged from the old.

Ashok Bhavnani
Architect

Ashok Bhavnani of the firm Bhavnani and Johanson (now Bhavnani and King) was chosen to design and build the new Paper Mill Playhouse. Bhavnani, from India, has lived in the United States for many years and has practiced his profession entirely in this country.

Bhavnani was selected because of his extensive background in theatre design. He had designed for the Shuberts and for many regional and community theatres and cultural centers across the country, including the McAliff Theatre in Baltimore and the Oklahoma Theatre in Oklahoma City.

In designing the new Paper Mill theatre, he brought with him consultant acoustician Peter George and lighting designer Nananne Porcher of Jean Rosenthal Associates, and her partner, Clyde Nordheimer.

Elevation showing new construction with integrated portions of the old playhouse.

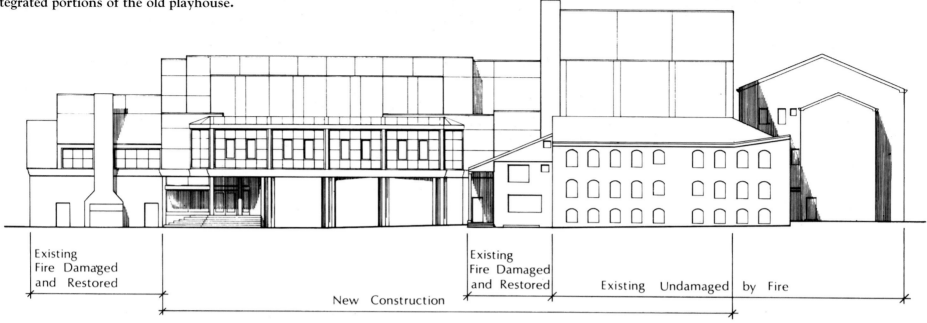

Existing Fire Damaged and Restored

New Construction

Existing Fire Damaged and Restored

Existing Undamaged by Fire

Jersey Economic Development Authority approved a plan enabling the theatre to obtain $2.5 million by issuing bonds with an interest rate of 70 percent of the prime lending rate. The rest would have to come from foundations and from fund-raising events. Local organizations were among the first to help out. In May 1980, the Exchange Club of Westfield held a champagne party to raise money for the Paper Mill's reconstruction. In his opening remarks, the co-chairman of the event, Douglas Schwarz, said, "There isn't one person here tonight who hasn't felt the loss of the Paper Mill." Other local groups followed with contributions.

A national search for an architect for the new building finally chose New York-based Ashok Bhavnani. Robert B. Heintz and his company were the associate architects and did much to assist in meeting the requirements of the local planning board. Heintz had been the designer of the addition to the Playhouse under construction at the time of the fire. He would later build another corner addition to that same section, as well as redesign the carriage house alongside the Paper Mill to form the present-day restaurant. Although the stage and auditorium areas had been gutted by the fire, Bhavnani's first consideration was to salvage the theatre entrance and lobby to retain the feeling of the old theatre. In the exterior, Bhavnani tried to visually accommodate the original entrance by designing the new theatre roof line in progressive rises from the older section. Inside, the restored lobby would be given paneled walls, the fireplace would be retained, and the warmth of the old entrance recreated. Above, a new and much larger gallery was designed for the Playhouse's art exhibitions.

The design for the interior of the theatre allowed for a considerable improvement in size, working

Trustee Ulysse J. Le Grange,
Angelo Del Rossi,
Ann Attridge of the
Schering Foundation, and
Trustee Allen G. Hegarty.

Above: Henry Gadsden, Chairman of
the Board of Trustees 1979–1980, was
the first to champion the rebuilding of
the Paper Mill and organize the effort
to obtain widespread support. Below:
Robert Heintz, Associate Architect.

efficiency, comfort, and attractiveness over the old playhouse. The new stage would be enlarged and would now have a proscenium forty feet wide—almost the width of the old theatre itself. The seating section was to be widened by twenty-five feet on either side and designed in a fan shape, moving the last row of the orchestra forward twenty-five feet closer to the stage and creating good sight lines from all seats. The balcony would extend over only a third of the orchestra, allowing better acoustics, and would be highlighted on both sides by glass-enclosed promenades leading to the art gallery. Both the orchestra and the balcony would be raked to the maximum allowed by the building code, adding improved visibility for all members of the audience. The theatre would now accommodate 1,192 seats.

From left: Angelo Del Rossi, Gov. Brendan Byrne, Eddie Bracken, Peter Shapero, and Floyd Bragg join in the groundbreaking festivities. In the background, Kitty Carlisle Hart and Monsignor Harrold Murray.

The Paper Mill Playhouse billboard announced the countdown on reconstruction. The skeleton Paper Mill staff during rebuilding comprised, left to right: Angelo Del Rossi; Albertina Reilly, Public Relations; Rita Donald, Children's Theatre Coordinator; Christine Agresti, Box Office Treasurer; Jim Thesing, Director of Development; Wade Miller, General Manager.

New seating access would be added for the handicapped, as well as an infrared sound amplification system to accommodate the hearing-impaired. An elevator would be installed and a secondary public entrance added on the river side of the building. Bhavnani increased the size of the orchestra pit to accommodate thirty-six musicians; the old pit had held only sixteen.

Backstage everything would be greatly improved. The stagehouse was now designed to accommodate 100 lines for flying sets and drops. There was to be a stage manager's station, and catwalks leading to areas above the ceiling for sound and lighting control. Lighting designer Nananne Porcher, of Jean Rosenthal Associates, theatre consultants, was brought in, along with Rosenthal partner Clyde Nordheimer, to plan the lighting installations. Peter George was the consultant acoustician.

Among those as determined to rebuild as Angelo Del Rossi was the chairman of the Paper Mill board, Henry Gadsden, who set about organizing the many aspects of the work that needed to be considered. He met daily with Del Rossi to better understand the plan for the new theatre. Board meetings were called and weekly fund-raising strategies were discussed. When all was ready, the intention to rebuild was formally declared to the press. Then, suddenly, Mr. Gadsden passed away. It was a major loss and everything stopped.

But, only for a short time. Trustee Floyd Bragg succeeded as chairman of the board and, together with Harriet Perlmutter, co-chaired the Building Committee, which was given the task of coordinating and raising the $5 million necessary to rebuild the theatre. Board member Ulysse J. LeGrange, new to the area, became a prime fundraiser for the cause. He and Del Rossi visited many of the major companies throughout the state and they became a very successful team. Associate architect Robert Heintz took on the difficult job of accommodating community zoning laws and obtaining appropriate permits.

After all approvals and permits were in order, ground was finally broken in July 1981. In spite of sweltering heat, it was a festive affair with about 150 people in attendance. Mayor Maureen Ogden and actress Kitty Carlisle were among those who spoke at the gathering. Architect Ashok Bhavani displayed his model of the proposed theatre, and actor Eddie Bracken, producer Angelo Del Rossi, and various trustees and staff donned hard hats along with the workers. Many toasts were made. It was a happy moment for everyone who had ever been connected with the Paper Mill Playhouse. Later in the year, on October 5, a major money-raising event was held by the Playhouse. It was legitimately called the Gala Night of Stars, for Ginger Rogers, Ann Miller, Sandy Duncan, Alfred Drake, John Gavin, Jerome Hines, Celeste Holm, Allan Jones, Barbara Meister, Betsy Palmer, Don Stewart, and Richard Thomas—all of whom (with the exception of Alfred Drake) had performed at the old Paper Mill theatre—returned to offer their services in getting funds for the rebuilding.

Early on, Henry Gadsden, who had been past chairman and chief executive officer of Merck and Company, had called in Allen Hegarty, recently retired as director of engineering for that firm. Upon Gadsden's death, Hegarty took over as chairman of the theatre's building committee and went to work organizing the project. On the construction site as the building progressed, he became the clerk-of-the-work.

Actress Kitty Carlisle Hart, a loyal friend to Paper Mill, speaking at the groundbreaking ceremonies.

No one was more diligent or persuasive, and through patience and push, Hegarty kept the job going and brought it in on time.

During the months of construction there were many problems that had to be addressed. The site of the Playhouse is on wetlands, so there were environmental concerns and drainage problems that had to be resolved. Bhavani's original design had included a higher roof, which was not approved by the community Building Department, and as a result acoustical adjustments had to be made. The original plan was to give the theatre natural acoustics but, because of the lower roof, plans were made to allow for enhanced sound. Within two years, the Playhouse would use microphones for all productions.

The work went on until the eleventh hour, but on October 30, 1982, the new Paper Mill Playhouse opened with a gala celebration.

Constructing the larger, greatly improved auditorium was equally as complex as building the new stage.

What a terrible shock it was for all of us when we heard the Paper Mill Playhouse had been burned down. However, when I first saw what an improvement the new theatre was over the old one, I felt that instead of punishing the offender, they should have given him a medal.

JEROME HINES

The new stage offered the best in technical facilities.

The new auditorium.

From ashes, the new Paper Mill Playhouse.

Opening Night Gala

October 30, 1982

The new Paper Mill Playhouse opened with a star-studded gala. Theatregoers arrived for a black-tie dinner and show. Guests convened at a reception, then went to the new theatre to see the American premiere of *Robert and Elizabeth*.

After the show, the festive group walked to a huge heated tent erected on a green near the theatre. Governor and Mrs. Thomas H. Kean were honorary chairpersons of the event and Betsy Palmer was mistress of ceremonies. Mr. and Mrs. Jerome Hines served as advisors to the Gala committee. Three former governors were in attendance, Brendan Byrne, Robert Meyner, and William Cahill. Secretary of State Jane Burgio, Senator John Ewing, Millburn Mayor Earl Cryer, and former Millburn Mayor Maureen Ogden joined in the celebration. There was dancing, and tours of the new theatre. Adding glamour and glitter to the affair were dozens of celebrities, most of whom had appeared in Playhouse productions before the fire.

Robert Johanson, director of the production, and producer Angelo Del Rossi escort the leading lady, Leigh Beery, into the gala reception.

Helen Hayes and her son, James McArthur.

Lillian Gish

Angelo Del Rossi, left, talks with Ginger Rogers, and Joshua Logan.

Most of us...knew that so important a body in New Jersey's cultural universe wouldn't disappear. We set to work to raise the curtain again. [This] will be the beginning of a new chapter in Paper Mill's history. It lights its stage once again.

JOELLA BEINFOHR
Gala Chairwoman

Mr. and Mrs. Robert Horton, Imogene Coca, and King Donovan.

Mistress of Ceremonies Betsy Palmer talks with George Grizzard, left, and Angelo Del Rossi.

Rebirth: The First Season

NOVEMBER 3 - DECEMBER 19, 1982

ROBERT & ELIZABETH
A NEW MUSICAL

PAPER MILL PLAYHOUSE

The stars of *Robert and Elizabeth*—Broadway leading lady Leigh Beery and newcomer Mark Jacoby, who would go on to star in Broadway's *Ragtime*, *Show Boat*, and *Phantom of the Opera*.

Robert Browning's theatre troupe gives him an enthusiastic send-off as he goes to meet Elizabeth Barrett.

ON OCTOBER 30, 1982, THE NEW Paper Mill opened its doors with *Robert and Elizabeth*, a very successful British musical based on *The Barretts of Wimpole Street*. This was its first major production in America, and it was quite a spectacle. Directed and choreographed by Robert Johanson with musical direction and vocal arrangements by Jim Coleman, the fourteen sets were designed by Paul Wonsek and the 226 costumes by Guy Geoly. At the party following the premiere, Helen Hayes exclaimed: "I liked it better than *CATS!*" (the big hit musical that had just opened on Broadway).

The second production in this season of rebirth was an outstanding comedy.

In 1965, I saw You Can't Take It with You *on Broadway with Rosemary Harris and a great company of actors directed by Ellis Rabb. When I was pondering what play should follow* Robert and Elizabeth, *I asked Rabb if he would be interested in directing a new production of* You Can't Take It with You *for Paper Mill. He was. That was the beginning of a wondrous production.*

But who could we get to play Grandpa, the central character in the piece? Thus began the casting game. We tried and tried but were unable to find that one person, the one on whom we could build the whole play. Then the theatre miracle happened. Separately, both Ellis and I thought of Jason Robards. His response was: "I think it's a great idea. Let's do it!" Casting was no longer a problem. Within days, I was getting calls from everyone and soon Jason was joined by Colleen Dewhurst, George Rose, Elizabeth Wilson, Maureen Anderman, Rosetta LeNorie, Alice Drummond, Bill McCutcheon, Nicholas Surovy, and other wonderful actors.

It was just the right play for us to do. It was a very big hit and audiences came from everywhere to see it. We moved the production to the Kennedy Center and then to Broadway, where it had a very successful run, and was later taped and aired on PBS.—Angelo Del Rossi

You Can't Take It with You.
From left: Jason Robards,
George Rose, Colleen Dewhurst,
Elizabeth Wilson.

The cast of *You Can't Take It with You*. The Paper Mill production of this classic American comedy went on to the Kennedy Center in Washington, D.C., and to a run on Broadway, and then was videotaped for *Broadway on Showtime*.

You Can't Take It with You. **Above:** Jason Robards backstage with Ann Kaufman (left) and Kitty Carlisle Hart, widows of the playwrights.

Above: Shaun Cassidy (left) and Milo O'Shea in *Mass Appeal.*
Below: Barry Nelson, Elaine Stritch, and Gwyda Don Howe in *Suite in Two Keys.*

The third show, *Suite in Two Keys,* was by Noel Coward in a favorite style, combining various sketches under one banner. Its two parts were *Come into the Garden, Maud,* and *A Song at Twilight.*

Next was *Mass Appeal.* During its run, New Jersey suffered a major blizzard that reduced the Paper Mill audience to a few stalwart theatregoers. The storm conditions also reduced the cast by fifty percent. For a cast of two, that presented serious problems. Shaun Cassidy, undaunted by being the only performer, gave his small audience an evening to remember by singing, dancing, and storytelling. It wasn't the show they had come to see but it proved to be a very personal theatre experience.

Following this production, Paper Mill completed its first "new" season with *The New Moon,* and *Man of La Mancha,* with Jerome Hines in his great portrayal of Don Quixote.

Robert Johanson

Robert Johanson became artistic director of the Paper Mill in 1984. Prior to the fire, he had directed three very successful musicals at the theatre: *Shenandoah*, The *Sound of Music* and *The Student Prince,* and had reopened the new Playhouse with *Robert and Elizabeth.* Angelo Del Rossi recognized that: "Here was a talent with the vision that our new theatre needed—a creative energy to develop new works and produce established theatre pieces with invention." Under Johanson's leadership, *Show Boat* and *Crazy for You* would be televised nationally on PBS; new versions of classic operettas would transfer to the New York City Opera and also be televised. *The Wizard of Oz* would transfer as an annual event to the Theatre at Madison Square Garden. Many new works would be developed and produced, and musicals that had languished and practically disappeared would be brought successfully back to life, most notably *Follies, Mack and Mabel, Fanny,* and *Children of Eden.*

Describing his life, Johanson says: *I grew up outside Wilmington, Delaware, where I was writing, directing and starring in my own productions from sixth grade on! Some teacher actually let me get 35 kids out of class to rehearse such epics as* The Dupont Story *and we would put them on for the whole school. I had a Cecil B. DeMille complex even then.*

After graduating with a fine arts degree from Ithaca College, I moved to New York and ten days later was cast in the new Broadway musical Shenandoah. *I performed seven different roles for over 1,000 performances, leaving the show every summer to go to Maine to do Shakespearean rep—playing Romeo, Prince Hal, Ariel, Lear's Fool—and directing Moliere. Then I was asked to direct* Shenandoah *for a summer tour. This brought me to the Cape Playhouse, where Angelo Del Rossi produced in the summertime. The show was a success and he asked me to remount the production at Paper Mill; the rest, as they say, is history. During those dark years when the theatre had burned down, I worked at the St. Louis MUNY Opera, which seated 12,000 people and featured massive casts and scenery; directed* Canterbury Tales, *which moved to Broadway; artistic-directed the Next Move Theatre in Boston, doing such plays as* Under Milkwood *and* The Miser, *and brought many productions to theatres all over the country. By the time Paper Mill was ready to reopen, I had directed almost every major musical somewhere, experienced the classics, kept up my acting and singing, and worked with a lot of amazingly talented people. It was as though I was always—all my life—in training for this huge responsibility of artistic director at Paper Mill.*

People ask, "What does an artistic director do?" What doesn't he do! You are responsible for every last detail that goes on stage, from choosing the play and the creative team to selecting every actor, every costume, every prop, the poster design, rewrites, kids, animals—everything. It's on your head. The most important thing is to select a great group of people who can help you do all these things. We've had truly gifted collaborative artists at the Playhouse who have made it possible to produce six shows each year on the Paper Mill scale, as well as all the special programs that make up the activities of the year. This teamwork makes what we do possible.

Robert Johanson with Elizabeth Roby (left) as the adult Jane Eyre, and Blythe Ausfant who played Jane as a girl.

The New Jersey Ballet

An additional highlight of the first season was the return of the New Jersey Ballet, joined by the New Jersey Symphony, to its "home" at Paper Mill on December 22, 1980. The ballet's production of *Nutcracker* is an annual year-end event at the Playhouse. Under artistic and executive director Carolyn Clark and artistic advisor Edward Villella, the company also performs spring and summer programs. It has presented such ballets as *Who Cares?* and *Stars and Stripes Pas de Deux* by George Balanchine, *Rodeo or The Courting at Burnt Ranch* by Agnes de Mille, and *Death and the Maiden* by Robert North.

Edward Villella and premiere danseuses.

Pas de deux in the Dance of the Sugar Plum Fairy.

The Chinese Dance

Broadway in the '80s

A season at Paper Mill can be compared to walking down a theatre street near Broadway, seeing the marquees announcing a new musical, a drama, a revival, and a comedy—a variety of theatre experiences for the audience and challenging opportunities for the playhouse.

ANGELO DEL ROSSI

When the Paper Mill Playhouse reopened in 1982, Broadway was in a creative slump. Unlike the 1930s, when even the Great Depression and the resulting lack of financing couldn't keep creative talent from having its moment before the footlights, the Broadway theatre was largely dull and listless. Plays were almost nonexistent, and revival after revival of once-great musicals was lackluster. Sandy Duncan and George Rose, two of Paper Mill's favorite performers, were an exception in the successful *Peter Pan* on Broadway, which had opened in September 1979 and ran longer than the original production. The Jerome Robbins-directed *West Side Story* (1980) was highly praised, as was the limited run of *Camelot* (1980) with Richard Burton.

For most of the 1980s Broadway was awash with British imports, primarily the work of Andrew Lloyd Webber. *Cats* opened in 1982 with Betty Buckley (who would awe Paper Mill audiences in its 1998 production of *Gypsy*) playing Grizabella. Later from Webber would come *Song & Dance*, *Starlight Express*, and *The Phantom of the Opera*. Two other imports, *Les Miserables* and *Me and My Girl*, were successes. *Cats*, *Phantom*, and *Les Miserables* are still drawing crowds today.

The American musical had no intention of dying, however. *Sugar Babies*, which had opened in 1979, starred an unbeatable duo, Mickey Rooney and Ann Miller. Its burlesque quality proved to be a sen-

sation. *Dreamgirls*, stunningly staged by director-choreographer Michael Bennett, opened in 1981 and ran for four years. *Barnum* (1980), with its circus setting and an outstanding performance by Jim Dale, did well, as did *Woman of the Year* (1981) starring Lauren Bacall, and *A Day in Hollywood/A Night in the Ukraine* (1980) guided by Tommy Tune, with additional music by Jerry Herman. *42nd Street*, based on the 1933 movie, was 1980's biggest hit and drew more than one tear from its opening-night audience when producer David Merrick announced that its director-choreographer, Gower Champion, had died earlier that day. These few successes, however, had been costly. The economics of the theatre were staggering and producers were having a difficult time of it.

Broadway's doldrums only raised spirits at the Paper Mill Playhouse, where revivals became new extravaganzas: *Annie*, *Fiddler on the Roof*, *Guys and Dolls*, *Evita*, *Damn Yankees*, *Barnum*, *Jesus Christ Superstar*, and *La Cage Aux Folles* were among Paper Mill's hits during the 1980s. And Broadway came to the Playhouse—to star in its productions and to lend other talents. The legendary George Abbott came to direct *Damn Yankees*, and choreographers, composers, lighting designers, and stage managers all found that life in the theatre could be just as fulfilling in Millburn, New Jersey, as on the Great White Way. After all, the Paper Mill Playhouse was truly "only forty-five minutes from Broadway."

Paper Mill in the '80s and Beyond

The first season in the new Paper Mill Playhouse was both memorable and significant. It established without a doubt that although the fire had destroyed a theatre building, it had not destroyed a theatrical company. The new productions were not just equal to the best of the past—they were better. That first season also indicated many of the directions in which Paper Mill would continue to grow, and confirmed the excellence of the people who would lead it in those directions.

With a new stage, a large and comfortable theatre, and state of the art sound and lighting equipment, Paper Mill was prepared to lead regional theatre into a new century. Broadway cast a shadow toward Millburn, but again and again the artistic staff at Paper Mill would creatively reshape traditional musicals in productions that equaled or outshone the originals. Operettas, classic revivals, comedies, and farces also were staged with the same kind of theatrical skill and imagination.

Angelo Del Rossi already had become a familiar and respected leader in the theatre community. He continued to capture the attention of leading theatre luminaries such as George Abbott, Stephen Sondheim, Maury Yeston, and Jerry Herman, who willingly turned to Paper Mill to introduce new work or bring new life to their previous successes. Young actors and actresses would find their way to Paper Mill on their way to stardom on the national stage, and dozens of established stars would return with delight to appear in Paper Mill productions time and again. Robert Johanson became increasingly the essential center of Paper Mill's creative excellence as he created new works, revisited the old, and adapted classic literature for the stage.

In the three decades following this pivotal first season, the reborn Paper Mill Playhouse would wrestle with the economies of theatre and with its obligations to a continually changing audience. The staff would become ever more engaged in outreach initiatives that offered the magic of the stage to broader communities. Paper Mill's not-for-profit status would continue to keep ticket prices at a level that was affordable to audiences across a wide economic range. The challenge of meeting production costs became increasingly difficult, but a loyal following of subscribers continued to offer support and to participate in experimenting with the new age of American theatre. Throughout these years of continued growth and development, the Paper Mill production team staged the theatrical spectaculars represented in the pages ahead.

I still remember the excitement. I was ten years old, and I was going to a show for the first time. The Paper Mill was doing another production of *The Desert Song*.

Just as vividly, I remember the fire—the tragedy followed by triumph as determined supporters rebuilt the old house better than before.

I was delighted to increase funding as governor and see in response Paper Mill develop into the finest subscription theatre in the country. I remember the excitement of *Show Boat* as it was taped for national television on the Great Performances series.

Paper Mill Playhouse and New Jersey are truly perfect together.

THOMAS H. KEAN
Former Governor of New Jersey

The Later Operettas

PAPER MILL PLAYHOUSE HAD PUT ITSELF on the musical map by presenting lavish operettas in the early days of its history. After the fire a whole new audience discovered this unique genre in Paper Mill's reinterpretations of the old favorites. Robert Johanson explains:

My first exposure to staging operetta came with The Student Prince. *I didn't know anything about operettas except for some of the old tunes. Boy, was I in for a surprise. First, the veteran cast taught me so much. Allan Jones, the dashing Ravenal in the 1936 film of* Show Boat, *played Doctor Engel, who sings the nostalgic "Golden Days." The song recalls the days of student life, which an older teacher reminds the young Prince to cherish. When Allan sang the song, it was a reminder to all of us of the golden days of beautiful romantic theatre music long forgotten in the wake of rock musicals and the last days of disco. There wasn't a dry eye in the house.*

Another revelation was Judith McCauley. Operetta heroines are very difficult to portray believably. They can be campy, silly, and obnoxious, but Judy has a gift for making them real, sweet, and truly admirable. She is such a lovely person, that when the male chorus serenades the leading lady, there is no question of their true affection for her. I've worked with Judy more than any other actress and I've seen her magic inspire cast after cast. This love for her is directly communicated across the footlights and has brought great heart to all the productions she has starred in.

The wonderful thing about operettas is their true theatricality. They are meant to be experienced in a theatre—live—with spectacular scenery and costumes and large robust choruses thrilling us with the glory of their sound. The plots are usually a bit ridiculous, but if they're played sincerely and sung beautifully, they are a great escape. Also, it doesn't hurt if they have sex appeal. This was our great discovery in the "new" Paper Mill.

Left: Allan Jones, Judith McCauley, Harry Danner in *The Student Prince*.

Allan gave the cast a scare at one performance. He made his first entrance, received warm entrance applause, and abruptly left the stage. The surprised actors made up dialogue and covered till he came back on about a minute later and continued. He had forgotten to put in his teeth!

Below: Judith with cadets.

The most stunning operetta score belongs to Romberg's *The New Moon* (opposite page)—a swashbuckling adventure on the high seas. This show brought Judith McCauley together for the first time with the young and dashing baritone Richard White. From their first performance together the sparks began to fly. The sex appeal of this duo was undeniable.

Richard would carry Judy off into the sunset at the end of each performance. A patron going up the aisle after the curtain call was heard to say, "Oh, if only I could get my husband to do that!" They went on to ignite the stage in *Desert Song*, *Show Boat*, and *Carousel*, and returned separately in many other musicals.

The New Moon

The New Moon had two unforgettable solos for Judith McCauley: the dramatic "Lover Come Back to Me" and the glorious "One Kiss."

Battle aboard *The New Moon*. The show boasted baritone Richard White, with Norman A. Large (swinging on the rigging) as the tenor, Philippe, who sings "Softly as in a Morning Sunrise." The leading men dueled with swords as well as high notes! And they led the male chorus in "Stouthearted Men," shaking the rafters and meriting two encores. Inset: Christopher Hewett and Larry Grey as the comic villains.

Michael Anania
Resident Scenic Designer

The first show Michael Anania designed at Paper Mill was the spectacular *Desert Song,* with its rocky canyons, grand palazzos, mysterious harem and, of course, the desert. He was asked back the next season to design three shows: *Guys and Dolls, Inherit the Wind,* and *Show Boat.* His creativity, attention to detail, and great versatility were just what the Paper Mill needed and he was invited to be Resident Scenic Designer—a position he has filled ever since. He has designed over 65 productions himself and overseen all the others, as well as all of Paper Mill's special events.

Anania graduated from Boston University in 1973 and freelanced as a designer while teaching at Emerson College and also serving as resident designer for the Lake George Opera Festival. He first worked with Robert Johanson on the 1980 Broadway transfer of *Canterbury Tales* from Equity Library Theatre, and they did many other productions together before he joined Paper Mill, where his work has been greatly praised.

Anania's scene designs have been seen on the many televised Paper Mill–New York City Opera productions, and in a great number of other productions: Broadway's *A Change in the Heir, Run for Your Wife,* and *The View from Here;* Off-Broadway's *Back to the Boulevard* with Liliane Montevecchi, directed by Tommy Tune; the New York City Center Theatre opera version of *Desire Under the Elms; Leader of the Pack* at the Bottom Line; the New York City Opera's *La Boheme, Wonderful Town, Most Happy Fella, 110 in the Shade, A Little Night Music,* and *Pajama Game;* and in Central City Opera presentations for ten years.

Michael Anania's rendering for the palazzo in *Desert Song* (above), and the actual set (right). This, his first design assignment at Paper Mill, was the beginning of a long association.

As for Michael Anania's sets, perhaps we at the *Star-Ledger* should just put in permanent type "Michael Anania has done a magnificent job, employing taste and style," and just pull it out every time this wizard designs a show.

PETER FILICHIA
Newark Star Ledger

Michael Anania's set for *Windy City*, a musical based on *The Front Page*, was part of the American Exhibit that won the Gold Cup, the highest honor awarded, at the Prague Quadrennial, an exhibition of the international theatre community's latest work in scenic design.

VICTOR HERBERT'S
NAUGHTY MARIETTA
April 1–May 10, 1987

THE STATE THEATRE OF NEW JERSEY
PAPER MILL PLAYHOUSE

Victor Herbert's exuberant *Naughty Marietta* received a major overhaul in the 1987 production. Allan Jones (right) was featured as a puppeteer who takes in a runaway, Marietta (Marianne Telese), and disguises her as a life-size marionette. A beautiful old-world puppet show was created for the interpolated "Isle of Romance," and Allan's rendition of the added "Toyland" was beautifully heartbreaking. It was the last song he would ever sing on the Paper Mill stage.

The Italian Street Song

Naughty Marietta, Grand Finale—"Ah, Sweet Mystery of Life"

Candide

Candide, Leonard Bernstein's brilliant modern-day operetta, took the audience around the world. It featured Robert Johanson as Candide and the star of the Broadway revival, Maureen Brennan, as Cunegonde.

Patrick Quinn as the very vain Maximilian.

Sal Mistretta, right, as Voltaire with a disguised Patrick Quinn.

Maureen Brennan yearns to "Glitter and Be Gay."

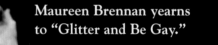

Jack Harold

Robert Johanson as
Candide and Maureen
Brennan as Cunegonde.

This production of *Candide* brought
Paper Mill to the attention of the
National Endowment for the Arts. When the
Endowment evaluated all the theatres
across the country that presented operas
and musicals and rated them for artistic
excellence, Paper Mill was ranked second
in the nation, surpassed only by the
Metropolitan Opera in New York City. This
high ranking secured funding for the
theatre for the next several years.

April 3 — May 12, 1991

THE STATE THEATRE OF NEW JERSEY
PAPER MILL PLAYHOUSE

The 1991 mounting of Franz Lehar's *The Merry Widow* was the eighth and most successful production of this operetta at Paper Mill. *The Merry Widow* is unique in that each act takes place at a different party. It was essential that each party outdo the one that preceded it, which provided a great challenge for director Robert Johanson and choreographer Sharon Halley, and especially for the designers: Michael Anania, sets; Gregg Barnes, costumes; and Mark Stanley, lights. This was quite costly and the theatre was aided by the generosity of the Howard Gilman Foundation, which provided funding for all the new costumes. This venture with Paper Mill was the first in what has become a long and wonderful association. Thanks to Mr. Gilman, as the curtain rose on each act there was an audible gasp from the audience.

ACT ONE—The Marsovian Embassy Ball. Black, white, and gold—majestic and handsome, based on Viennese and Hungarian palaces. All the men want to marry the wealthy and very eligible widow, played by Judy Kaye.

ACT TWO—A garden party at the widow's French villa. The colors and paintings of Monet were the inspiration for this set and costumes.

Judy Kaye was a magnificent Merry Widow. Her "Vilia" will long be remembered, as well as her high kicks as she joined the line of can-can dancers (with two encores). Not many operatic divas can do that!

ACT THREE—The lavish art nouveau Maxim's. restaurant. No red had been seen in the show until now. The effect was stunning.

Merry Widow: Much ado about a fan!

The young suitor Camille de Rosillion (Mark Janicello) writes "I love you" on the fan belonging to Baroness Zeta (Halley Neale).

The fan keeps turning up in the most unlikely places.

The dashing Count Danilo (Richard White, center) with Baron Zeta (Merwyn Goldsmith) and Njegus (Peter Bartlett).

The Paper Mill operettas became so successful, they caught the eye of Beverly Sills, who took three of them to the New York City Opera, where they played many seasons. *The New Moon* was televised on PBS Great Performances, and *The Merry Widow* on PBS Live from Lincoln Center.

Beverly Sills with Angelo Del Rossi (left), Robert Johanson (second from right), and Musical Director Jim Coleman.

Gregg Barnes
Resident Costume Designer, 1991–1998

Gregg Barnes first came to Paper Mill to design the revival of *Fanny*. He had worked with Michael Anania on the opera version of *Desire Under the Elms* at New York's City Center. His work earned an invitation to do some Paper Mill productions. His second project at the Playhouse was *The Merry Widow*—a lavish rethinking of the perennial favorite. All the costumes were designed and built from scratch, a major undertaking. After that great success, Barnes became the resident costume designer and designed over 45 shows. His work has graced many theatres and productions, including The Arena Stage, The Old Globe, The McCarter Theatre, Syracuse Stage, Berkshire Music Festival, Walnut Street Theatre, ESIPA Albany, *Side Show* on Broadway, the Radio City Music Hall Christmas Spectacular, the *Kathy and Mo Show, Suds, Pageant,* and New York City Opera's *Cinderella*. Gregg Barnes also teaches costume design at New York University's Tisch School of the Arts. He is the recipient of the prestigious Irene Shariff Award recognizing his entire body of work, including the Paper Mill productions.

Above: Costume for the Merry Widow's first entrance. Left: Ball gown design. Right: Count Danilo's costume.

Costumes at Paper Mill

Prior to Gregg Barnes becoming the resident designer, costumes for many large musicals were rented from the Eaves Costume Company. Eaves was the largest rental house in the New York area, having absorbed the stock of Brooks Van Horn, its competition for many years. The company was run by the Geoly brothers, Guy and Danny. Guy Geoly coordinated many shows for Paper Mill. He chose the best costumes from their elaborate stock, and beautifully designed additional pieces as needed. Some of Geoly's most successful shows were *Candide, The New Moon, Carousel,* and *Desert Song*. However, eventually the Eaves Company was sold to another organization and became private stock. A resident designer became imperative, and Gregg Barnes fit the bill.

Not all shows can be dressed in new clothes—costumes are very expensive to create. But Barnes had dealt with many costume warehouses, from the Old Globe and Warner Brothers to Malabar in Canada, the Washington Opera, the Arena Stage, and Goodspeed Opera House. Drawing on such sources, often costumes came from all over the country to join Barnes' original designs in fulfilling the requirements of a particular show.

Folk dancers in *The Merry Widow.*

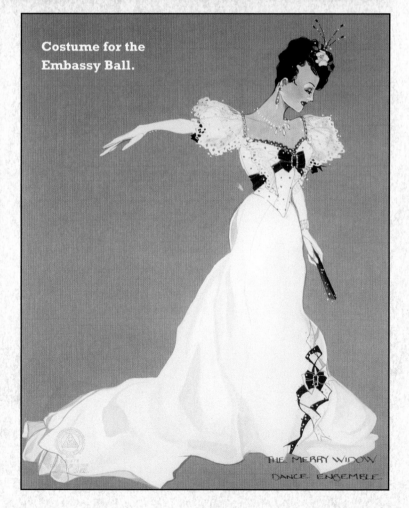

Howard Gilman was a man who had a great impact on the world of art, theatre, dance, and the environment. He became a dear friend to the Paper Mill after seeing *Jesus Christ Superstar,* and provided the funding for the spectacular costumes for *The Merry Widow*. His support, given every season until his death in 1998, is continued by the Howard Gilman Foundation under the guidance of Natalie Moody.

Howard Gilman will always be remembered as the principal angel for several Paper Mill productions:

> *The Merry Widow,* 1991
> *Camelot,* 1991
> *Great Expectations,* 1992
> *Chess,* 1992
> *Phantom,* 1993
> *A Tale of Two Cities,* 1994
> *Peter Pan,* 1994
> *The Prisoner of Zenda,* 1995
> *Comfortable Shoes,* 1996
> *Jane Eyre,* 1997
> *Children of Eden,* 1997
> *Wuthering Heights,* 1999

Costume for the Embassy Ball.

Romantic Musical Revivals

I define the word "revival" to mean
"breathe new life into," as opposed to "resuscitate."
Whether it is a complete reconceptualization
or an inspired casting choice,
there is always a way to find new life
in classic musicals. I also believe, however,
we must honor the author's intent and vision,
and strive to enhance and enlighten that work.
—Robert Johanson

My Fair Lady

LONG BEFORE BROADWAY HAD discovered the revival craze to the point of creating special Tony award categories for them, Paper Mill Playhouse had been mounting sumptuous and thoughtful productions of some of Broadway's greatest and not so great efforts. Almost every production was newly designed and created for the Paper Mill stage. Only occasionally, in the interest of finances, were sets and costumes rented once the new theatre was in operation.

Some of the greatest and most beloved musicals ever created came from the pens of the men who defined the modern American musical theatre: Richard Rodgers, Oscar Hammerstein, Alan Jay Lerner, and Frederick Loewe. There have been multiple productions of their most famous shows, and the 1980s and '90s saw many excellent revivals.

My Fair Lady. Below Judy Blazer played Eliza and Simon Jones was Professor Henry Higgins. Above: George S. Irving as Alfred P. Doolittle, Eliza's father. Opposite page: Professor Higgins' and Colonel Pickering's (Tom Toner) first encounter with Eliza, in Covent Garden. Inset: The transformed Eliza.

One of the remarkable moments in Larry Carpenter's production of My Fair Lady occurs in the scene where Eliza, having left Higgins's house in a rage (I'm assuming, of course, that you know the basic plot), has wandered back to Covent Garden where she and the story started.

Because she is so elegantly dressed and because she speaks so well, none of the people with whom she was intimate only six months earlier recognize her. They are all a little intimidated by her.

…The scene in Covent Garden (which ends with Eliza's father singing "Get Me to the Church on Time") is one that Alan Jay Lerner added to George Bernard Shaw's "Pygmalion," and it shows how sensitively he was attuned to the original play. I have never seen it acted as poignantly as it is by Judy Blazer, who is a heavenly Eliza, singing and acting the role radiantly.
—Howard Kissel

Even though *My Fair Lady* boasts a very large cast, quite often the brief cameo appearance of the Queen of Transylvania at the end of Act I is played by a made-up chorus girl. Director Robert Johanson said, "We need an extra here—someone regal and mature like our head usher Connie—hey! Why not get Connie?"

In the "old house" I had ushered, worked in the box office, and was an occasional wardrobe extra. Returning to Paper Mill Playhouse in 1983, I was shortly thereafter made Head Usher. One evening, I was summoned out of the theatre to see Roy Miller. As I stepped into the lobby, I couldn't imagine what kind of problem I might be facing.

The "problem" was a proposition. Would I be willing to play the part of the Queen of Transylvania in My Fair Lady? Would I! The next thing I knew I was standing at the top of a grand staircase surveying my guests for the Act I finale.

In a gorgeous purple gown that hugged my ankles and a train that loved to tangle around my four-inch heels, I was convinced that the "Queen" would tumble down the staircase instead of descending with head held high. I am relieved to report that I made it safely through all performances, stopping at the bottom to lift the chin of Judy Blazer, as Eliza, then once again ascending those dreaded steps. It was a favorite time for me.

—Connie Pearson

Carousel

Judith McCauley and Richard White gave perhaps their finest performances at Paper Mill, as Julie Jordan and Billy Bigelow in Rodgers and Hammerstein's *Carousel*. With wonderful effectiveness Judy conveyed a character of heartbreaking simplicity whose still waters nevertheless ran very deep. Richard and his wife, Sharon Halley, the choreographer for the show, had just given birth to their first child, Amanda. When he sang the famous soliloquy in which Billy imagines what it will be like to be a father, his tenderness when he reached the part about "my little girl" was immensely moving. Audiences love a good cry in the theatre; this was a four-hanky moment.

Camelot

The Paper Mill production of Lerner and
Loewe's *Camelot* is beyond superb, perhaps
the finest musical we have ever seen in that
house of a thousand hits, brilliantly cast and
played, incredibly mounted and costumed.
Just an extraordinary evening in the theatre.

JERRY KRUPNICK
Newark Star-Ledger

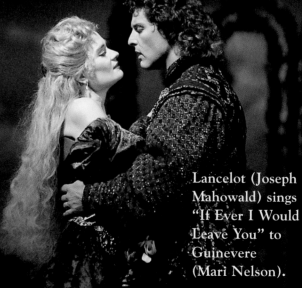

Lancelot (Joseph
Mahowald) sings
"If Ever I Would
Leave You" to
Guinevere
(Mari Nelson).

Gregg Barnes' costume design for Guinevere.

Above: Guinevere and King Arthur (James Brennan) face their destiny in Camelot. Left: Merlin (Larry Grey) is called away by Nimue (Julietta Marcelli).

James Brennan made such a hit in *Me and My Girl*, especially in the scene where he dons a king's robe and crown, that Paper Mill decided to ask him back the next year to play a real king—King Arthur. The director had always wanted to see Arthur played by someone sprightly and comic—a boy asked to assume a man's job—and, of course, touch your heart in the process. He gave a great performance.

Oklahoma!

Joan Mirabella and Marty McDonough dance the Dream Ballet.

Jamie Rocco, director:

At Paper Mill, I had the opportunity to direct a top-notch revival of Oklahoma. It was the first production to celebrate the fiftieth anniversary of Oklahoma's premiere. This was particularly exciting for me because I believe that Oscar Hammerstein is the father of musical theatre. His effortless blending of dialogue and lyrics created the blueprint for all musicals that followed. He knew how to talk to the heart of an audience and created many of the world's most beloved and emotional musical theatre pieces.

In Oklahoma!, I had always been disturbed by Laurey's snap decision to choose Jud over Curly as her date for the "box social." As I studied the play, it became evident that Laurey is truly and dangerously attracted to Jud. For the drama to work, I felt Jud had to present a real threat to Laurey's relationship to Curly. The audi-ence had to find this attraction potent and believable—thus, the casting of Robert Cucciolli as Jud against Richard White's Curly. As Curly, Richard represented an American ideal, the cowboy, tall, lanky and classically handsome, while Robert made Jud a brooding anti-hero, an outsider, dark and wildly physical.

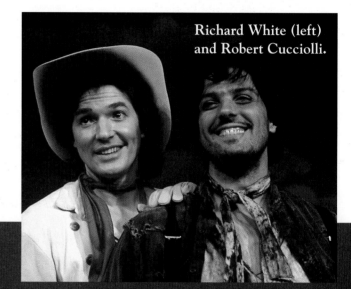

Richard White (left) and Robert Cucciolli.

Sharon Halley, choreographer for Oklahoma!

Choreography is much like any other art. I try to tell a story, set a mood, describe a feeling, and create an emotional response in the audience. The medium I choose to use is bodies in space—jumping, twisting, leaping, and spinning. Choreography to me is art in continuous motion.

At an intermission of Oklahoma!, a patron in the Paper Mill audience saw me and recognized me as the choreographer of the production. He had just seen the fifteen-minute ballet that ends the first act. His eyes were sparkling and he said, "Your ballet was just beautiful. I loved watching it. It was as if I were watching poetry, poetry in motion. Thank you." That was the best compliment I have ever received. I had done my job. I had entertained someone. I will remember that moment forever.

The Dream Ballet becomes a nightmare for Laurey.

Brigadoon

Tommy (Joseph Mahowald) and Fiona (Lee Merrill), the lovers in the tale of the village that appears from the mists every 100 years.

LERNER & LOEWE'S
BRIGADOON

Book and Lyrics by
ALAN JAY LERNER
Music by
FREDERICK LOEWE
The Romantic Musical Classic set in the Scottish Highlands
April 5 - May 28, 1995
Tickets on Sale Now!

THE STATE THEATRE OF NEW JERSEY
PAPER MILL PLAYHOUSE

NEW JERSEY STATE COUNCIL ON THE ARTS/DEPT. OF STATE.
THE NATIONAL ENDOWMENT FOR THE ARTS

The Paper Mill Playhouse is an extraordinary institution. Dangerously close, as the crow flies, to Broadway itself, it stages Broadway-style shows—usually actual Broadway revivals—but with a difference. A large house with a vast stage, Paper Mill, under its producer Angelo Del Rossi and artistic director Robert Johanson, often quite closely rivals the opulence of a Broadway production. But, sensibly, it never tries to stage a facsimile of the original, preferring to go largely its own way with the existing material.

CLIVE BARNES

South Pacific is sometimes thought to be unrevivable because it is not presently considered politically correct. However, the patriotism and racial prejudice depicted in the show are very accurate for their time. I felt it was crucial to place the audience firmly in the 1940s and the mindset of Americans stationed abroad. This production began with the island visible as the audience arrived. Planes occasionally flew over and a tropical breeze blew the American flag, which was waving stage center. A military drill was heard and the full company assembled for the sunset lowering of the flag. The pride in our nation's flag, the ideals and innocence, were palpable. The cast sang the "Star Spangled Banner" and, of course, the audience rose to its feet. It's very interesting to get a standing ovation at the beginning of a show. As the anthem concluded, the first strains of the overture were heard and South Pacific began. —Robert Johanson

Above: The sunset flag ceremony. Inset: Ron Raines as Emile le Becque. Left: Bloody Mary (Tina Fabrique) berates Cable (Mark McVey) as he consoles Liat (Marilyn Villamar).

Top left: Ngana (Samantha Robyn Lee) and Jerome (Jeffrey Songo).
Above: Nellie Forbush (Marguerite MacIntyre) washes that man right out of her hair. Far left: Tina Fabrique as the outrageous Bloody Mary. Left: "Honeybun" (Gary Marachek) and Nellie.

Gigi

Gigi was the only musical from the great composers Lerner and Loewe produced at Paper Mill that had not actually been a success on Broadway. Of course, it was originally an Academy Award-winning film, but it didn't all come together in the much later Broadway production. Paper Mill was determined to bring this great story and score to a more successful conclusion and the result was quite rewarding.

The first image was a phenomenal solo violinist, Jonathan Dinklage, playing a lush cadenza into the opening strains of one of Frederick Loewe's most beautiful melodies—"Gigi."

Gavin McLeod thanks heaven for little girls.

The key to a successful production of *Gigi* is having the right young lady to transform from a gawky teenager to a stunning beauty. Glory Crampton made the transformation exquisitely.

Left and above: Gigi's finale gown.

Glory Crampton, Anne Rogers, and Richard White celebrate "the night they invented champagne."

A persuasive case could be made that right now the best Broadway musical is not on Broadway. Heck, it's not even in New York. It's in New Jersey. The Paper Mill Playhouse specializes in Broadway-style revivals, normally of a winningly high standard. But, this time it has ebulliently excelled itself with a stunning staging of Lerner and Loewe's delicious musical *Gigi* which is far superior to any earlier Broadway manifestation.

CLIVE BARNES

Liliane Montevecchi lent her truly Gallic charms to the role of Aunt Alicia.

Gavin (Richard White) realizes that Liane (Mia Prince) is not "Thinking of Him."

Gavin McLeod and Anne Rogers "remember it well."

Paper Mill Recycles

Not every show requires multiple scenic and costume displays, but when Paper Mill produces one that does, it does so in the spirit in which the show was created, and has become a theatre well known for satisfying that requirement. One reason it is possible to mount such spectacular productions for a fraction of the cost of a similarly lavish Broadway show is that Paper Mill recycles.

The theatre builds almost all its scenery in its own shop in Raritan, New Jersey, and has a twelve-year reserve of scenery stored in its warehouse and in 134 semi-trailers. Recycling is also applied to costumes in Paper Mill's own stock, and those rented or donated from other costume shops around the country. Thanks to the talent and ingenuity of set designer Michael Anania and costume designer Gregg Barnes and their artisans, Paper Mill Playhouse has been able to repaint, reassemble, and restitch many set and costume components into beautiful new creations for a multitude of productions. In *Gigi*, for example, scenic

elements were pulled from twenty-one previous Paper Mill productions, and costumes from six regional houses, several New York City shops, as well as Paper Mill's own stock. So Natchez, Mississippi, and the Land of Oz became the Champs Elysées.

In addition to recycling, out and out trading has proved very effective as well. When New York City Opera expressed interest in presenting Paper Mill's *Merry Widow,* an ingenious business plan was worked out. Michael Anania's set was traded for the Opera's set and costumes for *Brigadoon,* designed by Desmond Heeley. Everyone was happy.

Sharon Halley's choreography evoked the style of the famous Belle Epoque novelty dancer Loie Fuller, who actually patented her lighting and costumes.

The role of Loie Fuller was performed by Andie Mellom.

Collaboration is a very important part of a successful musical. The relationship between the director and the choreographer is very important. They must understand one another's views of the show. They must agree on a point of view and how to achieve it. They must agree on the style and be capable of expressing that style. And last but not least, they must agree on a way in which to work together, making mutual accommodations for rehearsal space, schedule, and a great deal more. If these things do not happen the company can become confused and very unhappy. It usually makes for a very unpleasant working situation and a mediocre show.

At Paper Mill I have had the pleasure of working with a longtime friend and associate for over twenty years, Robert Johanson. Because of our long association through many shows and theaters, we have a working relationship that helps to surmount almost any problem. We also have a trust in each other's talent and eye. Gigi is a perfect example of our collaboration. Robert discusses the feel and the look he is going for. He gives me the music he has been listening to and then lets me alone to create. We often don't see each other during a rehearsal day until the end, when we check to see where we are. When a number is done I ask him to watch. Hopefully he is never too surprised at what he sees. I remember asking him to watch a particular transition in Gigi, going from a scene in an apartment to a hotel on the beach. I wanted to invoke the feeling of the tide with the movement of the dancers. He watched and said, "That's great, but we have to do it faster." He was right, and the transition worked beautifully. —Sharon Halley

Show curtain designed by Michael Anania.

SHOW BOAT

Show Boat

*Paper Mill's reputation
for musical theatre is extraordinary.*

Jac Venza
Executive Producer,
PBS Great Performances

S*HOW BOAT*, with book and lyrics by Oscar
Hammerstein II and music by Jerome Kern,
is one of the masterpieces of the lyric stage and
is often referred to as "*the* American musical."
The first musical to advance the plot through its
songs as well as the dialogue, it marked the
beginning of the true musical drama in modern
theatre. To date, there have been four productions
of *Show Boat* at Paper Mill Playhouse, in 1950,
1952, 1985, and 1989.

By far the finest staging was the 1989 production starring Eddie Bracken, Richard White,
Rebecca Baxter, Shelly Burch, Lee Roy Reams,
Lenora Nemetz, P. L. Brown, and Ella English.
It was directed by Robert Johanson and choreographed by Sharon Halley, with sets by Michael
Anania, costumes by Bradford Wood and Gregory
A. Poplyk, and lighting by Ken Billington. It
was televised on the PBS Great Performances
series October 27, 1989, and received two Emmy
award nominations, for outstanding musical
variety program and outstanding costume
design. Prior to *The Three Tenors* it was the most
viewed program in the history of Great Performances, and the only *Show Boat* ever staged
especially for television.

Shelly Burch as Julie in the 1989
production of *Show Boat*.

The musical, based on Edna Ferber's epic novel, spans over forty years and takes us with Captain Andy and his troupe of players up and down the Mississippi River on the show boat *Cotton Blossom.*

Ravenal (Richard White) meets Magnolia (Rebecca Baxter) and they "make believe" they're in love, above. At right: Captain Andy (Eddie Bracken) and his wife, Parthy (Marsha Bagwell) discover that it's much more than "Only Make Believe." Above right: Frank (Lee Roy Reams) and Ellie (Lenora Nemetz) are the second-rate song and dance team on the show boat.

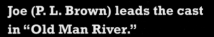

Joe (P. L. Brown) leads the cast in "Old Man River."

"Can't Help Lovin' that Man" is sung by Queenie (Ella English), left, with Joe, and by Julie (Shelly Burch), right, with Magnolia (Rebecca Baxter).

The second act opens at the Chicago World's Fair where two of the biggest attractions were "Little Egypt" and the world's largest Ferris wheel.

Ellie (Lenora Nemetz) describes "Life Upon the Wicked Stage."

Shelly Burch sings "Bill."

The musical ends back at the *Cotton Blossom* in the 1920s. Gaylord and Magnolia's daughter Kim (also played by Rebecca Baxter—center) is now the new star of the show boat.

A Landmark Production

There was so much material written for the original *Show Boat* and subsequent films that every major production is quite different. Paper Mill's *Show Boat* included for the first time a New Year's Eve chorus in the Trocadero that had been cut from the original, and "Ah Still Suits Me"—a showstopper for Joe and Queenie. It also restored the original Charleston for Kim, which develops out of a reprise of the famous "Why Do I Love You?"

Eddie Bracken and former New Jersey Governor Thomas Kean at the PBS taping.

Queenie and Joe in "Ah Still Suits Me."

One of Thirteen/WNET's most important missions is to partner with the great cultural institutions of the metropolitan area and to celebrate the artistic riches of our region. When we collaborated with Paper Mill Playhouse on their marvelous revival of *Show Boat* so it could be televised for our series Great Performances, we were able to share an unforgettable production with viewers from coast to coast. In fact, the success of that collaboration has led to televising Paper Mill's production of Gershwin's *Crazy for You*.

BILL BAKER
President, Channel Thirteen-WNET

Eddie Bracken

Eddie Bracken, the irrepressible hero in innumerable movies, had appeared on the Broadway stage in his teens and found his love for the theatre long before Hollywood discovered him. That love has brought him back to the theatre many times in his long career, and Paper Mill Playhouse has been the luckier for it. He first appeared at Paper Mill in 1969 in *You Know I Can't Hear You When the Water's Running* and the following year in *Plaza Suite*. In 1976, he returned to do *A Funny Thing Happened on the Way to the Forum*. He played Cap'n Andy in both the 1984 and 1989 productions of *Show Boat*. In 1992 he played the wonderful Wizard in *The Wizard of Oz* and in 1993 appeared in the Ray Cooney farce *It Runs in the Family*. In 1997 he delighted audiences in *No, No, Nanette,* and in Paper Mill's sixtieth year he appeared in *Follies.* Mr. Bracken is regarded with affection as truly a member of the Paper Mill family, and he is always available to assist in fund raising and to help in hosting guests and fans of the Playhouse.

Left: Eddie Bracken as Cap'n Andy.
Right: In an off-stage moment, Bracken entertains with a song.

Dramas and Comedies

Why go to Broadway for substandard fare when Paper Mill offers a menu to inspire the most demanding theatre gourmet?
—Simon Jones

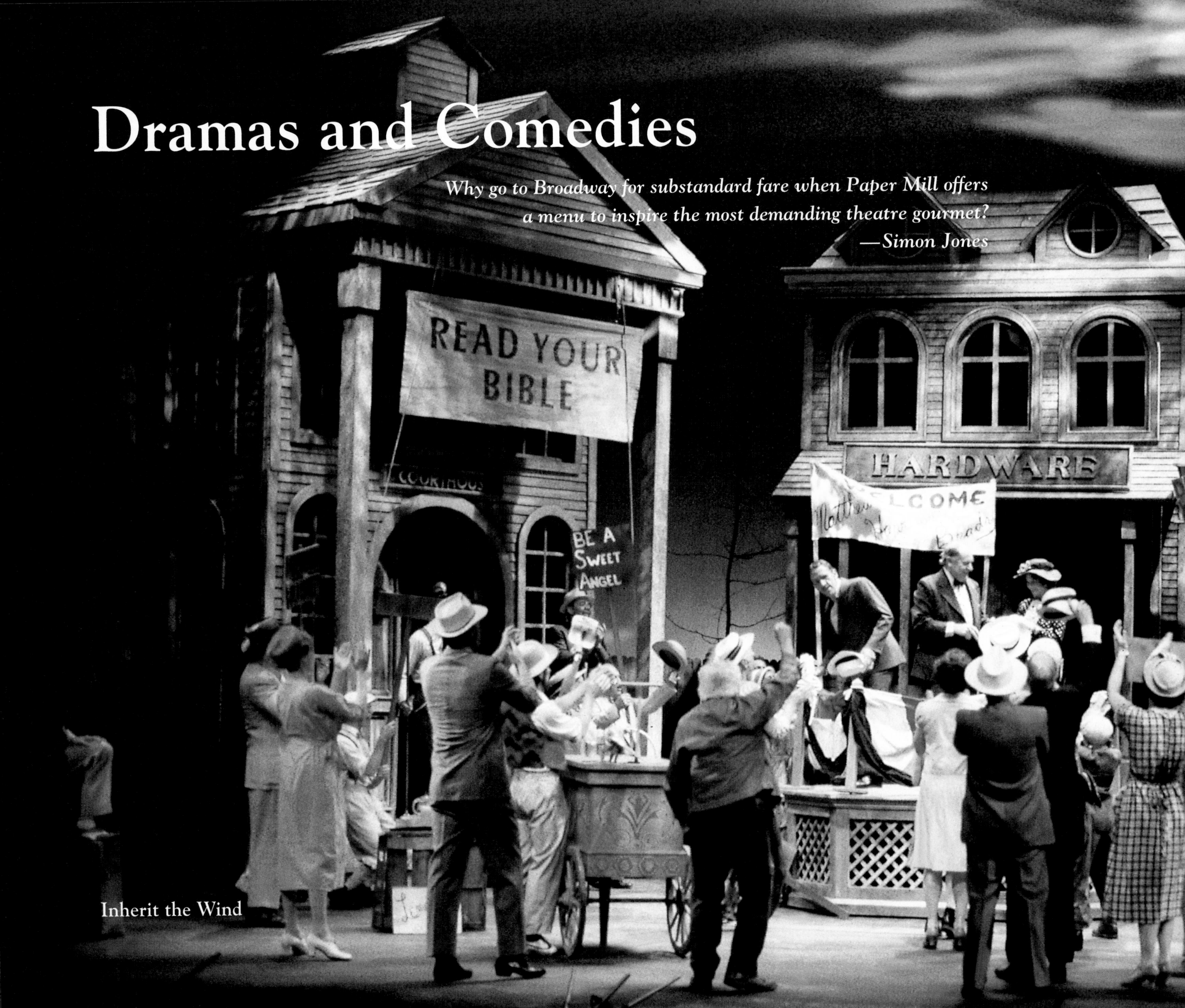

READ YOUR BIBLE

BE A SWEET ANGEL

HARDWARE

WELCOME

Inherit the Wind

NOT ALL PAPER MILL SHOWS ARE MUSICALS. THERE HAVE been many outstanding dramatic productions, from *You Can't Take It with You* to *Inherit the Wind, Sunrise at Campobello, Death of a Salesman, Amadeus*, and many more. There also have been both heartwarming and rollicking comedies, as well as hilarious fast-paced farces.

Inherit the Wind, 1985, dramatized the famous Scopes "monkey" trial that was held in Tennessee in 1925, over teaching evolution in public schools. This production won the Showtime Award for Excellence.

Robert Vaughan (standing) played defense attorney Clarence Darrow opposite E. G. Marshall as prosecutor William Jennings Bryan.

Sunrise at Campobello

Ron Parady brought the character of FDR to life. Kathleen Chalfant played his wife, Eleanor, with equal vividness.

Sunrise at Campobello, 1987, told the story of the early life of Franklin Delano Roosevelt, including his battle against polio and his return to politics. Ron Parady (seated) with Kathleen Chalfant (back row), Delphi Lawrence (left) and the Roosevelt children played by David Seaman, Joyce Bartok, Shane Patrick Flynn, Charles William Brady III and Judy Prescott.

Death of a Salesman, 1998 (opposite page), Arthur Miller's heart-wrenching American classic, shows the despair of an aging traveling salesman as he recognizes the emptiness of his life and ends it in suicide.

Death of a Salesman

Salesman Willy Loman was played by Ralph Waite; Lisa Richards was his wife. Sons Biff and Happy were acted by Rob Sedgwick and Sean Runnette.

A memorable, gripping production of one of America's most respected dramas. Ralph Waite masterfully mixes the old, cocky Willy with the devastated current one.

PETER FILICHIA
Newark Star-Ledger

Amadeus, 1984
The operatic drama about Mozart and Salieri, who may have murdered him.
Front row, left to right: Jack Harrold, Michael Tartel, Sally Flynn, John Thomas Waite,
Mary Jane Frankel, Bob Gunton.

Salieri and
Constance—
Bob Gunton
and Sally Flynn.

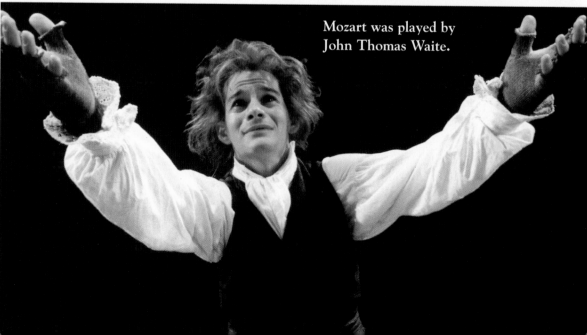

Mozart was played by
John Thomas Waite.

Comedies Galore

The Neil Simon Trilogy

Three comedies of American life based on the playwright's family and his emergence into adulthood were staged by Paper Mill in successive years: *Brighton Beach Memoirs* (1987), *Biloxi Blues* (1988), and *Broadway Bound* (1989). The part of Simon's alter ego, Eugene, was played by Mark Riffon in all three productions.

Above left, *Biloxi Blues:* Mark Riffon as Eugene in the Army.
Left: A family dinner in *Brighton Beach Memoirs*.
Above: Riffon and Barbara Caruso in *Broadway Bound*.

Lend Me a Tenor, 1991
From left: Kathryn Meisle,
David Sabin choking
Jeff Brooks, and
Marjan Haroldson.

The Foreigner, 1986
From left: Bob Denver, Jane Connell, and Greg Germann.

Jean Stapleton in
The Showoff.

The Showoff, 1984

Orson Bean as the
blundering showoff.

The Mask of Moriarty, 1998

Paxton Whitehead as
Sherlock Holmes, Moriarty's
indomitable opponent.

The Cocktail Hour, 1990.
Burt Edwards, mixing a drink, with
Ivar Brogger and Phyllis Thaxter.

Steel Magnolias, 1990

The Guardsman, 1984
Lawrence Luckinbill and Lucie Arnaz.

The British Farces

Farces, primarily bedroom farces, have been a popular entertainment in British theatre for years but have been produced much less often in the United States. Most farces involve highly improbable plot situations that usually concern sexual philandering, and very often the characters, through their own foolishness, are in the position of trying to protect their reputations or those of others. Invariably, characters just miss being discovered by one another in a fast-paced flow of entrances and exits through doors and windows leading to adjacent rooms, closets, corridors, and balconies. Names are disguised through layers of lies and misunderstandings, and there is often some innocent who must try to get everyone out of the mess they're in.

In 1986, Paper Mill Playhouse produced Ray Cooney's *Run for Your Wife*, starring David McCallum. Cooney, the artistic director of England's Theatre of Comedy, is the author of numerous highly successful farces and has directed, produced, and acted in a variety of others. The shows have been a great success at the Paper Mill. Cooney himself directed *Two Into One* with Tony Randall and Paxton Whitehead and *It Runs in the Family* (in which he also appeared), featuring Eddie Bracken. Cooney's *Out of Order*, starring Paxton Whitehead, has also been presented at the Paper Mill.

Two Into One, **1988**
Below: Paxton Whitehead and Millicent Martin.
Below, right: Tony Randall, Millicent Martin, and Beulah Garrick.

It Runs in the Family, 1994
Above: Alexandra O'Karma and Reno Roop.
Right: author Ray Cooney, Robert Mandan,
Harry S. Murphy, and Eddie Bracken.
Below: David McCallum and Kay Walbye in
Run for Your Wife, 1986.

Reno Roop and John Seidman (the dead body) in another hilarious scene from *Out of Order*, 1997.

Some of my happiest times in the theatre have been spent at the Paper Mill Playhouse. It's always a thrill to get that phone call from Angelo saying, "Ray, I think it's about time we did another of your silly plays."

RAY COONEY

Guys and Dolls

Classic Broadway

Just what is a Broadway musical? It isn't merely a musical that plays on Broadway. Operettas, cabaret works, shows created abroad have been produced on Broadway. They are not of the genre. Broadway musicals are a unique kind of theatre, the outgrowth of a taste, a tradition. There is a Broadway sound, a Broadway look, a Broadway feel to them.

—Martin Gottfried

SOME OF THE GREATEST EVENINGS of entertainment are from the razzle dazzle Broadway musicals. In the new Paper Mill Playhouse these classic shows were given spectacular productions. The voltage used just to light up Michael Anania's Times Square set for *Guys and Dolls* must have drained half the electricity from Northern Jersey.

Sky Masterson (Larry Kert) gives a lift to Adelaide (Lenora Nemetz), Sarah (Susan Powell), and Nathan Detroit (Jack Carter).

One of Broadway's greatest directors graced the Paper Mill at age 99 to rewrite and redirect his great hit, *Damn Yankees*. George Abbot, respectfully called "Mr. Abbott" by everyone, owns a half-dozen Tony Awards a and a Pulitzer Prize, and has such hit shows to his credit as *The Boys from Syracuse*, *Where's Charley?*, *Pajama Game*, *Pal Joey*, *On the Town*, *On Your Toes*, and *A Funny Thing Happened On the Way to the Forum*. He shared some thoughts about Paper Mill: *I went out to Millburn and saw their production of Candide, and I was very impressed. It was a marvelous production, superior in every way. The facilities there are first rate, and so are the people. I felt Damn Yankees could be done there and done right. Many of the productions at regional theatres—and*

Orson Bean

Susan Scott Flynn leads the Yankees in "Shoeless Joe."

Mr. Abbott with Alyson Reed and Orson Bean.

Damn Yankees had a cast and crew of more than sixty.

I think Paper Mill is maybe the best—are very well done. The productions are less expensive and the shows attract the middle class, the most intelligent people, the teachers—people who can't afford to go to Broadway. Tickets were $4.00 when I started in the theatre, but now....

The cast I'm working with here is just great. Today, the kids can sing and dance. Twenty, thirty years ago they did just one thing or the other. Today's people are well-rounded, better equipped than actors a generation or two ago. I would put the kids here in any Broadway show....

Nowadays, I yell at the actors from the house during rehearsals—I don't jump up on the stage the way I used to. I have an aversion to "Method" actors. Method actors struggle successfully at such difficult tasks as pretending they are trees in full bloom, but they never learn to say a final T.

Whatever Lola—played by Alyson Reed—wants, Lola gets in *Damn Yankees*.

FRANK BUTLER · ANNIE OAKLEY

CHIEF SITTING BULL

Some Broadway musicals are pure Americana: the Wild West antics of Annie Oakley; the exciting history of the birth of our nation; the great showman, P. T. Barnum; Mark Twain's hero, Huck Finn; a pacifist family during the Civil War; America's greatest humorist, Will Rogers. These and many more American subjects have made great stories for great musicals.

Shenandoah was presented in 1977, 1979, and in the production shown here, 1989. From left: Timothy Ford, Michael Piontek, Walter Charles, Malcom Gets, Ron Gibbs.

Annie Get Your Gun, 1987. From left: Anthony DiLeva, Larry Grey, Judy Kaye, Richard White, Ken Kantor.

Shenandoah. Dulé Hill and Tricia Witham sing "Freedom."

During Barnum, each performer had to learn a circus skill. There were many rigs set up on the stage—trapeze, wire for tight-rope walking—and in the house there were ropes attached to the ceiling, descending to the floor. The actors climbed to the top where they would be spun around just like in the circus. One evening, Angelo Del Rossi was challenged to climb. Removing his jacket he went hand-over-hand to the very top. There are good looks, charm, and a great body under that business suit! —Judith McCauley

In *Barnum*, Judith McCauley (top left) not only sang stratospheric high notes as the songbird, Jenny Lind, she also twirled fire batons in the circus section. P. J. Benjamin (above) played the great showman P. T. Barnum.

Barnum, 1986.
The world-famous General Tom Thumb was portrayed by Ray Roderick.

David Gunderman as Huck Finn and Lawrence Clayton as Jim in *Big River*.

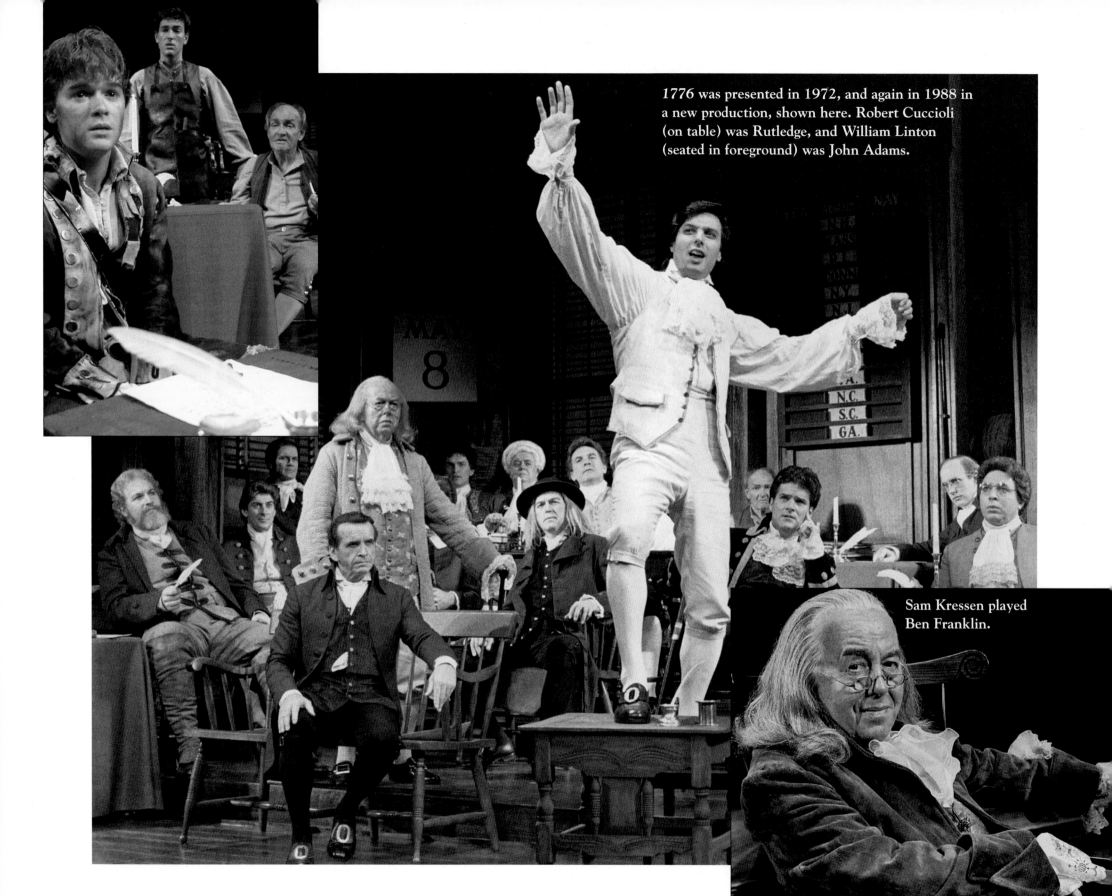

1776 was presented in 1972, and again in 1988 in a new production, shown here. Robert Cuccioli (on table) was Rutledge, and William Linton (seated in foreground) was John Adams.

Sam Kressen played Ben Franklin.

Will Rogers' Follies, 1998.
John Davidson played the title role.

This show says wonderful things about life and family. You can understand how people saw Rogers as a hero. So much of his "act" was really how he lived his life. That down-home charm, which I think he worked very hard to achieve, really impressed and moved, as well as entertained, people.

JOHN DAVIDSON

West Side Story, 1991.

Some of the great musicals are best remembered for their incredible choreography, and from time to time Paper Mill presents a loving re-creation of this outstanding work: Jerome Robbins' exciting dances for *West Side Story*, Tommy Tune's *My One and Only*, Michael Bennett's *A Chorus Line*, Gower Champion's *42nd Street*, and Donald Sadler's *No, No, Nanette* are only a few examples.

West Side Story

My One and Only, 1987.

A Chorus Line, 1991.

No, No, Nanette, 1997.

For theatrical time-travelers, the Paper Mill Playhouse, New Jersey's gift to Broadway often provides that special magic carpet called nostalgia. And its current trip takes us happily back to *No, No, Nanette*. This *No, No, Nanette* is the memory of a memory of a memory—but it's very much worth a trip to Millburn, N.J. And thanks for the memory.

CLIVE BARNES
New York Post

Donald Sadler (left) in rehearsal with Lee Roy Reems.

The cast of this Paper Mill revival of *No, No, Nanette* was studded with veteran stars—Eddie Bracken, Helen Gallagher, Kay Ballard, Lee Roy Reams, and Virginia Sandifur. Donald Sadler re-created his Tony-award winning choreography and directed as well.

I am most grateful to the Paper Mill Playhouse for reviving No No Nanette with the loving care and taste which prevail in all their productions. It was a perfect re-creation. It was also wonderful to be reunited with my longtime friend Helen Gallagher, who had created the role of Lucille Early in the original production (winning a Tony Award for Best Actress). Working with Helen at Paper Mill, where she now did the Ruby Keeler role, was a very special joy. Each night, when she finished doing the tap number "I Want to Be Happy," she would say, "Thank you, Ruby." —Donald Sadler

Helen Gallagher and Eddie Bracken in *No, No, Nanette.*

Helen Gallagher and chorus.

Miss Gallagher gave another outstanding performance in the Paper Mill production of *Side by Side by Sondheim,* 1985.

Let me tell you about the ghost that roams backstage at the Paper Mill. It comes in the form of a mouse who sat on my dressing table for four nights to watch me make up. The mouse appeared only at *my* table and that left me to wonder if it could have been the ghost of Patsy Kelly coming to check on me!

KAYE BALLARD

Kaye Ballard (at left) in *No, No, Nanette*. Lee Roy Reams (at right) played Billy Early. He also directed the Paper Mill production of Gower Champion's great musical *42nd Street*.

Below: The finale of *42nd Street*. Opposite page: The male chorus, John Scherer, center.

La Cage aux Folles, 1998.

La Cage aux Folles took gender roles to the extreme. This produciton featured a stunning performance by Lee Roy Reams as ZaZa, the most famous drag queen of St. Tropez. His able partner, Georges, was played by Walter Charles—who had formerly played ZaZa on Broadway.

From left: Leigh Beery, Walter Charles, Lee Roy Reams.

Walter Charles (left) and Lee Roy Reams.

My first appearance at the Paper Mill was in *La Cage Aux Folles*. We were a sellout hit and it was the most satisfying and rewarding time in my professional career.

LEE ROY REEMS

Lee Roy Reams with "The Cagelles."

Obviously, song-and-dance musicals are what most audiences immediately think of as pure Broadway, but there have been more contemporary musicals that have treated various subjects with very successful results. *Man of La Mancha* soars out of the deepest prisons to touch the heart with its "impossible dream." Paper Mill presented this modern classic in 1971, 1972, and 1973 with Jerome Hines, and in 1997 with Philip Hernandez (below).

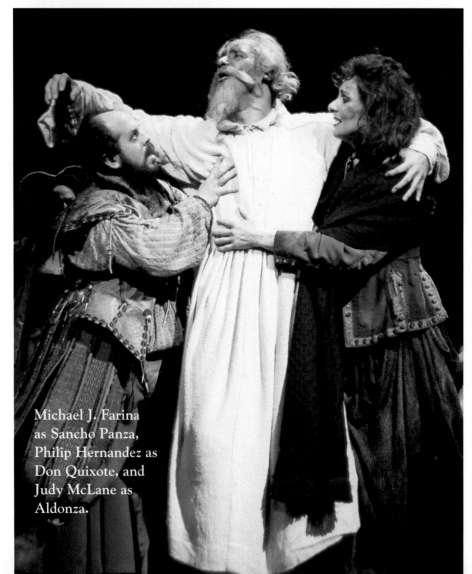

Michael J. Farina as Sancho Panza, Philip Hernandez as Don Quixote, and Judy McLane as Aldonza.

Evita portrays the electrifying rise of Eva Peron. The 1997 production provided a great showcase for the amazingly talented Judy McLane, one of Paper Mill's favorite contemporary actresses. Her dynamic and powerful voice and charismatic acting brought her instant recognition from her first performance as Florence in *Chess* to Nancy in *Oliver*, Luisa in *Nine*, Lily in *Dr. Jekyll and Mr. Hyde*, Aldonza in *Man of La Mancha*, and Eva Peron.

Sweeney Todd, 1992, offered thrills and chills of a different variety in the performances of George Hearn and Judy Kaye as the Demon Barber Sweeney and his accomplice in crime, Mrs. Lovett. Robert Johanson (far right) played her demented assistant Tobias.

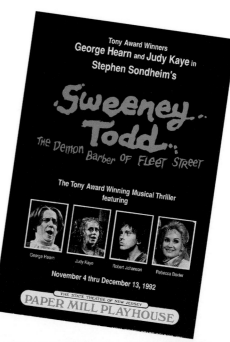

I was able to fully realize my own particular vision of Dreamgirls by having the luxury of working with a top-notch cast and an incredible creative team at Paper Mill Playhouse. The production was, in part, a salute to Michael Bennett's original spectacle, which was very cinematic. However, in rethinking the show for Paper Mill, I focused on its most vital element—the story of three women who get caught up in the frenzy of fame and how it ultimately affects their professional lives and personal relationships. The success of this version at Paper Mill in 1995 presented me with the thrilling opportunity to direct the premiere production of Dreamgirls in London's West End in 1999.

—Mark S. Hoebee

What the present director has seized upon is that what Eyen and Krieger created is really a pop opera, and he has staged it not as a ballet with songs, but precisely as such—operatically stressing the interplay between recitative and aria, the danced choruses and interludes.

CLIVE BARNES
New York Post

From left: Deidre Lang, Angela Robinson, and Tanya Holmes.

Hair Design

Hair design includes wigs and hairpieces, and styling, coloring, and cutting to create just the right look for a production. Howard Leonard has designed numerous shows for Paper Mill, as well as Broadway and films. One of his biggest shows was *Dreamgirls*.

I got the start of my hairdressing career at Paper Mill in 1976 while dancing in their production of Panama Hattie, *which starred Ann Miller. The hairdresser she had brought from the West Coast returned to Los Angeles without telling anyone. Since the company manager knew I had been helping the girls in the company with their hair, he asked me to do Ann's hair for the show for the rest of the run. That was a turning point in my life. This seemed like an opportunity not to be taken too lightly.*

It was many years and more than twenty-six shows later when Fate stepped in and I returned to Paper Mill. They needed a hair designer, and a friend suggested me for the job. Since then, Paper Mill had provided me with some of my most memorable moments.

Shows like Dreamgirls *had several design challenges, from the sheer number of wigs (98) to designing all of the hairstyles to conceal the microphones and transmitter packs.* Nine *required 1960s* Vogue *styles,* Call Me Madam *1950s elegance, while* Jane Eyre *and* Wuthering Heights *required hairstyles from a different century. The production of* Follies *was a chance to work with Ann Miller again, as well as many other grande dames. Each lady needed her own special touch to ensure that she not only looked different from the others and that her style was appropriate for her character, but also that no one else outshone her. With each new show comes a new set of challenges: sometimes size, sometimes personalities, sometimes styles. No matter what the challenge, at the end is the reward of working with great people on great productions.*

—Howard Leonard

"Hosanna" in *Jesus Christ, Superstar*, 1988.

Robert Johanson

The complete rethinking of Andrew Lloyd Webber and Tim Rice's great rock opera *Jesus Christ Superstar* was one of the most successful efforts in the history of Paper Mill. It was presented in four seasons, 1976, 1977, 1988 and 1989. It sold out every time.

The 1988 production was co-directed by Charles Blaisdell and Robert Johanson, who played the title role, with choreography by Susan Stroman. This was a project Johanson took very seriously: "The story of the last days in the life of Jesus are known to all. It is a moving, gripping, puzzling series of events leading to what could be the single most dramatic event in the history of man—the Crucifixion. The importance of this moment to millions of people could not be taken lightly, and even though the story is presented in the context of a rock opera, it was imperative that we envision the life of Jesus, his followers, and his detractors, and find the humanity in all of them. I asked Charles Blaisdell to join me on this journey. He guided us all in the spiritual truths of the story."

Magic, Blaisdell explained, *has many qualities. Jesus Christ, Superstar is a journey into the scope and depth of Spiritual Magic, the immeasurable region of religion and myth, in all time and places.*

This is the most thrillingly theatrical experience of the New Jersey stage season. Paper Mill's production is vivid and focused, an accelerating wheel of precisely gauged effects. Each image, action, and lyric is cut and polished to a diamondlike clarity. The show flashes past in a controlled succession of sensory bursts.

BOB CAMPBELLL
Newark Star-Ledger

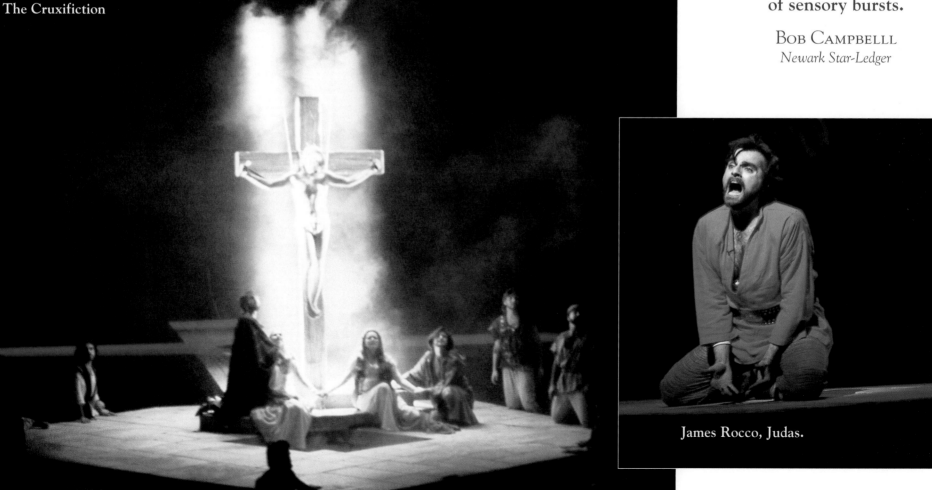

The Cruxifiction

James Rocco, Judas.

The Last Supper

The temple and the moneychangers.

We began with a late 1960s counterculture rock opera. Its score had phenomenal appeal to youth in an explosive decade of unabashed idealism and social liberation. Its story rang with resistance to militarism, to social conservatism, to religious hypocrisy and materialism. Its first productions had been rock concerts, which metastasized into grotesque, aweless, and cynical trashings of the Gospel Story. For many in that generation this was truth about religion; for others it was sacriledge.

Our challenge was to tell The Greatest Story Ever Told in a way that expressed the core of three great religions simultaneously—Judaism, Christianity, and Islam—but was true to the core of all spiritual traditions of all peoples. The heart of our challenge was to experience "Universal Truth," not just entertainment, spectacle, education, or authenticity, although Truth for us included all of these.

We began with the spiritual roots of Judaism, the mysticism of the Kabbalah. The Torah is foundational to three great religions, and Jesus comes to "fulfill" it. Our Jesus was Everyman, awakening from his heritage, culture, and personality, embracing Everyman's individual universal prophetic destiny, fulfilling ageless law by realizing Self to be Redeemer…to be One with God…to be God. We saw Jesus' Way—His striving, losses, suffering, metamorphosis, passion, sorrow, physical resurrection, and ascension—as Everyman's Way, as Everyman's aspiration and transfiguration.

This meant that twelve disciples simultaneously expressed twelve Hebrew double letters, twelve tribes of Israel, twelve zodiacal signs, twelve forms of movement, twelve spectrum colors and musical tones: Twelve, the ancient Hebrew "Highway of the Stars." This meant that every character was both personal and universal—an extraordinary challenge for performers.

Our production unfolded on a huge inclined cross, symbol of the Four-Lettered Name of God, YHVH, with a stone rose blossoming at its base, symbol of the Fiery Fifth Letter of Redemption rising within the name of God—Jesus. Temporal reality, places, and events flew in and blew out like Prospero's "insubstantial pageants," while cross and stone remained. Reality was shaped almost entirely out of light—light and "thin air."

The infinite, patient care with which characterizations, actions, and production were layered in precise, ritual correspondence to the mystical core of the Torah accounted for the staggering power, jubilation, tragedy, and apotheosis experienced by audiences and performers alike.

Within the universal structure, Robert Johanson literally lived, died, and ascended as us all. His Jesus sounded every note, from cantorial hymns of praise and sorrow, to operatic grand manner, to the immediacy of rock, to the simplicity of folk song. His experience of unfolding spiritual destiny began in the personal and self-satisfying, struggled through the death of mortality itself,

faced responsibility chin-to-chin with God, understood, suffered, forgave, and was transfigured.

Within this universal structure, doubt as well as affirmation took ritual shape: Pilate's juridical doubt, Herod's superstitious doubt, Simon's political doubt, Peter's self-doubt, and Judas' doubt that a "man I know to be a man" can become more than a man, can become one with God—can become God.

The unit set was a series of sloped interlocking platforms that appeared to float in space and a huge 30' x 20' cross behind, also sloped, used for entrances and acting areas. The cross was a constant symbolic reminder of the suffering of Jesus Christ.

MICHAEL ANANIA
Set Designer

Mary Magdelen and the ensemble in "Hosana."

I'll never forget our performance on Palm Sunday. Just as we reached the Hosanna number, the ensemble dancing out with palms, the fire alarm went off and the theatre had to be evacuated. There we were, Judas, Jesus, and all the disciples in costume standing out in the parking lot with the audience. Suddenly people were surrounding Robert, as Jesus, asking for his autograph. Very strange. The disciples moved in and steered him away from the mob. Everyone seemed to be afraid of me. Life imitating art? We got the "all clear"—it was a false alarm—and went back in, starting once again with the palms on Palm Sunday. —James Rocco (Judas)

Robert Cuccioli, Pontius Pilate.

These were not performances of a musical play; these were public rituals of personal redemption. When our Superstar played on Passover, it was for Jews an ideal representation of the "sufferings of the Messiah sitting as a beggar at the gates of Rome," identified not with the mighty but with the outcasts of humanity. And when Superstar played on Easter, it was for Christians an ecstatic realization of resurrection and ascension to divinity. For each audience participant, the ritual confirmed and fulfilled his or her faith; to none was it alien or untrue.

The performances were uniquely thrilling perhaps because performers and audiences alike were challenged to rise to impossible heights, to trust truth over fact, to renew time-honored techniques of comedy and tragedy, and to sing new songs to new music which yet intone temple secrets thousands of years old.

—Charles Blaisdell

Angelo Del Rossi got caught up in *Superstar* too. He was determined to get the end of the show just right. The offstage hammering of the nails into the cross was not to his satisfaction. It did not sound authentic. He would frequently go backstage, grab the hammer himself, and pound the nails properly. He was also determined that the final moment be correct. One of the most stunning effects ever seen at Paper Mill was the Ascension in the last moment of the play. The cross fell away and thousands of tiny stars slowly descended as the levitated body of Christ rose into the heavens. Angelo was constantly concerned that the stars were coming in too fast; they had to appear at just the correct speed for the magic moment to happen. He was right. When the tempo was correct the audience experienced the feeling of being lifted out of their seats. There was always an awed hush after the last beat of the music and then the cheering began.

Joseph and the Amazing Technicolor Dreamcoat

Paper Mill enjoyed great success with this early Andrew Lloyd Webber/Tim Rice Bible musical with a twist. In 1984, Joseph was played by David Gaines and Liz Larsen was the narrator. The show was so popular it was repeated for a summer run the next year. Then 15 years later the show was expanded to include a contemporary mega-mix of all the tunes for a grand finale. This version starred Patrick Cassidy and Deborah Gibson.

Above: Patrick Cassidy as Joseph (1999).
Inset at left: Davis Gaines as Joseph (1984).
Bottom left: Eric Martsof as Pharaoh (1999).
Below: Patrick Cassidy, Deborah Gibson, and the company (1999).

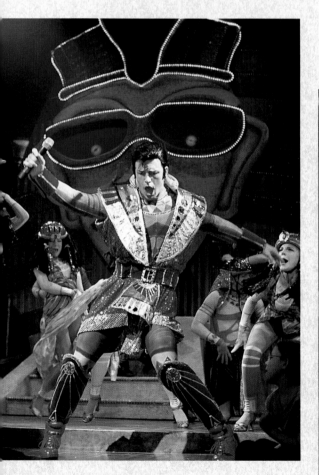

Crazy For You

In 1999, Paper Mill presented a rousing re-creation of the international hit Gershwin musical *Crazy for You.* This too was taped for PBS Great Performances. The Paper Mill production was directed by James Brennan, and Angelique Ilo recreated Susan Stroman's award-winning choreography. Tom Helm was musical director, and the cast included Jim Walton, Stacey Logan, Jeb Brown, Bruce Adler, Jane Connell, and Larry Linville.

SUSAN STROMAN began choreographing at Paper Mill Playhouse with *Sayonara, Roar of the Greasepaint, Jesus Christ Superstar, Shenandoah,* and *Rhythm Ranch.* Her choreography for the Broadway production of *Crazy for You* won a Tony award, and she won a second Tony for the revival of *Show Boat.* She was warmly welcomed back for Paper Mill's *Crazy for You,* which preserved her work for posterity.

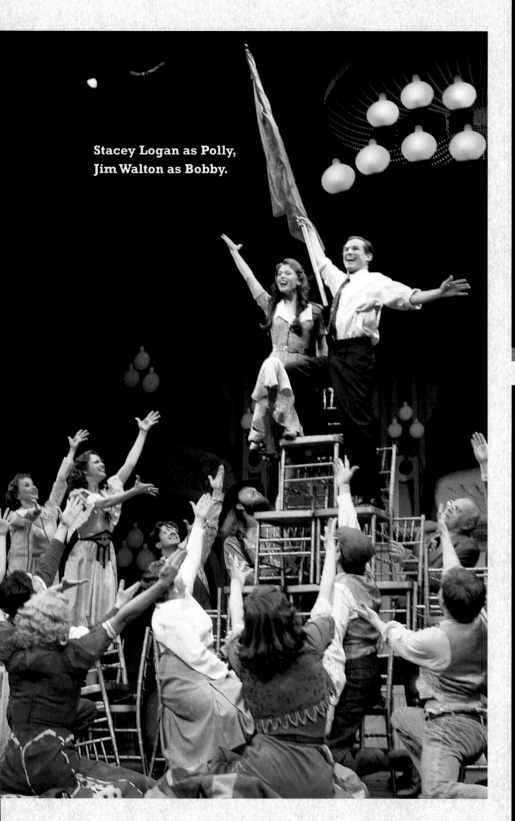

Stacey Logan as Polly,
Jim Walton as Bobby.

Sandy Edgerton as Irene Roth is
astride Jeb Brown as Lank Hawkins.

"Shall We Dance?"

Crazy for You finale.

Larry Linville and Jane Connell.

Mia Price as Patsy teaches the men of Dead Rock to dance.

BETTY BUCKLEY
GYPSY
DEBORAH GIBSON

SEPTEMBER 9 TO OCTOBER 25, 1998

Forget *The Lion King.* Forget *Chicago.* Drop everything, rent a car—hell, buy a car—and head straight for Paper Mill Playhouse in Millburn, N.J. where Betty Buckley is starring in Gypsy.

TERRY TEACHOUT
Daily News

In the great backstage musical *Gypsy*, the role of the most famous stage mother of all time, Mama Rose, was extraordinarily rendered in 1998 by Betty Buckley (top). The exceptional cast featured Leonard Wolpe as Herbie (above) and Deborah Gibson as Louise (standing left, with Buckley).

Deborah Gibson as Gypsy Rose Lee in three moments of the show-stopping "Let Me Entertain You."

The Blanche and Irving Laurie Foundation

The support and encouragement of the Blanche and Irving Laurie Foundation has enabled Paper Mill Playhouse to breathe new life into many classic pieces of musical theatre, including *Gypsy* (1998), *Oklahoma* (1992), *My Fair Lady* (1993), *South Pacific* (1994), *Brigadoon* (1995), *Call Me Madam* (1996), *No No Nanette* (1997), *Follies* (1998) and *Crazy For You* (1999). Under the leadership of Gene Korf, the Foundation's support and its love and respect for the American musical have allowed Paper Mill to produce these masterpieces with the highest artistic standards and in the manner intended by their creators, and to introduce these masterpieces to a whole new audience.

Above: Joe Machota as Tulsa sings "All I Need Is the Girl." Above right: Alexandra Kiesman in the part of Baby Jane. Right: Louise (Deborah Gibson, on left), Dainty Jane (Laura Bell Budy), and Miss Cratchett (Dorothy Stanley).

Dorothy Stanley (center) played the stripper Tessie Tura, and Anna McNeely (right) was Electra. Jana Robbins (left) played Mazeppa and stood-by for Mama Rose. Twenty years earlier at Paper Mill Playhouse, she had portrayed Gypsy (below) with Dolores Gray (on left) as Mama Rose.

Concerts & Special Events

Special concerts began shortly after Paper Mill was founded. They present artists who broaden the Playhouse menu of voice, dance, and music. Originally a summer feature, they have expanded to programs throughout the year. Today, modern dance, and jazz, popular, and country music help attract new audiences to the theatre. In addition to the artists pictured on these pages, the performers have included the Chinese Golden Dragon Acrobats and Magicians of Taipei; the Pilobolus Dance Theatre; the Lar Lubovitch Dance Company; the New Jersey Ballet; the Manhattan Rhythm Kings; the Preservation Hall Jazz Band of New Orleans; the Kingston Trio; the Duke Ellington, Count Basie, and Glenn Miller orchestras; drummer Buddy Rich and his band, and Lionel Hampton and his orchestra. Individual performers have included Nancy Dussault and Karen Morrow in concert with the Metropolitan Symphony Orchestra; comedian David Brenner; flutist Ransom Wilson, and vocalist Rosemary Clooney. There also has been a series of plays for children, and such special programs as *Paper Mill Salutes the American Musical.*

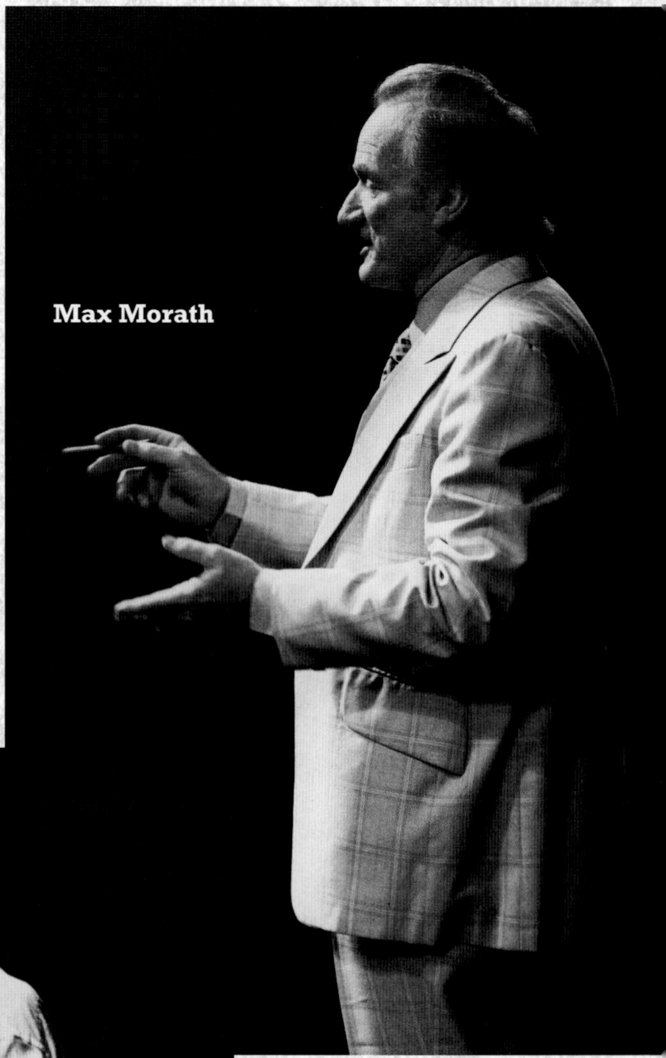

Max Morath

Dizzy Gillespie

Carlos Montoya

Louis Armstrong

Gerri Mulligan

The Shirelles

Judy Collins

163

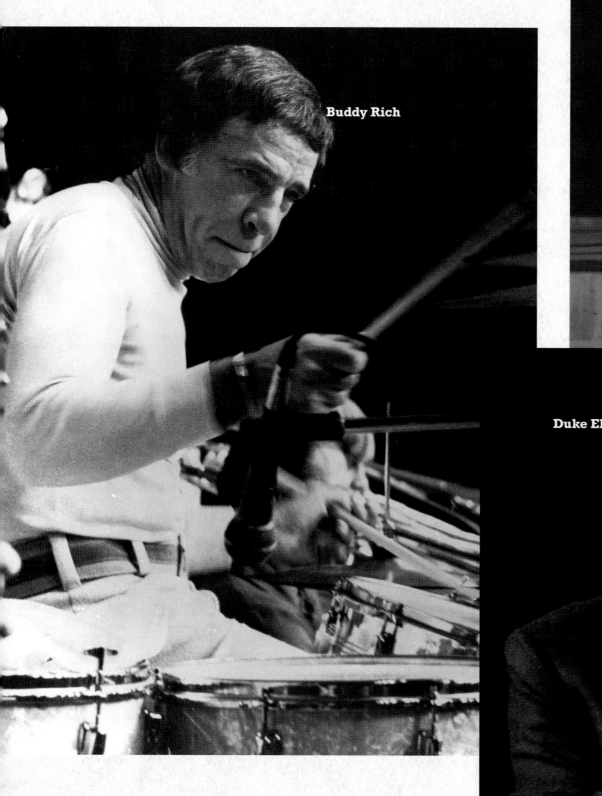

Buddy Rich

George Shearing

Duke Ellington

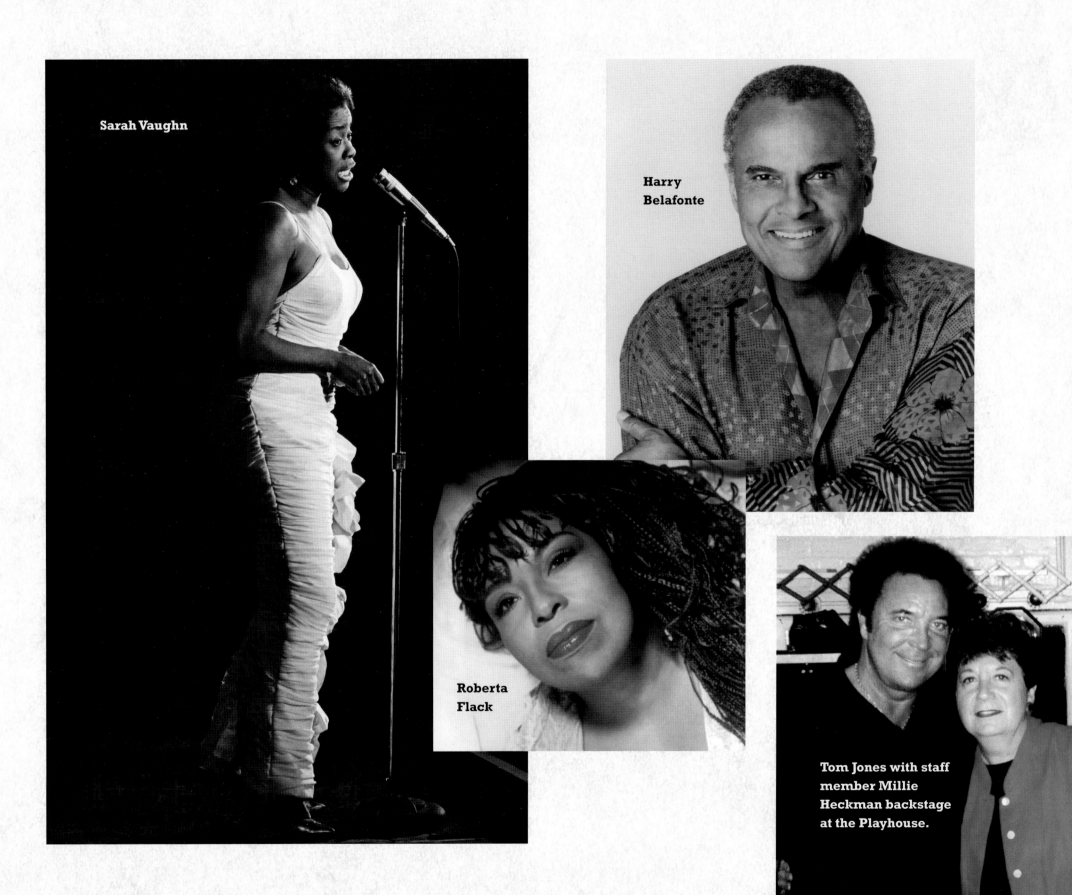

Sarah Vaughn

Harry Belafonte

Roberta Flack

Tom Jones with staff member Millie Heckman backstage at the Playhouse.

Tap Dogs

The McGuire Sisters

Dave Brubeck

Herbie Mann

Kathie Mattea

Lar Lubovitch Dance Company

New Works and World Premieres

The arts are an integral part of every civilized society and every proud state. Certainly Paper Mill is an integral part of New Jersey and truly makes us proud.
—Christine Todd Whitman
Governor of New Jersey

THE GREATEST CHALLENGE FOR ANY theatre is developing and presenting new works. Musical theatre is the most difficult because of the great number of diverse elements that must synthesize into a successful whole. Twelve world premieres were staged between 1987 and 1999 in the reconstructed Paper Mill Playhouse. This, at first, was largely made possible by a grant from the Artistic Focus Fund of the New Jersey State Council on the Arts. This support was part of Governor Thomas Kean's initiative to make New Jersey "second to none" in the arts by bringing attention to the state for its national arts contribution. The nationwide broadcast of the Playhouse's production of *Show Boat* was made possible by this fund, as was the development of new works through Paper Mill's Musical Theatre Project.

The staged reading phase in the development of the musical *It's A Wonderful Life*. Right: the chorus. Above: the featured performers, James Brennan and Roxanne Parker.

The Musical Theatre Project, 1985–1991

In this developmental program, new plays started as fully rehearsed, staged readings presented before several invited audiences at Paper Mill. Audience reactions and critiques gave the authors and creative staff a chance to assess their work. All of the dialogue and music had to be presented, and the authors could not participate in the performance—such as the composer serving as musical director—so that they could watch and fully experience their creation. The challenge was to understand how everything worked, not just selected highlights as at backers' auditions. This was an important step toward an ultimate full production.

From the staged readings, some projects were selected to go on to a workshop phase. They were mounted in a rehearsal room with minimal sets, lights, and costumes, but with choreography and musical arrangements added to a full staging of the work.

Again, invited audiences were asked to respond, and much was learned toward refining the material and envisioning a physical presentation of the piece. This evaluation was crucial to deciding whether to spend hundreds of thousands of dollars on sets and costumes in a full-scale, onstage production.

The first musical from the Musical Theatre Project to be given a full production was the hauntingly beautiful *Sayonara*, based on the James A. Michener novel, with book by William Luce, music by George Fishoff, and lyrics by Hy Gilbert.

**Above: June Angela as Hana Ogi.
Left: June Angela and Ako with Takarazuka girls.**

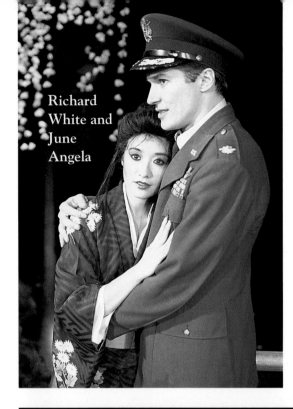

Richard White and June Angela

I've had the joy of working on many shows at Paper Mill. But my favorite, which has a wealth of fanciful memories, is Sayonara. As a choreographer, I do a great amount of research on the period of the story, the geographical area, the culture, the music, and, of course the pertinent dance style. This show involved a traditional Japanese fan dance that segued into a Taiko drum section and ended in a production number in the style of the famous Takarazuka troupe of Tokyo. I learned Kodo drumming, and then set about rehearsing the female dancers for weeks in simultaneous dancing and drumming. At the end of each day, hands were sore and bleeding. Each morning we would begin again with hands bandaged in white tape.

In one section, the girls jumped from drum to drum, and every so often someone would miss completely. In one performance, Yasuko did just that. She could not get back into the line of flying, leaping dancers, but suddenly she threw herself down center stage and began pounding out the rhythm on the floor like a drummer possessed. At the climax there she was, looking like the star of the number. It was truly cross-cultural. She was "saving face" by not giving up, but like an American Broadway star, she was seizing the moment and finishing with great exultation and expertise. —Susan Stroman

June Angela with the Taiko Drummers.

Rhythm Ranch was a charming homage to country-and-western musicals of the Roy Rogers-Dale Evans genre. The show was directed by Philip McKinley, with choreography by Susan Stroman. She discovered many western-theme ideas that would later be developed further in *Crazy for You*.

Robert Cuccioli with gauchos.

Norma Mae Ling with the cowboys.

Beyond a Reasonable Doubt

This dramatic, although nonmusical, play was developed through the new works project. It was written by Nathan Mayer, a former judge who explored the drama of plea bargaining. The Paper Mill production starred Karen Valentine and David Groh, (below).

Mikado, Inc.

One of the zaniest and most delightful projects in the new works program was *Mikado, Inc.* Based on Gilbert and Sullivan's *The Mikado*, it used Sir Arthur Sullivan's melodies but had the audacity to feature new lyrics by Albert Evans and a new book by Jane Waterhouse and Robert Johanson. The result was quite a lot of fun, and far different from the traditional operetta, last presented at Paper Mill in 1948.

In this modern-day version, staged in 1990, Mikado is the name of the largest corporation in the world, with new headquarters in Hohokus, New Jersey.

Marsha Bagwell as Katisha with Jason Ma as Pish-Tush, Michael Mulhern as Pooh-Bah, and Philip Wm. McKinley as Koko looking on.

Jason Ma, center, with company.

If you want to know who we are,
We are gentlemen of Japan:
On many a vase and jar,
On many a screen and fan,
We figure in lively paint:
Our attitude's queer and quaint—
You're wrong if you think it ain't, oh!
(lyrics by W. S. Gilbert, 1885)

If you want to know who we are
We're a company from Japan!
We make many a VCR
We make many a truck and van!
We travel in suits and ties,
But never believe your eyes—
We're Samurai in disguise!
Ah!
These ties are a great disguise!
(lyrics by Albert Evans, 1990)

Mia Kort, Christine Toy and Ann Hasada

Three little office temps are we
Mixing the coffee and the tea
Losing the only bathroom key!
Three little office temps.
(lyrics by Albert Evans, 1990)

Three little maids from school are we,
Pert as a schoolgirl well can be,
Filled to the brim with girlish glee,
Three little maids from school.
(lyrics by W. S. Gilbert, 1885)

Mikado, 1948

Right: Philip Wm. McKinley as Koko with the modern Samurai. Below: Koko (Clarence Nordstrom) in the 1946 *Mikado*.

Christine Toy and James Rocco.

In the original *Mikado*, Nanki Poo is a wandering minstrel; in *Mikado, Inc.*, Frankie Poo (short for Puccelli) is an aspiring rock singer who becomes the "voice" of Mikado, Inc.—the "Micro Chap." He has been discovered at the Meadowlands by "The Boss," Madame Katisha, who takes quite a fancy to him. He doesn't take to her, however, preferring the delicate Yum Yum. This makes The Boss quite unhappy!

After many complications involving cybernauts, a mysterious teahouse, cherry blossoms, and missing helicopters, the CEO of Mikado himself—sort of a reclusive Howard Hughes—arrives in a zeppelin and puts everything right.

Marsha Bagwell sings the Boss's song.

I am the boss and what I want I
always get!
If I look cross, well folks you ain't
seen nothing yet!
I am the leader of the pack—
When I attack—stand back!
(lyrics by Albert Evans)

Paper Moon

In 1991 the New Jersey state arts budget was suddenly cut in half across the board. However, during her term in office Governor Christine Todd Whitman and the Arts Council have been working to strengthen support for arts again. At the time of the cut Paper Mill lost a large portion of its funding. This meant the end of the Musical Theatre Project and the Artistic Focus Fund. As a result, new theatre projects had to be funded by outside producers or somehow done to fit within the tight budget for each season.

The first outside partnership was with Roger Berlind, for *Paper Moon*. He provided enhancement funding to cover the extraordinary costs beyond Paper Mill's normal operating budget.

This musical by Martin Casell, Larry Grossman, Ellen Fitzhugh, and Carol Hall was based on the film *Paper Moon*, which starred Ryan O'Neal, his daughter Tatum, and Madeline Kahn. In the Paper Mill version, Gregory Harrison and the young Natalie di Luca played the unlikely duo who con their way through the Depression of the 1930s. Christine Ebersole gave a standout performance as a tawdry vaudevillian. Although the show had many highlights, it did not transfer to Broadway as was hoped, but was presented in many theatres around the country.

Above: Natalie di Luca and Chandra Wilson.

Left: Christine Ebersole and Gregory Harrison.

Above: Clint Holmes and the band.
Left: The family of *Comfortable Shoes* (clockwise
from top left): Scott Irby-Ranniar, Clint Holmes,
Nancy Ringham, Adam Wade, LaChanze.

Comfortable Shoes

The next new project was one that was small enough
to be funded from within the Playhouse's existing operating budget—*Comfortable Shoes*, by Clint Holmes
and Nelson Cole. Holmes came to Paper Mill with a
rough outline and ten songs for an autobiographical
musical about his life growing up in a mixed marriage.
His mother was a white British opera singer, his father
a black jazz musician. Robert Johanson became inspired by the story and began developing the material
with Clint and Nelson.

What was originally intended to be a one-man
show with a band and back-up singers was expanded
to a larger story that included the roles of the parents,

Clint's wife, his younger self, and other people in his
past. The result was extremely entertaining and very
moving. The audience leapt to their feet every night
before the last song was even over. Many producers
were interested in taking the show further, including
to Broadway. Clint unfortunately chose a producer
who ultimately was unable to succeed at what he
promised and this beautiful show was shelved.

Up, Up, and Away—
The Songs of Jimmy Webb

Everything happened to this musical revue! Technical
difficulties delayed set construction; three costume
designers and two hair designers dropped out because
of personal problems; ice and snow kept the audience
away; cast members were in auto accidents; the flu
daily knocked down crew and musicians. And one of

the stars, Judy McLane, fell through a trap door during rehearsals and landed on her head in the orchestra pit. She missed eight performances, but ultimately recovered. Nevertheless, the show went on!

Its reception was quite polarized—audiences and critics either loved it or they hated it. Robert Johanson, who directed and appeared in the show, was quite surprised: "I got more mail on this one than almost any other and the comments were equally divided: 'Thank you for doing something different—a compelling evening of great music—beautifully sung,' to 'This could possibly be the worst show I've ever seen at Paper Mill!' Now, I know that due to circumstances beyond our control the show had not jelled as well as we would have liked, but I never expected a show of this kind to produce 'hate' mail. I shiver to think what would happen if we did something really disturbing."

New musical works are always unpredictable, and challenging, but Paper Mill remains committed to encouraging their creation. Additional productions in the Musical Theatre Project are listed in Appendix II.

Judy McLane and Kelli Rabke

From left: Associate Producer Roy Miller, Executive Producer Angelo Del Rossi and the company of *Up Up and Away* meet with composer Jimmy Webb (second from right) after a performance.

It was ironic that I would perform such demanding physical roles at Paper Mill, dying in *Evita,* murdered in *Oliver,* beaten up and raped in *Man of La Mancha,* but finally sustain an injury in an intimate four-person musical review!

JUDY MCLANE

I can recall such spectaculars as
To Kill a Mockingbird,
The Prisoner of Zenda and
particularly, Robert Johanson's own
version of *Great Expectations*. He has
become wondrously skillful at getting
the dramatic scenes properly
highlighted in these adaptations,
which, in effect, as novels, really have
to move with the dissolving speed of
the cinema rather than the more
leisurely dramatic pace of the stage.

CLIVE BARNES
New York Post

Literary Adaptations

IN 1991 THE PAPER MILL MOUNTED A stirring production of Harper Lee's *To Kill a Mockingbird*, adapted from her novel by Christopher Sergel. This proved to be very successful for several reasons. The large size of the theatre suited itself to epic drama in both the scope of production and the size of the cast; the many students who attended special matinee performances had an opportunity to see a novel they were reading in school realized in front of their eyes; but most important, the general audience experienced a beloved book brought to life by marvelous actors.

For the trial scene, many local patrons of the theatre were the spectators, so the scene was filled

with over sixty people and appeared very realistic. Emily Ridgway, a Short Hills resident and longtime supporter of the Playhouse, participated. She was known as the "Cookie Lady" and every performance brought in freshly baked cookies that she handed out to the trial spectators and the actual audience at intermission. She made a lot of new friends that way.

Left: George Grizzard gave a riveting and sensitive portrayal as Atticus Finch. Tiffany Kreissler played his daughter, Scout. Above: Dill (Daniel Reifsnyder), Scout, Jem (Jesse Bernstein), and their neighbor, Miss Maudie (Katherine Houghton).

The response to *Mockingbird* was so overwhelming that Robert Johanson immediately began to think of other novels that would make effective stage productions: My *favorite English novel is* Great Expectations. *I reread it and imagined the scenes and characters leaping onto the stage as I turned each page. I'd found our next project. It was important to me to try to* embrace *the entire scope of the novel. In the case of* Great Expectations, *it has many plot threads which ultimately culminate in the stirring conclusion. So often, in the film versions, characters and entire story lines are dropped or changed drastically and I figured other people were like me—they wanted to see the book as they imagined it, as true as possible.*

Mr. Jaggers (Richard Woods) announces Pip has "great expectations."

Pip—Michael James Reed

Young Pip arrives at Satis House to be "raised as a gentleman."

On opening night the actor playing Mr. Jaggers delivered the famous line "I have come to tell you—you have great expectations!" and then fainted and had to be rushed off to the emergency room. I was sitting in the back of the theatre, and suddenly found myself running backstage, picking up the stage manager's book, and walking out onstage saying, "We will continue!"—picking up where we left off. Now the problem was, I really wanted to watch the show—so during Act Two, I went out to see the burning of Miss Havisham, the boat collision on the River Thames, and then here comes the prison scene and I'm thinking, "Where is Mr. Jaggers? Oh no! I'm Mr. Jaggers!" I rushed down, jumped on the stage and continued once again.

Boat collision on the Thames.

Young Pip (Daren Edward Higgins) speaks to Miss Havisham (Elizabeth Franz), the jilted bride.

To work on shows of such magnitude was simply awe inspiring. I remember the first night of tech rehearsals and Robert walking around like a little kid showing me the wonders of the sets that we would call home for the next six weeks. I was speechless and breathless with excitement. I took glee in the next two adaptations I did, watching the actors have the same reaction when they first arrived at Paper Mill, realizing that indeed, these shows were going to be big!

MICHAEL JAMES REED

Charles Dickens
A Tale of Two Cities

FEBRUARY 16 — MARCH 26, 1994

THE STATE THEATRE OF NEW JERSEY
PAPER MILL PLAYHOUSE

Charles Darney is convicted by the People's Tribunal.

The common people of Paris, oppressed and impoverished by the aristocracy.

The five most successful British novels, in order, are: Dickens's *Great Expectations* and *A Tale of Two Cities*; *Vanity Fair* by Thackeray; *Jane Eyre* by Charlotte Brontë, and *Wuthering Heights* by Emily Brontë. Having done *Great Expectations*, it was only natural that Robert Johanson's next adaptation would be *A Tale of Two Cities*. Eventually, dramatizations of the two Brontë novels would follow, but Johanson says he doesn't think he'll ever tackle *Vanity Fair*.

In *A Tale of Two Cities*, local talent was used again to people the stage. Emily Ridgway, the "Cookie Lady" from *Mockingbird*, volunteered to be a victim of the guillotine. Here was a real trouper—a lady in her late seventies who got her head chopped off every night!

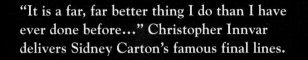
"It is a far, far better thing I do than I have ever done before…" Christopher Innvar delivers Sidney Carton's famous final lines.

Michael James Reed who played Pip in *Great Expectations*, portrayed Charles Darney in *A Tale of Two Cities* (above). In both plays he appeared opposite Nancy Bell (Estella in *Great Expectations*, Lucie in *Tale*, above), and both times he got the girl at the end. By their third production together, the romance was more than theatrical: it developed offstage and led to marriage.

Costume design for Charles Darney.

Costume design for Lucie.

When I look back on the very first day of rehearsal for *Great Expectations,* if someone had tapped me on the shoulder and said, "See that guy over there, Michael James Reed? You're gonna marry that guy," I would have called them crazy.

NANCY BELL

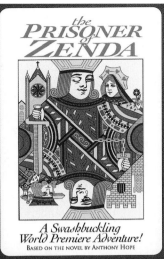

As a break between Dickens and the Brontés (who were to come next), Paper Mill presented *The Prisoner of Zenda*, adapted by Peter Manos from the Anthony Hope romance. Michael James Reed was once again opposite Nancy Bell, but this time as the villain.

Both male leads played two parts. Michael James Reed was Robert, Lord of Burleson, and the villain, Michael, Duke of Zenda. Jonathan Wade was Rudolph Rassendyll and Prince Rudolph.

Confrontation: Archvillain Rupert (Tito Enriquez) vs. Rassendyll (Jonathan Wade), posing as Prince Rudolph.

Princess Flavia (Nancy Bell) displays her marksmanship.

The Duke threatens Princess Flavia.

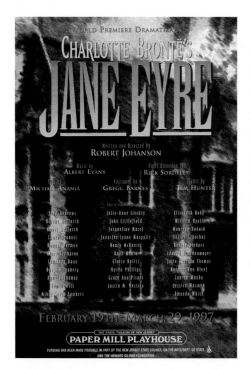

Two sisters living in the middle of the desolate Yorkshire moors produced two of the greatest books of all time. Both books contained autobiographical material, and both revolutionized the writing of fiction. *Jane Eyre* by Charlotte Brontë gave the world its first full-blooded female character—a plain, intelligent, passionate woman very much like Charlotte herself. Experiences in the novel, such as the horrible conditions at Lowood School and serving as a governess, were taken directly from Charlotte's experience.

Jane Eyre was portrayed by Elizabeth Roby and St. John Rivers by John Littlefield.

Blythe Ausfant, Glory Crampton, and Natalie Van Kleef.

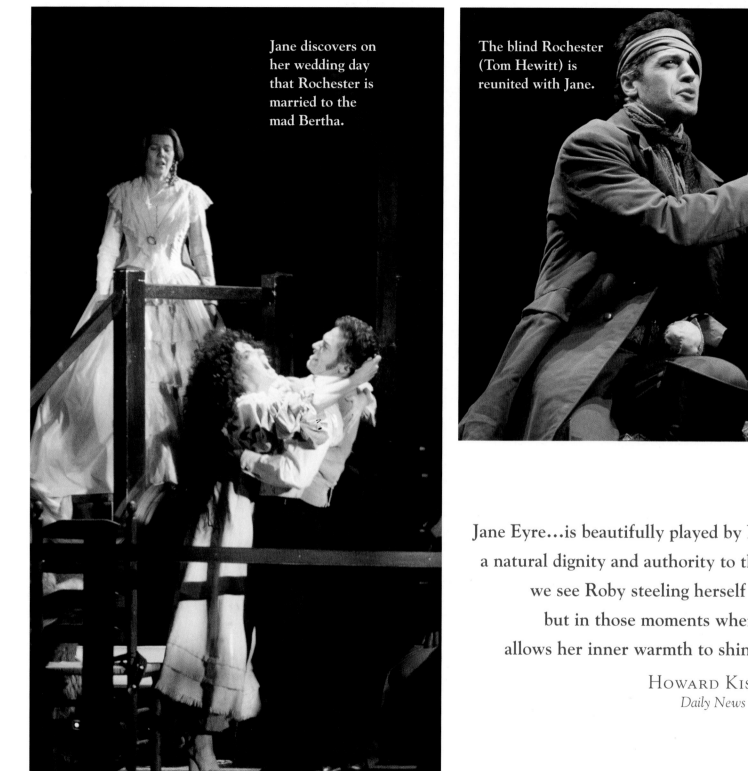

Jane discovers on her wedding day that Rochester is married to the mad Bertha.

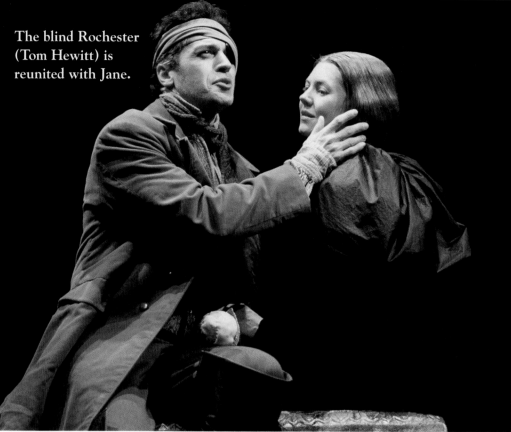

The blind Rochester (Tom Hewitt) is reunited with Jane.

Jane Eyre…is beautifully played by Elizabeth Roby, who brings a natural dignity and authority to the role. For the most part, we see Roby steeling herself against misfortune, but in those moments where she relaxes and allows her inner warmth to shine, the effect is radiant.

HOWARD KISSEL
Daily News

Emily Brontë's *Wuthering Heights* could not have been more dissimilar from her sister's novel: A brutal story of rough characters as wild as the moors themselves, bent on revenge and the destruction of each other. The Paper Mill productions undertook to tell the entire story of both novels. Almost all the film versions have ignored the second half of each story; the famous Laurence Olivier *Wuthering Heights* actually stops half way through the book.

Right, and above right: Heathcliff was portrayed by David Ledingham, Catherine by Libby Christofersen. Far right: Costume design by Gregg Barnes.

Mark H. Dold as Edgar, Elizabeth Roby as Isabella in *Wuthering Heights*.

Young Critics Program

This is one of the many educational outreach programs at Paper Mill. It encourages analysis of plays and their performances. Professional critics hold seminars about writing theatrical criticism. The students then see a show and write their own critiques. Here are some examples from the Young Critics at Rosa Parks Arts High School, written after attending *Wuthering Heights*.

The play, Wuthering Heights, was very good. I could now add this play to my list of favorites. I recommend all those who enjoy plays involving love and who love pieces written by the Brontës to view that production. If I had to rate this production on a scale of one to ten, I would give it an eleven.—Lakeisha Baker

Wuthering Heights is a great story of two families that learn a lot from each other. It was the first time I've heard of this story, but I found it to be very exciting. I fell in love with the characters immediately. Paper Mill did a great job. I expected a lot less, but got more than I hoped.—Taisha Moran

The first half was touching and it was sad to see Catherine die. Still the show was very powerful and very magical and very melodramatic.—Herman Irving

Jodie Lynne McClintock (right) as Nellie Dean.

I was completely enthralled in the performance from the moment the lights went down. I loved the set design, the lighting and the feelings they created. The gloom in parts of the show and the overflowment of joy in others was evident. But it was the story itself that was the most extraordinary. This was a tale that left you feeling for each character—understanding their thoughts and feelings and their wanting to reach out in some way. I was left crying over the loss and disappointment of the families, but smiling over young Cathy's great joy at the end.—Tiffany Herroeth

Shows That Took a Second Look

Mack and Mabel

SOME SHOWS ARE CONSIDERED FLOPS in their initial Broadway or London engagement. Why some plays work and others don't remains a constant mystery. If it were easy, the theatre would not be the challenge it is, and of course, the triumphs would not be so great. Paper Mill has had great success in shedding a more favorable light on some shows that were originally considered less favorably, as well as shows that initially enjoyed success but saw very few subsequent productions.

One such show was *Mack and Mabel* by Jerry Herman and Michael Stewart, the creators of *Hello, Dolly!* This show had everything going for it in its initial 1974 tryout: two big stars, Robert Preston and Bernadette Peters, the much-awarded director Gower Champion, producer David Merrick. It was a show of great merit, yet all the pieces didn't quite come together. Paper Mill took a second look, going back to work on the property with Jerry Herman. (Michael Stewart had died shortly prior to this revival.) Jerry is the only songwriter to have three Broadway shows run over 1,500 performances: *Hello, Dolly!*, *Mame*, and *La Cage aux Folles*.

The restored *Mack and Mabel* opened theatrical doors for the return of this almost forgotten musical.

It was revived in London, where it won many awards, and now productions of it occur all over the world.

Lee Horsley and Jane
Metz, Mack and Mabel.

Mack and Mabel *was the most difficult failure
for me. I'm not afraid to say I love it best. It's my
best work. Bringing it back has been a fourteen-
year dream. I was taken out to Paper Mill for the
first time to see Candide (another show rescued
from failure), and I was truly dazzled. I dragged
Mike Stewart to the next Paper Mill production,*
Annie Get Your Gun. *After Act One Mike
turned to me and said, "I think we've found
a home." To this day and for the rest of my
life, I believe that Mack and Mabel should
be a staple of our musical theatre....I vowed
that I would not stop until I'd made it into what
it deserved.*—Jerry Herman

Making a silent movie,
"Whatever Happened to Mabel?"

Fanny

Fanny was a Broadway musical also produced by David Merrick. When it initially opened out of town, the show ran four hours. Cuts were made based on how certain performers were being received instead of necessarily the best choices for the material. The love interest between Fanny and her lover, Marius, was reduced to a fraction of its original intent in favor of featuring the character men, Walter Slezak and Ezio Pinza. These men carried the show for a re-spectable Broadway run, but the property itself languished due to many imbalances. At Paper Mill, the script was returned to the original source material of Maurice Pagnol's stories, with the emphasis properly revolving around the title character. However, the two character men, this time José Ferrer and George S. Irving, were still equally effective and their argumentative, exasperating, deeply felt friendship will long be remembered at Paper Mill.

Easily the best musical of the spring is found way off Broadway at the Paper Mill Playhouse. Harold Rome's 1956 musical *Fanny* has been given a splendid revival.

DAVID PATRICK STEARNS
USA Today

I used to try to time it so that I could peek into the theatre regularly about halfway through Act One. This was the scene where Marius runs off to sea and his father, played by José Ferrer, sees him boarding ship from his upstairs bedroom. He rushes down through his house, out into the streets, and onto the end of the dock, which juts out into the audience. The boat has sailed. José calls from the bottommost depths of his feeling: "Marius! Marius!" The production was full of these raw emotional moments, passionate and human. It is one of my favorite productions.

—Angelo Del Rossi

The leads in *Fanny* are those endearing old goats César and Panisse, and they are endearingly portrayed by José Ferrer and George S. Irving. Ferrer still sings with a resonance and acts with his trademark incisiveness, while Irving is a joy in every way.

ANGELO DEL ROSSI

Fanny (Teri Bibb) watches a confrontation between César and Panisse.

Singin' in the Rain

Something quite surprising happens during the first act finale of *Singin' in the Rain*, which is being given an enthusiastic, glitzy revival at the Paper Mill Playhouse. It's not because the audience applauds the gracefully cascading rain that drenches the set in which the hero sings and dances the title tune. After all, rain, which in life is often as inconvenient as it is necessary, boggles the mind of a theatergoer susceptible to special effects: The water falling on the stage is real. It soaks the actor, who is also real and must return to the stage a few minutes later as dry as a bone. Even while you wonder how it's being done, you respond to its emotional impact within the show's loveliest production number. Michael Gruber does what Mr. Kelly never had to do in the film, that is, dance and sing at the same time, which takes not only talent, but a sturdy constitution. —Vincent Canby, *The New York Times*

Never in my whole career have I ever experienced anything quite so thrilling and invigorating as the rain sequence in Singin' in the Rain. This truly theatrical moment was a twofold gift: First, to have the opportunity to recreate such a memorable moment out of one of the greatest MGM musicals, one designed, as always, in the inevitable Paper Mill fashion—breathtakingly beautiful. Michael's set, Tim's lighting, and Gregg's clothes thoroughly transported me back to the decadent elegance of early Hollywood. Second, after the sheer physical endurance required to perform that first act—a marathon that has proved to be the greatest challenge I've ever had to face—how appreciative I was to cool off under the torrential downpour of a well-placed water spout. Except for the occasional bad behavior of a certain black umbrella, the number went off without a hitch, an amazing feat considering how complicated it was. Once again, I praise the incredible crew of the Paper Mill whose technical and emotional support, not to mention a good drying off each night, gave me seven weeks of absolute bliss.—Michael Gruber

Michael Gruber and Daniella Panessa.

Above, and top right: Michael Gruber and Randy Rogell, "Cosmo."

Deborah Jolly (Lina Lamont) is upset making a silent movie in *Singin' in the Rain.*

Chess

Steve Blanchard wins the championship match.

Chess was a blockbuster double album by Tim Rice, Benny Andersson, and Bjorn Ulvaeus. Onstage, it has never had the same script twice, but the new production at Paper Mill Playhouse is an exciting, dynamic version which tells a human story set against a glittering but violent international background.

This Chess is the best of the many productions I've seen. It's chief glory is its presentation of a human story presented on a human scale.

TED OTTEN
Trenton Times

Judy McLane and Keith Rice.

Everyone has their own vision of great books they have enjoyed. When I saw the Broadway production of The Secret Garden, I admired its artistry and really enjoyed the score, but found that the production concept didn't match my notion of the book. I wanted to try a completely different approach to the words and music at Paper Mill Playhouse. Little Mary has lost her parents, and her Uncle Archibald has lost his wife. Their minds are traveling in a labyrinthine maze of grief and confusion until they finally can let go and claim a new life through each other. We explored this mysterious journey through dark and shadow, as a true ghost story—lives haunted by their past and only escaped through the rejuvenating power of spring at the end of the play. Michael Anania and Gregg Barnes did an incredible job of re-conceiving the look of the show, and Mitch Dana's lighting pulled it all together. The cast embraced the new approach and the results were quite moving. The authors, Marsha Norman and Lucy Simon, had resisted seeing any production for several years, having been so close to it for so long on Broadway. When they attended this new version, they were like kids in a candy shop, alternatively laughing and crying as they greeted us afterwards and recapitulated every detail that was new: "The dinner party in India…the carriage ride…the emergence of the ghosts…the picture frame at the end!" We were very gratified.

—Robert Johanson

Cheri Bebout played Mary.

The Secret Garden

In designing the gowns for the ghosts, I used lace to give a light airy look and feeling, and pale appliquéd flowers to always suggest the presence of the garden. We found in dancing that adjustments needed to be made in the choreography to always maintain the floating gossamer look we wished to achieve.

GREGG BARNES

Keith Rice

Stephanie Douglas and
Cheri Bebout.

Robert Johanson

Nine

What a thrill it is to walk out on this stage in a house that has breathed such extraordinary creative new life into two of my works, *Phantom* and *Nine*. It really is quite unprecedented to have a theatre that continually does this kind of directing and reconception of pieces that redefine them. I'm really quite grateful for it.

—MAURY YESTON *from a speech at the 60th Anniversary Gala*

Guido's paramour (Glory Crampton).

Guido Contini (Paul Sheffler) and his wife Luisa (Judy McLane).

Michael Anania's superb set for the spa in *Nine*. Costumes by Gregg Barnes.

Rehearsals begin for *Phanton* with (from left) director Robert Johanson, lyricist Arthur Kopit, actor Richard White, composer Maury Yeston (seated), musical director Tom Helm, and choreographer Sharon Halley.

Phantom

Phantom boasts well-crafted melodic and visual moments of genuine beauty, plus a shining performance from Richard White that cuts across the theater like a lighthouse beam on a dark and stormy night. He's dashing, tender, wounded, funny, and always believable.

MICHAEL SOMMERS
Newark Star-Ledger

At the same time as Andrew Lloyd Webber was writing his *Phantom of the Opera*, Arthur Kopit and Maury Yeston were creating their show titled simply *Phantom*. Based on an earlier teleplay by Kopit, their work took a very different approach to the story, revealing the childhood of the Phantom and his relationship with his father. As luck would have it, the Lloyd Webber show reached Broadway first and became a phenomenon. However, the quality of the Kopit–Yeston version was not to be overlooked. So with a vigorous ad campaign to inform the audience that this was a different *Phantom*, the production was mounted and enjoyed much success.

Richard White as the Phantom and Marie Lawrence Danners as Christine.

Christine's singing debut at the bistro.

Patti Allison sings "A Diva's Work Is Never Done...."

Marie Laurence Danvers as Christine.

Gregg Barnes designed a magnificent dress for my final entrance in *Call Me Madam* but it was made of many pieces, and try as we would, there wasn't enough time for me to get into it. It broke my heart to abandon it, but it had to be replaced— by another beautiful gown!

LESLIE UGGAMS

Above: Leslie Uggams was the "hostess with the mostess" in Irving Berlin's *Call Me Madam*. Left (left to right): Michael O'Steen, Stephanie Douglas, John Scherer in Cole Porter's *You Never Know*.

Among the shows that weren't originally failures, but whose reputation had languished and were seldom performed, Paper Mill revisited three with special virtues. *You Never Know* featured a delectable Cole Porter score in his only six-character musical. *Call Me Madam* had the music of the great Irving Berlin and a wonderful starring role. *Animal Crackers*, originally written to feature the Marx Brothers, was that rare breed—a musical farce. Charles Repole directed all three of these productions.

Directing Animal Crackers at Paper Mill Playhouse gave me an incredible opportunity to be especially creative and invent staging that would reflect the uniquely clever style of the George S. Kaufman musical. Animal Crackers is a script rich in both absurd comedy and brilliantly farcical characters, with dialogue that virtually attacks the imagination. The talented production team that Angelo and Robert assembled was able to bring a fresh, clear vision to the piece. If I wanted Groucho to fly, he flew. If statues needed to come to life in the moonlight, they breathed. If I needed a harp to magically appear, it rose from nowhere center stage, with Harpo poised at the strings. Without such detailed care to the visual elements, the comedy of the piece could not—and would not— have been realized so clearly. Of the many gifts derived from working on a show like Animal Crackers, the most satisfying by far was the gift of laughter. It permeated the rehearsal hall, making the work enjoyable for both the cast and myself, and it was infectious. To this day, I believe it was the single most important factor in bringing the characters, the music, the wit of Kaufman to life on the Paper Mill stage.*—Charles Repole

Animal Crackers

The zany brothers, from left: Zeppo (John Hoshko), Harpo (Les Marsden), Chico (Robert Michael Baker), and Groucho (Frank Ferrante). The always-beleaguered dowager was played by Carol Swarbrick.

The Roar of the Greasepaint—The Smell of the Crowd, an allegorical musical with a superb score, was also seldom performed. This version, set in a post-apocalyptic Dr. Seuss nightmare world featured expressionistic sets by Michael Anania, inventive choreography by Susan Stroman and dynamic portrayals by George S. Irving as Sir, and Robert Johanson as the underdog, Cocky.

The Roar of the Greasepaint—
The Smell of the Crowd

The 1940's Radio Hour was not considered a success on Broadway, but certainly succeeded at Paper Mill with its realistic depiction of wartime America. It was set during an enacted radio broadcast on a snowy December night with a big band and great Forties tunes to warm everybody up.

The 1940's Radio Hour

Dorothy Stanley with (from left) Bob Walton, David Chaney, Larry Grey, John Scherer and Kenneth Kantor.

Applause

Another show that Paper Mill revisited was *Applause*, starring Stefanie Powers (left). This was a co-production with Fran and Barry Weisler. Gene Saks directed, and the choreography was by Ann Reinking.

❧

The "second look" revisions, reconstructions, and reinterpretations that Paper Mill has presented over the years have covered the entire range of theatre: operettas, dramas, comedies, revues, and musicals of all kinds. The scale of production has ranged from simple to complex to lavish, according to the dramatic needs of the show. And of course the degree of reinvention called for has varied. One of the most involved—and most interesting—productions was a complete re-creation of a story laid in the time of the Creation itself, *Children of Eden*.

Children of Eden:
The Evolution of a Production

EVERY PRODUCTION PRESENTED AT the Paper Mill Playhouse involves a concentrated effort on the part of the entire staff, but a show that originates at the Playhouse brings with it a certain tension and a special need to shape it into its best form. In the fall of 1997, Paper Mill staged *Children of Eden,* music and lyrics by Stephen Schwartz and book by John Caird.

The theme of *Children of Eden* is the relationships between parents and children. Set in the time from the Creation to the Great Flood, it uses the stories of the families from which the entire human race has descended—Adam and Eve, Noah, and their children. It deals with basic and eternal human difficulties and triumphs: family love and tensions, parental successes and failures, discipline, filial rebellion, sibling enmity, and most of all, the growth of love, wisdom, and understanding.

The evolution of the show had begun with an unsuccessful London production in 1991, followed by several small productions in the United States. Stephen Schwartz had maintained his faith in the show, and when it eventually came to the attention of Paper Mill, both its universal theme and Schwartz's stunning music had an irresistible appeal. What follows chronicles the process that brought *Children of Eden* to the Paper Mill stage.

Adam (Adrian Zmed), Father (William Solo), and Eve (Stephanie Mills).

In The Beginning...

In Fall 1996, Angelo Del Rossi and Robert Johanson meet with Stephen Schwartz to discuss and construct a production growing out of the original script and the themes that are the foundation of the show. Schwartz credits the original concept to his friend, Charles Lisanby, who designed the Radio City Music Hall Christmas and Easter Shows. Lisanby came up with the idea of the Creation story as the basis for a similar Radio City show for the summer months.

Stephen Schwartz says of his own development of the concept: *When I first started, I didn't really have in mind much more than a pageant. And then as it developed, it became clear that it was going more in the direction of a book musical, with Cain being sort of the antihero and turning into Noah's son, Japheth.... What appealed to me about the idea was that it was a way to deal with the issue of dysfunctional families and how dysfunction gets passed from generation to generation. And how that chain has to be broken at some point for everything to heal and for everyone to make a fresh start. It's just that rather than being three generations of a family in New Zealand on a sheep farm in 1860, it's the First Family, which happens to consist of God and Adam and Eve. My tendency as a writer is to find a story that is set in another time or another world, but which deals with contemporary issues or themes that are important to me. You just use the setting as a veneer, but basically you're dealing with issues that are contemporary, but also timeless.*

Del Rossi, Johanson, and Schwartz agree that Paper Mill Playhouse is the ideal place to create an entirely new production of *Children of Eden*, and work begins immediately. All Paper Mill staff

Kelli Rabke, Stephen Schwartz, Darius deHaas.

directly involved in production—including artistic, design, technical, financial, and marketing—outline each phase of the show's development and requirements. Budgets are drawn up to cover all costs and contingencies. Director Johanson has requested a cast of sixty (40 adults and 20 children), the largest ever assembled at Paper Mill. Special permission from Actors Equity Association—the professional actors' union—will have to be obtained to cast local nonunion children. If permission is granted, it will have quite a positive impact on that part of the budget. In the next weeks, decisions are made on the choreographer, stage managers, music director, lighting designer, sound designer, hair and makeup specialists, and other specialized production people, with assistants for almost all of them.

Casting

With a production team in place by Spring 1997, casting director Jessica Donovan sends out performer requirements in the form of official "breakdowns" that go to all the talent agencies. She then sets up days of audition appointments from the agent submissions for principal roles. There are also the required Equity and non-Equity chorus calls held for ensemble singers and dancers, and long hours of "creature" improvisations to find children of all shapes and sizes who will play animals in the Garden of Eden and on Noah's Ark.

The challenge of casting Children of Eden *was not just the sheer numbers of performers of all ages, but the artistic team's consensus that we have as many races represented as possible—especially within the principals who make up the "Family." The refreshing part of this long process (we began in May and were still casting in October) was that because this was a "new" work, we*

were unrestricted by the usual preconceived notions of a role. We could cast on talent, with less regard to "type."—Jessica Donovan

Auditions and callbacks continue throughout the summer with numerous ups and downs. The role of Father/Noah is offered to a performer who has to refuse because his off-Broadway show will move to Broadway. The search begins anew. There are also understudies and soloists to consider. Throughout these auditions, everyone looks at photographs and checks resumés. Director Robert Johanson is patient and instructive, explaining the music and his approach to the script. Serious contenders are asked to try songs from the show. Those being considered for principal roles read scenes with Assistant Director Patrick Parker. Johanson and Music Director Danny Kosarin make suggestions, Stephen Schwartz often coaches. Performers are called back in groups to dance for choreographer Dawn DiPasquale. Discussion follows every tryout.

Some sessions are long and tense—the chorus calls are mob scenes. Then there are the days that will be remembered forever. During casting for the role of Young Abel, a tiny eight-year-old boy energetically enters the large audition studio. He proceeds confidently to the table to meet the production team and goes down the line shaking hands, politely and professionally greeting each person. He takes his music to the pianist and strides to the center of the room. The artistic team sits up, poised to hear the usual current Disney standard. The music begins and the boy starts strutting and belting out, "Fly me to the moon, and let me play among the stars…"—complete with finger-snaps and imaginary microphone, a direct takeoff on Frank Sinatra. The child finishes with a sly wink of the eye and the entire table bursts

The tragic first brothers, Cain (Darius deHaas and Abel (Hunter Foster).

into spontaneous applause. He is genuinely pleased at the response. Robert Johanson says to his assistant, "We've got to have this kid in the show." He is cast in the part of a penguin, and later appears in other Paper Mill productions.

The casting deadline is near, and still no Eve/Mama Noah. The vocal demands of the role are astounding and the portrayal requires a particular quality of strength and a range to play impetuous youth to wise old age. Stephen Schwartz had very definite ideas about the character: *It was extremely important to us—and I'll speak for John Caird, my collaborator, because we talked about this quite extensively—that the character of Eve not be made out as she is, frankly, in the Bible: to seem like the sinner or the weak person or whatever; that her choices were made consciously and for good reasons and she's actually the stronger one, the more inquisitive one. It was also extremely important to us that the issue of eating the apple was all about pushing the boundaries of knowledge and had nothing to do with sexuality.*

With those requirements in mind, Jessica Donovan worked hard to find the right performer:

The character of Eve was probably my biggest challenge. Everyone had finally agreed on an actress and we lost her to Parade *in Toronto. I thought of Stephanie Mills—the original star of* The Wiz *on Broadway—who by then had been in semiretirement. I tracked her down in North Carolina; her sister-in-law was acting as her agent. By the time she flew in to audition, she was very nervous. When she opened her mouth to sing Eve's songs, the room was silent. She started to relax and thrilled us with her singing and her spirited interpretation. We all agreed she WAS Eve.*

After filling the pivotal role of Eve/Mama Noah, casting is completed with Broadway professionals for the other major roles: Adrian Zmed as Adam/Noah; William Solo as Father; Darius deHaas as Cain, and Hunter Foster as Abel. Kelli Rabke, who is cast as Yonah, had had her first professional leading role as Dorothy in the Paper Mill production of *The Wizard of Oz*. Several ensemble roles are filled by young people who have been part of Paper Mill's various programs: the summer conservatory and concerts, and Rising Star Award winners. Contracts are signed and returned and everyone is looking forward to starting rehearsals. But first, back to the business at hand.

Costumes

It is mid-September 1997, and the artistic team has gathered at the Costume Collection in New York City, where the majority of the costumes will be constructed. The primary purpose today is to discuss costume needs with the designer, Gregg Barnes. Present are Robert Johanson, director; Dawn DiPasquale, choreographer; Michael Anania, scenic designer;

Stephanie Mills.

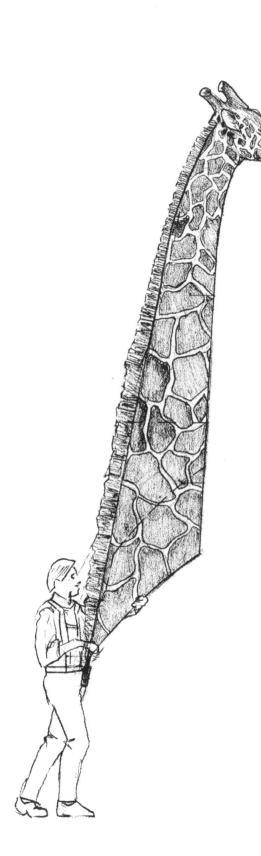

James D'Asaro, production manager; Monique Walker, properties manager; Donna Drake and Patrick Parker, assistant directors.

Barnes displays his preliminary designs with fabric samples for texture. The director and choreographer go over them with questions and explanations. Most of the show's children and many of the adults will represent animals during parts of the show and there is considerable discussion about what form their costumes should take. Should the porcupine have quills coming from his back? What kind of a bird is it, a stork? No, it should be more graceful. Will the elephants require three or four actors? Choreographer Dawn DiPasquale is concerned with the performers' ability to dance in the costumes and is asked to demonstrate some of the ideas she has been working on. The script calls for five actors to play the important role of the snake. What can they wear that will physically connect them, but allow them to move individually as well as in a unit? The discussions continue. Gregg brings out an animal book for suggestions.

Everyone agrees that seals would be great fun. Dawn knows just the two dancers to do the job. What color are the seals? Black will not show up well on the set. Will they have caps on their heads, flippers on their hands? Dawn is concerned that costumes not cover performers' faces. The participants consider each character and animal in relation to the physical qualities of the performers: hair color, skin color, height, build, and body shape. Some of the animals will be portrayed simply with hand puppets or paper sculptures, while others—unicorns, elephants, giraffes—will require elaborate headpieces and ingenious harnesses worn by actors who must be strong and adept enough to handle such complicated devices gracefully.

Gregg Barnes was so helpful. Early on in the design process, I went to his studio to demonstrate steps and the movement vocabulary I was working toward. He was wonderful in designing costumes that my dancers could move in easily, and also making sure that masks and pieces such as horns and tails didn't get in the way of partnering. Some of the masks and headpieces were challenging, but for the most part the dancers were able to make whatever adjustments they needed to cope with sight and balance issues without compromising my original vision of the choreography.—Dawn DiPasquale

In designing the costumes, Gregg looks for a timeless feeling. Researching folk costumes from all cultures, he finds amazing similarities, not just in the past but in today's world. A percentage of the pieces used can be bought from Indian, Chinese, and African shops, with Barnes and his staff building the remaining garments. Some animal costumes will have to be constructed by outside artisans. There is often a thin line between set, costumes, and props. Paper Mill's prop department will build birds on wires, as well as oversized frames and harnesses for the larger animals. It has been decided that the presentation of the animals as well as the physical locations will be representative as opposed to realistic.

Creating the First World

A few days later, the same group, plus lighting designer Jack Mehler, gathers at the Paper Mill Playhouse Theatrical Arts Center in Edison, New Jersey—commonly known as "the shop." It houses a few small offices, but most of the vast space is devoted to work and storage areas where carpenters and painters produce the sets and props. Shelves hold tens of thousands of items essential for "dressing" stage sets of all kinds.

Everyone is here to see a model of the set and to look over props for the show. In his small office with drawing table and dozens of books for research, resident scenic designer Michael Anania quietly moves a production from paper to visual theatrical settings. Starting with the script and music, he meets often with the director and, taking the director's ideas as the framework, incorporates his own understanding of effective theatrical presentation into the show's concept. Michael displays a draft of the set and explains his plans for the various lines of scenery. The

ACT I.2: EDEN

working stage space is 50 feet deep, with a proscenium arch 40 feet wide and 24 feet high. There are 78 separate lines—sets of cables and overhead battens to hold scenery and curtain. Anania says, "It's like designing a big machine and I love the chance to make the machine work."

Design, logistics, and complex details all must be considered and reconsidered. Should there be two lines of stars in the sky? Is there room to get the whale in? Where will the ramp and stairs be placed, and how and when should the great center disk turn and tilt? Noah's Ark is enormous. and there are apt to be problems moving it, and moving the actors around it. After settling dozens of questions, everyone moves to the warehouse to consider props.

A few chairs are set in the center of the vast space and everyone sits as if in an audience while the props people display their wares. The atmosphere is quite jovial as the assistants run back and forth

"Ritual" and "Circle" are two words that most influenced the scenic design for Children of Eden. A magic space was created to give the cast of sixty a place in which to come together and tell their story. The shape of the space became circular—actually two spaces, a circle within a circle—further adding to the look of a ritualistic space. The center sloped disk, which could revolve, became the main storytelling area. The surrounding circle took the form of a curved ramp that enfolded the main playing space and allowed the ensemble to observe, and at times participate in, the action on the main disk from a higher vantage point. As scenes progressed, different scenic elements were added to the space to change location, but these pieces always had to become a part of the ritualistic circle of life. —Michael Anania

Treasures in the Paper Mill Theatrical Arts Center: backdrops; costumes; chairs, tables, and assorted furniture to fit any historic period. Complete sets of tableware and linens; chandeliers and street lamps; swatches of fabric; rugs, paintings, plumbing fixtures, bicycles, suits of armor, trees, benches, marblized columns—and myriads more.

showing comets with flying tails and stars and planets on sticks and poles. The group likes the fish in blue and gold best. The birds are too heavy, they should be made from paper. Now they look at worms, now the whale, now tree branches and apple blossoms. They check swatches of fabric and hand puppets of small animals. Little by little, decisions are made—subject to change, of course. A rich full day.

A week later, another major production meeting is held, this time at Paper Mill. A roomful of production people are in attendance including set, lights, sound, costumes, props, stage manager, production manager, director, choreographer, and their various assistants. The first discussion involves final dates for designs and costumes, approvals on sound, lighting, and scenery, labor costs on load-ins, orchestra and technical rehearsal schedules, reduced rehearsal hours for children, and, of course, a pep talk on budget by the money people. Nothing can be constructed until the various budgets are approved.

Robert Johanson now talks through the entire production, describing the story, music, and movement while scenic department assistants change the set model as each scene unfolds. Every item is explained—lighting, makeup, props, costumes, whether microphones would best be placed in some performers' hair. The group ponders how to display the "mark of Cain" on the actor in that role. It has to appear suddenly, in a dramatic instant. It is humorously suggested that the actor be permanently but gently branded and the mark covered with makeup for other scenes. A few laughs help—this is a long and intense meeting.

The afternoon continues with talk of how best to set up various scenes near and on the Ark, a major piece of the set in the second act. When Yonah

releases the dove, can it fly out over the audience? Should stars come out in the sky for that scene? Should there be a moonrise in the earlier "Ring of Stones" scene? Lighting designer Jack Mehler has been asked to come up with a rainbow effect for the final scene. Detail after detail is covered, up to and including curtain calls. Everyone will now go away to make changes and revisions.

Staging an Epic

It is a week before rehearsals begin. Budgets were approved, so sets and costumes are well under construction at their various shops. Robert Johanson and Dawn DiPasquale, with their assistants Patrick Parker and Beth Dukleth, meet at Robert's home for a day of planning the actual staging of performers' movements. Michael Anania and his two assistants have brought the revised set model and proceed to explain the workings of the scenery. The majority of the set changes will be executed by the actors, so the team must carefully plot each move and track every performer's path.

Patrick produces a stack of quarters (depleting his entire laundry supply), each of which has been labeled with the name of a performer and color-coded to denote principal, soloist, dancer, child, etc. Everyone gets down on the floor. Pieces of the set model are laid out to represent the stage area and the performer-coins are placed in appropriate spaces. For hours they are moved around to work out the movements of each person throughout the show, visualizing the look of everyone in full costume, the props they carry, the best groupings, exits, entrances, and set moves.

"If we move the center ramp back, it works fine except when we do the whale."

"I'll let stage management know that the ramp

will have to be brought forward at that moment so the whale can pass."

"Where do we have the snails?"

"I think it will look better if we have a whole school of fish instead of their being broken up."

"Now we have five snails, the mommy, the daddy, and three babies downstage right."

"Okay, then let's put all the fish down left."

"What's the most magical way for the snake to enter and exit?"

"Who will take the planets from the children?"

"Can the worms get on stage ahead of the bees?"

"Take Kelli out of the 17 spot and put her at number 8."

"All props have to be cleared by the time the turntable moves."

"Do we have anyone left on stage to remove Adam and Eve's cloaks?"

"Can the duck come out of the trap in the first animal ballet?"

"No way, a duck is not a burrowing animal."

"What if we make it a bunny?"

And so it goes throughout the day, moving quarters, moving ramps and pillars on the model, trying to cover the smallest details in preparation for rehearsals; time is of the essence. The enormous size of the cast makes blocking their movements somewhat like planning a battle, no—a major invasion.

R-Day: October 9, 1997

The first day of rehearsal begins at 10:00 a.m. at the Wein Rehearsal Studios in New York City. This is one of the few facilities large enough to allow Paper Mill to realistically map out the dimensions of its stage, which is larger than most theatres on Broadway. It is easier at the beginning to rehearse here than to transport the performers, most of whom live in Manhattan, out to the theatre in Millburn every day. In a few weeks, the entire production will transfer to the Playhouse to begin technical rehearsals.

Present on this first day are the producing and artistic staff, theatre department heads, composer Stephen Schwartz, and the entire adult cast. A large U-shaped table has been assembled with the set model placed at the open end. Angelo Del Rossi welcomes the company and says how good it is to be producing a show with a composer who is living. The very "alive" Mr. Schwartz comments on how secure he feels in knowing it will be a success at the hands of Paper Mill Playhouse and Robert Johanson. Robert makes introductions and gives the cast an orientation on both the show and the theatre.

The cast proceeds to read through the entire show while Johanson uses the model to explain their locations as scenes progress. It is amazing how strong the first readings are, and characterizations are already emerging. Bill Solo (Father) is a bit surprised to find out he will be "flying" in one scene—heights

Rehearsal—Planets whirl as Father accomplishes the Creation.

Right: Rehearsal—Snakey doings.
Below: The Apple Tree in the Garden.

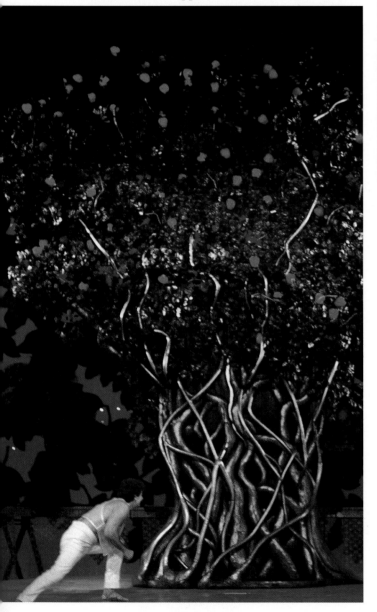

are not his forte. The read-through is accomplished, there is a short break, and then down to business. Robert begins blocking the Eden scenes with Father, Adam, and Eve; Dawn and her assistant set up in another studio across the hall and begin plotting "snakeography"—setting the movements for the five people playing the snake. Dawn herself is a beautiful dancer and it is lovely to watch her choreograph the others. The snake music has a lively quality to it and the performers fall immediately into the fun of it. They are using a long tube reinforced by hoops, which will temporarily represent the snake. They wrap it around themselves and crawl and slither with it. Conductor Danny Kosarin is teaches beautiful harmonies to the ensemble in a third studio. In the next few days, more of the same. Scenes and dances are mapped out. The animal ballet is begun, Act Two

blocking begins. Always there is singing and more singing. It's amazing how fast this all goes together.

The Saturday of the first rehearsal week is the march of the wee folk. All the children are on hand. Dawn gently leads each one through his or her paces. The children come in all sizes, shapes, and colors, as befits the children of Eden. A few parents are present, along with Sharon Hazard, the "child wrangler," whose task is not unlike a steer wrangler's—round 'em up and keep 'em in the pen. The older children seem responsible and have a working knowledge of music and movement. Some of the younger children are shy and need to be coaxed. When not rehearsing, they sit on the floor in corners playing cards (the boys) and discussing clothes (the girls). The really little ones find a lap to sit on and nibble snacks, vaguely watching rehearsal. All are amazingly quiet and well behaved. The wrangler gives the kids a little pep talk on not leaving the room without permission. One boy trips. Dawn expresses concern, which seems to be all that's necessary to get him back to work.

Because of our concept of having a non-ethnic-specific tribe telling this story (and also because the animals from the Ark would eventually become all of the animals of the earth), I began studying rituals and ceremonies represent-ing animals through their movements in African, Indian, Chinese, Native American, and other cultures, and then combining elements from each. I also watched a lot of nature shows and followed my poor cat around the house. A wonderful tool I discovered was the theory of "shape shifting" in religious ceremonies, that is, feeling the human body morph—in a way—into another creature. This was helpful in translating animal movements to our human physicality. —Dawn DiPasquale

William Solo rehearses the opening number with the company.

It has been a good first week. The company has united in their collective glee and the mass exodus from the studio begins for a well-deserved day off.

The Pace Increases

In the second week, more progress is made. The children are present only on certain afternoons—it can be quite overwhelming when the entire cast is on the "stage" marked in the rehearsal studio floor.

Director Johanson watches Dawn DiPasquale demonstrate a dance movement.

Midweek, there is a photo call for publicity and promotion shots, and on the last day, a "stagger through" of the entire show. The stage manager announces "places" and Robert gives instructions for a full run-through—"try not to stop." The cast applauds after each good performance. The snake is getting laughs. Darius' first-act solo is emerging as a show-stopper. This is the first time the children have witnessed these scenes and, when Cain kills Abel, the youngest little girl, Cassandra, terrified, bursts into tears and must be comforted. One little boy carries her about on his back trying to make her laugh. But soon it is the end of Act One and Stephanie as "old" Eve is making her "dying speech" and singing the show's title song. Now most of the children and a good many of the adults start to weep. The entire company joins in singing the Act One finale. The artistic team watches intently, with tears streaming down their cheeks. The sound is breathtaking as Schwartz's music soars to a climax. Tissues are passed out to all. They take a breather and get ready for Act Two.

Rehearsal resumes. The second act is a bit ragged. Robert spends a great deal of time on each performer, always with patience and humor. Copious notes are given by Robert, conductor Danny Kosarin, and Dawn. It is now evident to the performers where they still have work left to do. The creative team discusses where the "holes" are—some scenes still need tightening; perhaps the second act is too long and we should find places to cut. Director Johanson remembers: *Working with such a diverse cast on such rich and meaningful material was emotionally charged every day. From the youngest to oldest performer there was a span of nearly fifty years. So many cultural heritages to learn and grow from—so many differing generational philosophies of working and living. Truly a*

The fully realized Garden of Eden.

microcosm for a world in which we'd all like to live—surely what God had intended. The most moving day in rehearsal came when I learned that our little Sinatra, young Paul Iacono, was currently fighting his own battle with leukemia. He went regularly for treatments that could really knock him out from time to time, but he would bounce right back and rejoin rehearsals, sharing his bright and inspiring personality

The third week of rehearsals is mostly for polishing—only four days until the company moves to the theatre. The show has been staged entirely and now needs to be drilled and drilled. Mornings are devoted to trouble spots and afternoons to running the show for pacing and continuity. Designers, dressers, and stagehands trickle in during the week to watch the run-throughs, taking notes, tracking performers and props. At times, there are over 100 people in the large rehearsal room. The final studio run-through on October 30 goes surprisingly well. There are only a few mistakes, only a line or two needs prompting. The cast gathers to receive instructions about transportation to Millburn and about what will be expected of them over the long days of technical rehearsals. Everyone is dismissed, all rehearsal props and costumes are packed up. Apprehension and excitement are in the air—we'll be on stage tomorrow.

Yonah releases a dove form the Ark.

Adam tries to restrain Cain's attack on Abel.

Adam, bereft.

There are, you know, some people in the world who don't like musicals. Too silly and superficial, they say. No redeeming social value. Who needs another boy-meets/loses/gets-girl story? They (and everyone else) are urged to rush to the Paper Mill Playhouse to see *Children of Eden,* one of the most intelligent and profound musicals ever written.

PETER FILICHIA
Newark Star-Ledger

The Final Stages

Technical rehearsals ("tech") occupy five days of gruelingly long hours and frayed nerves. The technical crew has been hard at work all week in preparation for the actors' arrival on Friday evening. Scores of lights have been hung. The Eden show deck (stage floor) has been installed complete with turntable and winches. Grooves in the floor allow set pieces to be moved electronically. Backdrops are in place ready to fly in and out; special effects are being assembled. The dressing rooms are now full of costumes and the halls are filled with animal parts.

A long table has been set up in the middle of the auditorium. It will be home base for the production team for the next week. Everyone is equipped with headphones so designers, crew, and stage management can communicate with each other and, it is hoped, divert any impending technical disaster as the actors now attempt to perform with all the elements in place. The director has the crucial "god microphone" so he can communicate with the actors on stage and control the rehearsal progress. At the same time he is instructing the stage manager on cue timings and adjusting lights with the designer at his side. Robert Johanson is a master at the process.

The actors arrive and get into costumes, wigs, and body microphones. The sound designer will now hear the vocals amplified for the first time and many adjustments will be made. The huge array of props is distributed and the actors begin to learn the routes that will take them in and out of scenes. Meanwhile, the lighting designer has his work cut out for him. Lights are focused and refocused; colors wash across the stage as he searches for the right "look" for the scene; the spotlight operators learn which actors to follow when.

The underlying magic of Children of Eden is the telling of a vast, epic tale in a way that comes across as clean and succinct. Working from this idea of simplicity I took the end, Father's final gift of the rainbow, and laid out a path to get there. In the beginning, the colors of the rainbow are introduced as part of Creation. Then, during the course of the story, places which are mostly of Father's hand—like the Garden—use strong, simple rainbow colors, and places which are of the children's making use more complex combinations of shades and tints. The play also contains destructions, expulsions, curses, and floods that are by nature spectacular. I felt, however, that these too needed to resonate with simplicity, so I approached them in a ritualistic way, using broad strokes of pure white lightning and nearly surrealistic color shifts.—Lighting Designer Jack Mehler

The long hours and days of tech rehearsal go by. Dawn and Beth adjust spacing and patterns. Patrick and Donna run back and forth from production table to stage calming actors, choreographing set moves, and solving problems with quick costume changes. Robert is firmly at the helm, his director's eagle eye never wavering from the stage as things fall into place. The work is tense and harrowing. Voices and limbs get tired, props break, costumes are refitted and replaced, set pieces and actors collide and tempers flair. But somehow, in a very short time for such an ambitious production, the magic happens. By the fourth day the Creation opening number, with its whirl of planets and bodies and stars and trees occurs with no major catastrophe. There are gasps of astonishment and awe when the Apple Tree explodes, splitting in half and flying away during Adam and Eve's expulsion from the Garden. Eve's death and ascent to heaven, where she is reunited with Adam and Abel, is heartbreakingly beautiful. Then the massive Ark appears in the second act, seemingly hauled on by a few actors holding ropes. This time the flying rig does not rock and tilt and allows the scene to be played without that unmistakable quiver of fear in the voice of Almighty Father from above. The march of the animals to the Ark begins. There is an orchestra at last, and the dancers' bodies respond on an entirely new level. The final pose—and everyone bursts into applause. Dawn is in tears, "It works, it works!" Robert is finally smiling.

The opening Animal Ballet.

The Main Event

Children of Eden opened on November 5, 1998. The first-night audience cheered the beautiful production and the press gave it some stunning reviews. But that was hardly the end of the adventure. With a large cast and complex scenic and technical operations, no show runs without problems, most of which an audience never knows about. A few composite notes from stage manager Eric Sprosty's Performance Report, which covers everything, good and bad, during each performance, tell a harrowing tale.

RAIL: Upstage Dove line broke just before flight. God walked it down.

PROPS: One umbrella palm broken, another close to breaking. Piano in pit broke string (C two below middle C). Needs to be replaced by Wednesday.

CARPENTRY: Can you check and repair apple tree? Seem to be two holes in stage left netting.

WARDROBE: Michael H. is having an allergic reaction to the lion head. Can you look at it?

ACCIDENTS/INJURIES:

Paul I.—Fell on stairs in hallway during intermission.

Jeffrey S.—Hit right shin on disc during Animal Ballet.

Cassandra H.—Fell on exit from "Ain't It Good."

Jon Jon B.—Twisted right ankle leaving stage at curtain one.

Jim W.—Jammed left foot on platform offstage right that is not normally there.

Vince D.—Sciatic nerve, due to rake and snake

ABSENT/SICK:

LaTonya H.—still sick.

David B.—excused absence.

Trent K.—voice problems.

REPLACEMENTS/UNDERSTUDIES:

Beth D. on for David B. Jimmy S. sang "Wasteland" solos for Trent. Erica C. hurt knee, Jeffrey did both turtles. James J. as porcupine.

PERFORMANCE NOTES: Lynette's necklace broke on stage. Beads everywhere. Long intermission—Sheetal forgot to put on her microphone. Adrian only delivered one baby—brain lapse! Great Audience!

STANDING OVATION!

And so it went. During school-night performances the older children were doing their science projects in the dressing room; the little ones were napping between scenes. The day one of the actor vans from Manhattan was delayed in tunnel traffic was also the day two major reviewers arrived—of course! Marketing director Debra Waxman did her best to wine and dine them in the restaurant while waiting for the show to commence. One night during an early scene, Stephanie Mills fell on stage and hit her head. She picked herself up and tried to keep singing, but fainted into Adrian's arms and was carried off stage. The show came to a halt for about nine minutes. The audience waited patiently while ice and aspirin were dispensed and options were discussed. Ever the ultimate "pro," Ms. Mills was back on the stage (with a colossal headache) to finish the show for a cheering crowd. The usual winter colds and flu continually plagued the company, and there were performances when it was very difficult to get two of all the animals for their entrances into the Ark.

Darius deHaas and Kelli Rabke.

Father watches over construction of the Ark.

WHEN THE PRODUCTION CLOSED ON
December 14, it was hard to break up the group. No
one wanted to begin the parting. The experience
had been positive and uplifting. They knew it was
important work; it made them happy. Assistant stage
manager Becky Garrett said it succinctly: "It was a
very special company. Only Paper Mill and Robert
Johanson can do that kind of thing." And composer
Stephen Schwartz concluded happily:

*I think it's the best show I've ever done and I just
wanted to get it right. Which I think we have. And based
on the kind of response we've gotten, it certainly seems
we have. Now what will happen with it, will happen with
it. I'm just pleased to be here at Paper Mill.*

Epilogue

On January 14, 1998, the cast met for one more time at The Hit Factory on West 54th Street in New York City. They were there to make the Paper Mill Cast Recording of *Children of Eden*. Along with the entire cast were the major staff of Paper Mill Playhouse, dozens of technicians, public relations people, and Stephen Schwartz, who seemed delighted to the point of dancing a bit during the recording. It couldn't have been a happier ending.

American Premiere Recording

CHILDREN OF EDEN

Music & Lyrics by
Stephen Schwartz

Book by
John Caird

Based upon a concept by Charles Lisanby

RCA VICTOR

Children of the cast recording part of "Let There Be" for the CD.

Above: Allan Jones, Neva Small, Allan Seuss, and Kim Crisswell record the "Stars of Christmas" Paper Mill holiday album. Right: Two more Paper Mill cast recordings.

The Wizard of Oz

I find it most fitting that we open our tenth anniversary season in the new playhouse with a production of the timeless Wizard of Oz. The nature of this story touches the lives and hearts of all generations. I thank everyone for making our dreams at Paper Mill come true over the past decade and for challenging us to continue to chase our rainbows. ANGELO DEL ROSSI

IN 1992, **THE PAPER MILL PLAYHOUSE STAGED A** spectacular production of *The Wizard of Oz* to celebrate its tenth anniversary. The script was based on the books by L. Frank Baum and originally adapted by John Kane for England's Royal Shakespeare Company from the motion picture screenplay of 1939. As the sold-out audiences approached the Playhouse, they were greeted by a glistening Emerald City and entered the lobby via a yellow brick road. This was just the beginning of a magical journey concocted by Paper Mill's own theatrical wizards: director Robert Johanson and choreographer Jamie Rocco, working with the magic of Michael Anania's amazing sets, Gregg Barnes' lavish costumes, and dazzling lighting by Tim Hunter.

The challenge of bringing this large show to the stage required the work of five scenic shops and six costume houses. The show was so successful that it was optioned by the Theatre at Madison Square Garden and opened there four years later starring Roseanne as the Wicked Witch of the West. Subsequently the show toured the United States with such stars as Mickey Rooney and Eartha Kitt, continuing to bring revenue back to the Playhouse.

Eddie Bracken as the Wizard and Kelli Rabke as Dorothy leave Oz by balloon.

The integration of all elements of the production's design took constant planning over a period of six months. The show has 19 different settings, 755 lights, 273 colors, 240 special effects, and 175 costumes.   MICHAEL ANANIA

Above right: Michael Anania's model for the black-and-white Kansas.
Below: The actual set for Dorothy Gale's farm in Kansas.

When I was little, I always wanted to have special powers. I would go around blinking and clicking my heels waiting for something to happen. I think now it has. Being able to play Dorothy is truly magical.　KELLI RABKE

Over 300 hopefuls auditioned to play the girl from Kansas. The winner, young Kelli Rabke, made her Paper Mill debut as Dorothy, with Judith McCauley as Aunt Em (later Glinda, the Good Witch of the East) and Michael Hayward Jones as Uncle Henry (later the Winkie General). In perfect casting, a dog actually named Toto played Dorothy's dog Toto.

Munchkinland

The MGM film has indelibly imprinted the characters and themes of the *Wizard of Oz* in our minds. One of the magic moments was Dorothy's arrival in Oz, when black-and-white scenes burst into full color. Another was the emergence of the Munchkins from hiding. Creating those moments, and the many others that make the story so delightful, with equal charm and believability on stage is a real challenge, for the techniques of the theatre are far different from those of the movies. Paper Mill produced this great American fantasy Oz with such magic that it has gone on to tour internationally year after year.

Over 600 children and little people auditioned to play thirty Munchkins.

Norma, Joyce, and Gary Pratt

I am a longtime front-row subscriber at Paper Mill, but I attended shows back in the 1940s when I was just a kid. I was treated to a show on special occasions, like a birthday. During every show, I dreamed of some day appearing in a Paper Mill production. It took over fifty years, which proves dreams can come true. Just never give up!

It was an awesome experience when my son Gary (4'2"), his wife Joyce (4'4"), and myself (3'11"), were called to audition for the Wizard of Oz at Paper Mill. Each of us landed a part in the production. It wasn't long before all the Munchkins became one big happy family. Of course, I soon found out it was not all fun and games. We worked hard and long, and tech rehearsals were exhausting. Would I do it again? You bet! —**Norma Pratt**

Norma Pratt (center) with Munchkins.

My inspiration for the Munchkins was that of a fanciful garden of flowers, candies, and vegetables. In the movie, Glinda wears a huge pink dress; in our show she wears an upside-down tea rose—it's pink, and it's still very big, but it's a decidedly new look.

GREGG BARNES

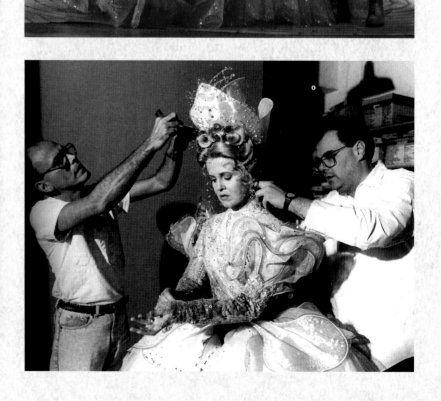

Elizabeth Franz, the Wicked Witch of the West, with Nikko (Derrick McGinty).

Tin Man Michael O'Gorman

Scarecrow Mark Chmiel

Cowardly Lion Evan Bell

IN THE SUMMER OF 1994, THE PLAYHOUSE followed its great *Wizard of Oz* success with another spectacular fantasy, the beloved *Peter Pan*. It ran for eight sold-out weeks and included many innovations to the Broadway musical made famous by Mary Martin.

Every young boy identifies with Peter Pan, probably more than any fairy tale hero. Girls have so many fantasies to choose from—Cinderella, Sleeping Beauty, Snow White—but for me at least, it was *Peter Pan. No wonder I felt a bit cheated when, as a child, I watched Mary Martin portraying the boy from Never-Never Land. Why was a girl playing Peter? As an adult I understand the conventions of theatre and appreciate Mary Martin's great gifts…but as a kid, I just didn't get it. I guess I may have harbored that feeling all these many years and felt compelled to play Peter so that other little boys could see a male playing their hero.*

—Robert Johanson

Mr. and Mrs. Darling—Christopher Innvar and Elizabeth Walsh—and family.

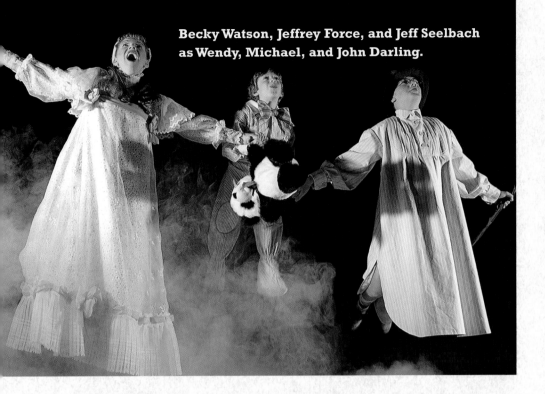

Becky Watson, Jeffrey Force, and Jeff Seelbach as Wendy, Michael, and John Darling.

FLYING BY FOY. The Foy company has flown more Peter Pans than anyone else, including Mary Martin in the original version. Here, David Hale of Foy helps the Darling boys learn to soar.

Never-Never Land

The production of *Peter Pan* presented several unique challenges. Never-Never Land needed to be like a gym, with high bars and a trampoline, and it had to move and revolve with apparent grace and ease. Since this unit weighs six tons, "grace" and "ease" took a lot of thought and planning.

BOB MURPHY
Scene Shop Foreman

Set sketch for the Never-Never Land show curtain.

Never land!

Playing Peter almost killed me! It is the most strenuous role in musical theatre. When you're not flying, you're fighting pirates, dancing with Indians, doing all sorts of aerobics, sliding down poles, climbing trees, singing twelve songs, most of it while wearing a very uncomfortable Foy harness. Near the end of the run, I sustained an injury which put me out of the show. I simply jumped 18 inches from the window seat to the floor of the nursery, but came down wrong and tore my calf muscle—I was hobbled. It's the kind of injury they shoot horses for. Of all the things I had to do in the show—this did me in.

—Robert Johanson

Ken Jennings as Capt. Hook's henchman, Smee.

Peter and the boys of Never-Never Land, triumphant.

Robert Creighton took over the role of *Peter Pan* and made such a terrific impression he was asked back the next season to play the Artful Dodger in *Oliver*.

Dana Solimando as Tiger Lily.

Tiger Lily costume rendering.

In designing the costumes for *Peter Pan*, the challenge was to arrive at a less traditional look for the inhabitants of Never-Never Land. The pirates became far more exotic as their origins became 16th century Morocco, 17th century Venice, distant Bangkok, or Shanghai. Likewise, the Indians began as a more fantastical blend of India and points west.   GREGG BARNES

Capt. Hook's pirates.

At the end of *Peter Pan*, Peter and Hook square off in a swashbuckling sword fight. It isn't often an actor gets to stand on stage in front of a packed house and point a sword at his director!

CHRISTOPHER INNVAR
Captain Hook

Oliver

Children and Animals

Madam, there's no such thing as a tough child—if you parboil them first for seven hours, they always come out tender. —W.C.Fields

Natalie di Luca in *Paper Moon*.

MANY PERFORMERS HAVE JOKINGLY groused, like W.C. Fields, about working with children and animals, but they know that audiences love seeing the little scene-stealers onstage. Paper Mill Playhouse audiences have seen some delightful performances, as well as mishaps, from pint-sized performers and their four-legged friends.

Gypsy—Uncle Jocko's Kiddie Show.

"Hello everybody. My name is June—what's yours?" My real name is Alexandra Kiesman. I played the role of Baby June in *Gypsy* and I had a really great time! It was magical— like theatre is supposed to be. I wanted the audience to see Baby June as this incredibly talented, energetic kid who really REALLY loved to perform on stage.

ALEXANDRA KIESMAN

Bulldog Stella played Bill Sykes vicious dog in *Oliver,* but in truth was a gentle creature.

Little David Watson who played the title role in *Oliver,* had an amazing experience. During a chase scene, he had to climb a ladder to the rooftops. He got going so fast that at one point neither his feet nor his hands were on the ladder and he plummeted almost twenty feet to the stage. He lay there with the wind knocked out of him and the curtain was brought down. The emergency squad was called and he was taken to the hospital. Now, the show had to go on. A little eight-year-old named Crystal-Eve was his understudy. She was crying hysterically in a corner. Robert Johanson remembers: *I said, "Crystal-Eve why are you crying?" "David…he fell… is he dead?" "No, he's going to be fine, he's just going for a checkup to be sure and now we need you. You know all the lines and all the songs don't you?"*

"Well…yes." "Do you think you can do it?" "I think so."—It was right out of 42nd Street. I maneuvered her to the stage, the curtain went up, and I introduced her to the audience. She was so tiny, but I told the audience she was ready to step in. We picked up with the next number where the entire company sings: "Consider Yourself One of Us" to little Crystal-Eve and she was just great. The audience cheered for several minutes before the show could continue and gave her a well-deserved standing ovation at the end, just as young David returned, perfectly fine.

❧

I was lucky to grow up in Mountainside, New Jersey, with theatre-loving parents. They would take me to shows at Paper Mill regularly and I was soon hooked. By age seven I was taking singing, dancing, and acting lessons in New York City. My first professional job, at age ten, was "The Milliken Show," an elaborate industrial that was produced annually at the Waldorf Astoria, where I had the prvilege of working with Ann Miller and Donna McKechnie. The following year I went to an audition for Paper Mill's production of The Sound of Music. I landed the role of "bratty" Brigitta and couldn't have been more thrilled to perform at the Paper Mill—it felt like home. Ten years went by before I returned as an adult performer in 42nd Street. Ten more years and I was fortunate to be cast in what would prove to be one of the most exciting shows I have ever performed in— Follies. Here I was, twenty years later, again sharing the stage with Ann Miller and Donna McKechnie. Growing up at the Paper Mill has been a wonderful experience for me, and I feel extremely fortunate to now be able to bring my children to these incredible productions.

—Jean Marie

Jean Marie (third child from left) in *The Sound of Music* with (at left) Barbara Meister and Jean Pierre Aumont. She grew up to be one of the tallest showgirls in show business, a great asset when she played in *Follies* (above).

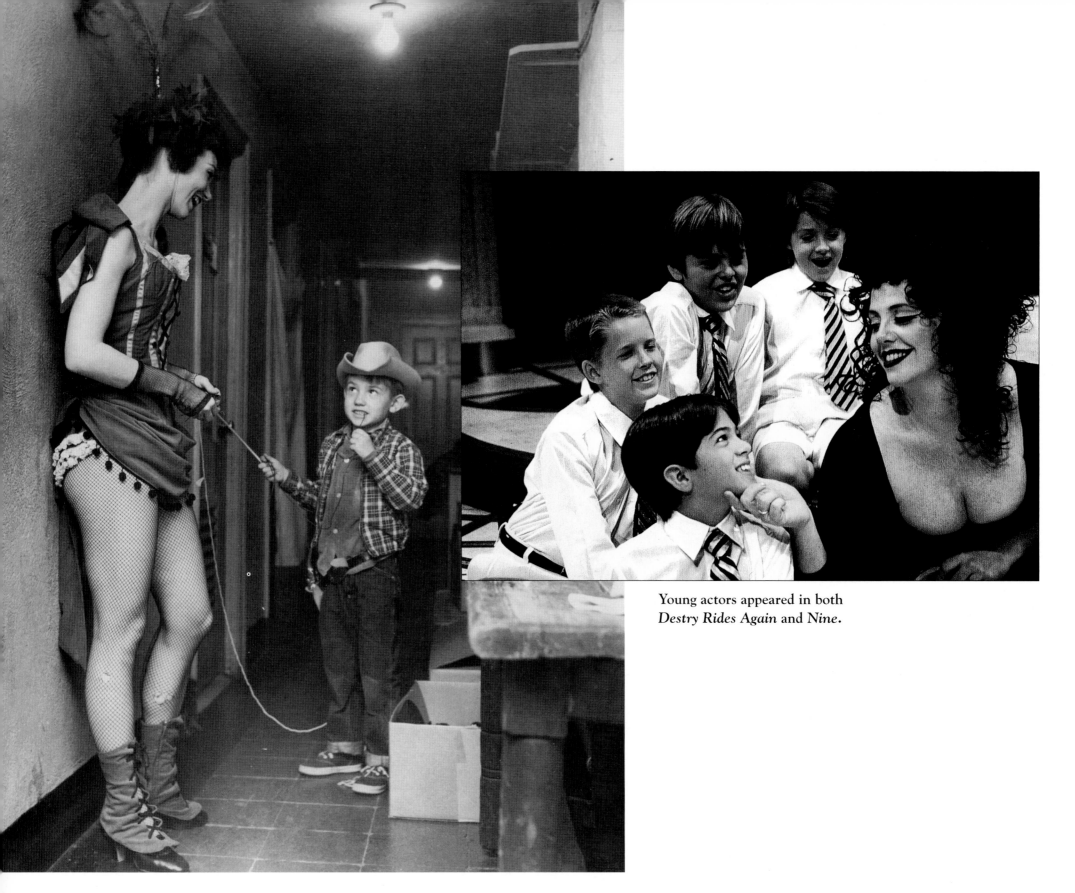

Young actors appeared in both
Destry Rides Again and *Nine*.

Grown-ups never understand anything for themselves, and it is tiresome for children to be always and forever explaining things to them.

—ANTOINE DE SAINT-EXUPERY, *The Little Prince*

Marcia Lewis with the orphans in a number in *Annie*, 1983. Above right: Tara Kennedy as Annie with her dog, Sandy.

The little dog who played Fanny in *Wuthering Heights* (seen below with Elizabeth Roby) was found in a shelter. She came to Paper Mill homeless, but immediately won everyone's heart and was adopted by one of the stage managers at the end of the run.

From left: Samantha Robyn Lee, Marguerite MacIntyre, and Jeffrey Songo in *South Pacific*.

As a sophomore in high school, looking back, the life I've had at Paper Mill seems so short, yet I've been performing there since I was in fourth grade. That year, I made my first stage appearance at Paper Mill with the New Jersey Ballet's production of Nutcracker. Then in 1994, I appeared in South Pacific, in in 1997 I was in Children of Eden. A year later I was cast in Gypsy as a newsboy. Having been performing at Paper Mill every year since 1993 is something I'm so glad to have done. Being on a professional stage, working with real directors and actors, and seeing my name in playbills next to actors who are stars in movies I watch is the best experience a kid could have. The acting, singing, and dancing skills I've acquired at Paper Mill affect the shows I do at school or in community theatre. Every time I go to an audition, the directors see my resumé and say, "Wow, Paper Mill, eh?"—Jeffrey Songo

Susan Powell as Laurey and Richard White as Curly shared the stage with Beau in some scenes in *Oklahoma*.

Gypsy was performed in September, a time of year when new lambs are born, and Deborah Gibson had to sing the tender "Little Lamb" to her new pet (right). The first "lamb" to arrive was a two-month-old black sheep as big as a bulldog. This was the only animal that had been found after a long search and it was very rambunctious. Would a stuffed lamb have to be the alternative? Suddenly, the lighting designer, Mark Stanley, remembered he had friends in Connecticut who raised test-tube animals for research. They were called, and indeed had a two-day-old lamb. The theatre purchased it, put a diaper on it, found Anna McKneely (who played the stripper "Electra" in the show) to take it home every night—and Deborah had her very little lamb.

Above: Scott Irby-Ranniar created quite a sensation in *Comfortable Shoes* at Paper Mill. He went on to create the role of Young Simba in the Broadway sensation *The Lion King*. Left: Both children and animals were onstage in many scenes in *Jesus Christ, Superstar*.

Robert Johanson on the burro that Philip McKinley and Lillian Graff rode in *Desert Song* (below).

In addition to a burro, *Desert Song* featured a camel that turned out to be quite cantankerous and had the worst breath imaginable. But the trouble it caused was all worth it because each night the camel got one of the biggest laughs in the history of the Playhouse. When the leading lady (Judith McCauley) was brought in on it blindfolded, she complained about her rough treatment and said, "And then you transported me on that horrible smelly elephant!" The camel, greatly offended, would slowly turn his head toward the audience with a deadpan look that outdid anything Jack Benny ever performed. The audience would laugh for several minutes as the camel just kept staring at them disgustedly.

In the *Wizard of Oz*,
Toto played—Toto!

When the stage manager walks by your dressing room and calls out,
"Ten minutes," there is a special feeling in the air at the Paper Mill
Playhouse. The feeling always gives me goose bumps!

—Paul Iacono, age 10

Paul Iacono waves goodbye
in *Will Rogers' Follies*.

More Than a Theatre

Every production at Paper Mill is an experience not to be missed; every community project is a new door open for a young person…to pursue a rewarding career in the arts.

—Lonna R. Hooks
New Jersey Secretary of State

Paper Mill is a cultural organization whose programs touch the lives of all generations, encourage the talents and education of young people, and offer wide-ranging access for people with disabilities. The expansion and progress of Paper Mill is made possible by generous support from individuals and organizations who believe in the theatre's mission and the social contribution it makes. I am proud of my association with this exceptional organization, and honored to play a role in its growth and development

JOHN MCEWEN
Director of Development

MORE THAN SIXTY YEARS AGO A troupe of thespians transformed an abandoned factory into the Paper Mill Playhouse "to create a greater interest in art, music, drama, history, literature, education, and theatre." No wonder Paper Mill has evolved into so much more than a theatre. It has become a haven and a springboard for aspiring actors and actresses. It has become a stage for literary forms. Paper Mill offers award-winning programs in which signed interpretation brings words to the hearing impaired and live real-time descriptions bring color to the otherwise blackened world of the blind. Children's programs excite the imagination of very young audiences. A variety of outreach initiatives invite young men and women to explore the endless possibilities of personal expression on the stage.

As one of the nation's most accomplished regional theatres, Paper Mill finds challenge in revitalizing and preserving the American musical as well as preserving classics and introducing new work. There are many aspects to that challenge. The composition and expectations of audiences are rapidly changing. The financial underpinnings of theatre are becoming ever more extravagant with burgeoning costs for costumes, for set fabrication, for marketing and insurance, and of course for the well-deserved

compensation of the talented actors and actresses who bring their performances to the stage. There is an ever-widening gap between the cost of productions and the income from ticket sales. The economics of modern-day Broadway extravaganzas well exceed the capacity of the regional theatre. In this climate, Paper Mill Playhouse strives to remain a stage larger than any on Broadway, one that will continually discover and nurture new writers, composers, and performers whose work will eventually charm audiences around the world.

Paper Mill emerged from the ashes of 1980 with magnificently generous support from a loyal family of corporations, foundations, community organizations, government officials and agencies, and—perhaps most important—loyal subscribers. Under Director of Development John McEwen, support has grown to the point that Paper Mill boasts the largest subscription base of any regional theatre in the country. The Paper Mill Guild, guided by Sharon Sandbach, nourishes the image of this very vital resource for the performing arts. Many other individuals and programs are also a part of this ongoing leadership and success. Here are some special highlights of Paper Mill's development, education, and outreach programs.

The Renée Foosaner Art Gallery
Established by Antoinette Scudder to show her art collection as well as her own paintings, the gallery at Paper Mill has become a showcase for artists throughout the region. Gene Carrington (left) was curator of the gallery until the fire of 1980. With reconstruction, Samuel Foosaner endowed a new gallery named for his wife, who was an artist. Each year some 500 artists exhibit original watercolors, oils, and pastels. A much-acclaimed international competition of miniature art draws over 1,000 entries annually. Consignment sales benefit the artists and Paper Mill. A later contribution by the Vincent and Anna Visceglia Foundation added a coffee bar to the gallery.

Above: Merrillyn Crane, Gene Carrington's successor and current gallery director, and assistant director Ray Lenhart prepare the annual International Miniature Art exhibition.
Left: An exhibition in the spacious, well-lighted gallery.

I n 1985, Paper Mill Playhouse was very fortunate to have Dr. William A. Tansey III agree to serve as a member of the Board of Trustees. He is an extraordinary individual who has enormous creative talent for developing exciting concepts and ideas. His passion for the arts inspires him to encourage others to share this experience which will improve their lives and give them pleasure and enjoyment that will fulfill them in a most enriching manner. This belief is no more evident than in the contributions he has made to the growth and development of Paper mill Playhouse.

Dr. Tansey was chairman of the committee for the development of the F. M. Kirby Carriage House and Baldwin Court. He raised funds of more than $1 million to complete these projects. They resulted in the transformation of the carriage house into a premier dining facility and the creation of a beautiful courtyard with a reflective fishpond, magnificent theatrical decorative arches, and a signature tower clock at the entrance.

Dr. Tansey has served as chairman of the Nominating and Planning committees and as a member of the Executive Committee. His joy in serving others is further demonstrated by his continuing support in public relations, outreach programs, and all the many other facets of Paper Mill Playhouse.

It was Bill Tansey's positive attitude and encouragement that excited and influenced me to publish this book for the Paper Mill Playhouse. It is with great pleasure that I honor my good friend for the fervor and care he brings to all his many projects and to the people whose lives he touches.

—David M. Baldwin

The F. M. Kirby Carriage House

The former residence of Frank Carrington on the east bank of the Rahway River is immediately adjacent to the main entrance of the Paper Mill. After Mr. Carrington's death there was considerable effort to preserve the charm of this eighteenth-century home. From ideas originated by Angelo Del Rossi and guided by Dr. William A. Tansey III, conversion to a comfortable, well-appointed restaurant was achieved. This very challenging project, designed and executed by Robert Heintz, was underwritten by Fred Kirby, a longtime generous supporter of the performing arts and especially of Paper Mill. The ultimate restoration was named the F. M. Kirby Carriage House. It has become the stage for quiet pretheatre dinners, festive receptions and opening night celebrations. As the personality of the restaurant has evolved, it has become a unique facility to embrace new visitors as well as seasoned members of the Paper Mill family.

Baldwin Court

Immediately following the inauguration of the Kirby Carriage House, David and Barbara Baldwin initiated and generously endowed the adjacent area in front of and alongside the Playhouse, the area now designated Baldwin Court. Under the creative guidance of landscape architect John Meeks, uneven macadam paving was replaced with handsome colonial Boston pavers and iron storm drain covers almost magically disappeared. Paper Mill's waterwheel emblem was fashioned with bluestone in the center plaza. A water garden against the side of the Carriage House became a quiet sanctuary near where long ago there had been a wishing well. Bluestone steps led to a small "secret garden" at the base of a giant sycamore tree that leans over the river.

A brick promenade along the river side of the theatre was framed by an iron arch at each end conceived by Michael Anania and Jana Thompson and

Angelo Del Rossi, Walker Kirby, and Fred M. Kirby at the opening of the remodeled Carriage House.

fabricated by Robert Minervini of Artistic Metal Works, a New Jersey family business of artisans. The main arch (at left and on title page) connects the theatre with the Kirby Carriage House. Silhouette images of music, song, and dance capture themes that are integral to Paper Mill's productions. The arch at the far end of the promenade has silhouettes of animal characters from fables, and a magician pulling a rabbit from a hat, an allusion to David Baldwin's enthusiasm for collecting items relating to theatrical magic of the past.

A large four-sided clock set on a geometrically imaginative column is the centerpiece for the entrance to Baldwin Court from the street. The entire space is itself a showcase of artistic talent, as well as a place where patrons of the theatre can wander before and after performances to reflect upon the show and enjoy one another's company. While the court was dedicated to David and Barbara Baldwin for their generous contribution, the whole project is evidence that visionary individuals with a commitment to the performing arts and to education can dramatically enrich the life of a theatre.

Paper Mill Trustee Dr. William A. Tansey III, Vice-Chairman Barbara Baldwin, David Baldwin, and John Meeks share a happy moment during the celebration of the completion of Baldwin Court.

> If audio description was not offered at Paper Mill it would be very difficult to adjust and the quality of my theatre experience would suffer. My sighted friends who have attended Paper Mill with me have applauded the amount of information delivered through audio description and the quality with which it is provided. I love this program and every theatre should have it!
>
> SALLY MYERS
> *Audio description program subscriber*

Access for Everyone

Long before Congress passed the Americans with Disabilities Act, Paper Mill made a commitment to ensuring that all individuals would be able to attend the theatre with dignity and independence. The Playhouse is proud to be one of the few theatres in the country to be completely accessible to individuals with disabilities.

With the guidance of advisory boards made up of community leaders with disabilities and others representing organizations serving people with disabilities, a wide range of access services were designed and implemented.

For those who have mobility impairments the theatre has elevators that take patrons to all levels of the theatre. Removable seats in the theatre allow those in wheelchairs to sit next to their companions.

Patrons with hearing difficulties are accommodated in several ways. An infrared amplification system carries sound from the stage to wireless headsets. For audiences of the profoundly deaf, Paper Mill hires American Sign Language (ASL) interpreters for both its mainstage and children's theatre productions. And for those who do not read ASL there is Open Captioning: A transcript of the dialogue scrolls up on a digital screen as the lines are being spoken by the actors onstage. On request, the theatre sends out scripts of

As part of Paper Mill's programs for the vision impaired, sightless audience members are given show costumes to help them "visualize" the styles and lectures presented in the production.

the production in advance to familiarize these patrons with the story and dialogue. Paper Mill Playhouse was the first theatre on the East Coast to offer this service, and only the third in the nation.

Paper Mill Playhouse also took the initiative in being the first theatre in New Jersey to make its programs accessible to individuals with visual impairments. Elevators and other facilities have Braille and raised floor numbers and labels. Pre-performance sensory seminars allow patrons to feel props and costumes being used in the production. During a performance, an audio description delivered through an FM system gives patrons a live, concise description of the action on stage. More than 3,500 people a year benefit from these services, which are made possible by the leader-

For the hearing impaired, Paper Mill offers signed performances of each production. Here Bill Moody, Laura Murphy, and Richard Chenault sign for a performance of *Chess*.

ship support of Merck & Company, the New Jersey Commission for the Blind and Visually Impaired, Everett and Bernice Hansen, and Carol Deem.

Dedication marked the opening of UMDNJ—University Hospital's Paper Mill Playhouse Infusion Program, an outpatient program for AIDS patients. Marc H. Lory, Vice President and Chief Executive Officer of the Newark Hospital (right) points out the new bronze plaque on the program's door to Angelo Del Rossi (second from left) and Irving J. Marsh, Chairman of Paper Mill's Board of Trustees (1992).

Leading the Way

Recognizing that whatever is good for theatre in New Jersey benefits the Playhouse as well, Paper Mill is active in several statewide organizations. Drawing on its experience as a leader in the area of arts access, Paper Mill founded the New Jersey Arts Access Task Force, a resource that assists state cultural organizations in making their facilities and programs accessible to people with disabilities.

Paper Mill is a founding member of the New Jersey Theatre Group, a service organization for the professional theatres in the state. And as a founding member of ArtPRIDE, an arts advocacy organization,

Paper Mill's leadership works to ensure that local and state officials adequately support the arts through appropriations and are aware of the importance of the arts to the economy and overall well-being of the state and its residents.

The Playhouse also helps to lead the way in raising funds for other community organizations. Through the generosity of cast, crew, musicians, and staff Paper Mill has raised more than $500,000 for AIDS research, and has presented benefit performances to support Broadway Cares/Equity Fights AIDS, the Hyacinth Foundation, and the infusion clinic at University Hospital in Newark, New Jersey.

Annually, Paper Mill works with the Make a Wish Foundation to help brighten the worlds of terminally ill children and their families by providing gifts and lunch at The Manor, followed by a limousine ride to Paper Mill for a performance of New Jersey Ballet's *Nutcracker*. And since 1994, Paper Mill's management and audience members have contributed annually an average of $2,500 and 2,000 to 3,000 pounds of food for the New Jersey Community Food Bank.

Business and Foundation Support

To carry out its not-for-profit mission, Paper Mill needs to raise an average of $3 million a year to maintain high artistic quality, keep ticket prices affordable, and implement its wide range of community outreach

One of our earliest and most active supporters has been the Paper Mill Playhouse. Since the first special performance of *West Side Story* in 1991, through other productions to today, Paper Mill has raised more than $360,000 for those in crisis and in need. On behalf of all those we assist, I am very grateful to the entire Paper Mill family for this very generous assistance. What we do together makes a difference.

TOM VIOLA
Executive Director
Broadway Cares/Equity Fights AIDS

John McEwen, Director of Development and Mary Ellen Waggoner, Associate Director of Development meet Elizabeth Dole (center) after her lecture.

programs. Sold-out houses provide only a portion of this amount; the rest comes from corporations and foundations, large and small businesses, government agencies, individuals, and membership support groups, all of whom recognize the social enrichment that derives from the performing arts.

The Howard Gilman Foundation, the Blanche and Irving Laurie Foundation, the Selma Morris Trust, the National Endowment for the Arts, the New Jersey State Council on the Arts, Arizona Iced Tea, Mercedes-Benz Tri-State Dealers, and Bristol-Myers Squibb Company all have played a leadership role in supporting the work of Paper Mill Playhouse. Many additional contributing organizations and businesses are included in the list in the Appendix IV.

Building Member Support

Another major, and far more personal, source of support is the Paper Mill "family"—the nation's largest theatrical subscriber base. These loyal theatregoers support the productions, workshops, and outreach

programs through raffles, auctions, receptions, and galas. They reach into their own pockets when necessary, and volunteer many hours to do what they can to make Paper Mill Playhouse a very special place.

The Playhouse also hosts a variety of fundraising events that celebrate the accomplishments of the theatre, introduce new supporters, and give members of the Paper Mill family an opportunity to meet the people whose work they support.

The Paper Mill Playhouse Guild

In the very early days of Paper Mill Playhouse, producer Frank Carrington encouraged the formation of a group of volunteers made up of women enthusiastic about the theatre and willing to spend time promoting it and enjoying an "insider's" role—meeting the stars and the directors, the set and costume designers, and being privy to the backstage workings of the theatre. Today's Guild is the same in many ways, but its contribution to Paper Mill is now of major importance. Annually, the Guild raises ap-

Standing, left to right: Paper Mill Vice President Barbara Baldwin; Millburn Mayor Elaine Becker; Angelo Del Rossi. Seated, left to right: Paper Mill Trustee Sharon Sandbach, Martha Kostyra, Martha Stewart, and Junior League of the Oranges and Short Hills President Laurie Finn enjoy lunch at the Kirby Carriage House.

proximately $100,000 through a gift shop on the lobby mezzanine, raffles, wine tastings, symposia, and a theatre tour to Europe. The members have been tireless in their efforts and unendingly enthusiastic in their support of the Paper Mill.

The Guild collaborates with the Junior League of the Oranges and Short Hills on a lecture series to help support the outreach programs of both organizations. Special guests at these activities have included Martha Stewart and Elizabeth Dole.

To honor the women who have significantly made a difference to the growth of the Playhouse and the development of the arts in New Jersey, Barbara Baldwin, Vice-President of Paper Mill Playhouse and her committee developed the annual Leading Ladies Luncheon. This event has honored such luminaries as actress Celeste Holm; Paper Mill benefactor Emily Ridgway; Executive Director of New Jersey Network and former Chairwoman of the New Jersey State Council on the Arts Elizabeth G. Christopherson; actress Judith McCauley; New Jersey Assemblywoman Maureen Ogden, and Millburn Mayor Elaine Becker.

Above, left: Angelo Del Rossi, actress Celeste Holm, Luncheon Chairwoman Barbara Baldwin, and actor Wesley Addy gather prior to The Leading Ladies Luncheon where Ms. Holm was honored. Above, right: Sylvia Baron, Paper Mill Program Editor Nancy Marino, and Jerry Baron at one of the theatre's fund-raisers. Below: Guild members Ethel Bear (right) and Helen Rosen wait on a customer at the Paper Mill Guild Gift Shop.

Paper Mill Outreach

Paper Mill's inaugural season, in 1938, included performances for young audiences, such as "The Adventures of a Brownie," and classes in various theatre skills, including dance and elocution. That original commitment to education in and through the arts continues today in the activities of Paper Mill's Education Department, which oversees nine programs of educational outreach, theatre classes, and performances for young audiences. In 1989, the Adopt-A-School Project was implemented by John McEwen, Director of Development, and Susan Speidel then the theatre's Development Associate. The success and expansion of the Project and the theatre's commitment to increase its investment in arts education lead to the creation of the Education Department with Ms. Speidel as its Director. The Adopt-A-School Project and other education programs seek to expand the interests and horizons of New Jersey students and to build an informed theatre audience for the future.

Newark Arts High School students perform in the 1998 Adopt-A-School Play Festival.

Adopt-A-School Project

The Adopt-A-School Project was founded in 1989 with forty students and three teachers from Newark Arts High School. The selection of Arts High for the pilot year of the program connected Paper Mill's present-day operations to its past. During the early 1930s the art deco auditorium of Arts High had housed many productions guided by Frank Carrington and Antoinette Scudder in their years with the Newark Art Theatre. During the pilot year, students attended productions at Paper Mill and met with many of the staff and performers involved in those shows. At the end of the year, discussions with the Arts High drama faculty led to plans for workshops and artist residencies. The plans evolved into a three-phase program that has become a standard part of the Newark Arts High School drama curriculum:

Observation. Students attend performances at Paper Mill Playhouse, receive study guides and participate in pre-performance seminars and discussions. Tickets and transportation are free of charge.

Participation. Students work with a theatre artist placed in residence at their school to create an original play, which is ultimately performed in a student festival at the Playhouse.

Analysis. Workshops dealing with advanced skills requested by the students and educators are presented in the school. These master classes allow in-depth investigation of performance skills, technical theatre crafts, the business aspects of theatre, and many other topics.

The Adopt-A-School project has expanded beyond Newark to include over 5,000 high school students and 200 teachers in high schools throughout the state. Ongoing support from the Prudential Foundation, the Geraldine R. Dodge Foundation, and the Schering-Plough Foundation has been the key to this expansion and to the growth of the program. The

Students from Newark Arts High School, including a young Savion Glover (dancing at right) perform in the first Adopt-A-School Festival in 1991.

Adopt-A-School project has received national recognition and was cited as a model arts partnership by the Kennedy Center's Alliance for Arts Education.

TheatreStart

Introduced in 1994 to provide an introduction to theatre for elementary and middle school students, TheatreStart features workshops in creative drama, in-school performances by touring companies, and attendance at a production at Paper Mill Playhouse. The program can adapt to any grade level.

Performances. For two performances, Paper Mill brings artists and theatre companies to the school for assembly programs. A third performance, at the Playhouse, features a professional touring children's theatre company in a performance that relates to other TheatreStart activities.

Workshops. Workshops that augment the performance experiences are presented in the school. They are designed to increase arts literacy and awareness and to build self-confidence and communication skills.

Alternative Program

The Alternative Program was developed to meet the specific needs of schools throughout New Jersey that provide educational intervention and incentives for "at risk" students. In this smaller-scale version of the Adopt-A-School program, students work one-on-one with an artist in residence in creative drama and movement exercises. All activities aim to build life skills and increase self-esteem. They include trips to the theatre, pre-performance seminars, and in-school workshops aimed at developing literacy, critical thinking, and communication skills.

Students from Edison High School during post-performance analysis and discussion in the Adopt-A-School Play Festival.

> Paper Mill has made a commitment to the education of students and to the training of future theatre professionals and audience members. The Rising Star Awards make my students feel valued, honored and understood. It shows them that there are other teenagers who share their passion, their commitment and their love for the theatre.

> JOHN HOUSLEY
> *Northern Valley Regional High School*
> *Recipient of the 1997 and 1998*
> *Rising Star Award for*
> *Outstanding Achievement by a Director*

Author Regina Barreca, actor William Mooney and film critic Bob Campbell discuss Humor in America at a 1993 Humanities Series Symposium.

Young Critics Program

The Young Critics Program developed from a conversation with a teacher from Rosa Parks Arts High School who noted that many of his students who were interested in theatre were also enrolled in a journalism or creative writing class. Students in this program come to the Playhouse without charge to participate in pre-performance seminars with a theatre critic or the director of a show and to view a performance. Afterward, they write a review that is shared with the cast and production staff of the show, and with their classmates in school. Examples of student reviews of *Wuthering Heights* are given on page 189.

Humanities Series

Beginning in 1990, Paper Mill has held symposia on a great variety of subjects, each in connection with a production at the Playhouse. During the run of *Singin' in the Rain*, Professor Richard Brown, host of "Reflections on the Silver Screen," led a discussion on the magic of Hollywood. In connection with *Gigi*, the topic was a history of the Belle Epoque, with a presentation in which resident costume designer Gregg Barnes discussed the clothes of the period and showed his costumes for the production. During *My Fair Lady*, the subject was "Pygmalion on Stage, from Shaw to *My Fair Lady*," with a panel of experts from colleges and universities in New Jersey. For *Oliver*, the program was "Food, Glorious Food," and those who attended were asked to bring a canned or boxed food item to benefit the Community Food Bank of New Jersey. This led to the creation of an annual food drive sponsored by the playhouse in which more than $25,000 and 30,000 pounds of food have been collected to date. There have been programs on Lerner and Loewe, Irving Berlin, Gershwin and Rodgers and Hammerstein, and special programs on the Brontë sisters, "From Page to Stage, A Look at Musicals Adapted from Great Literature," and "Poetry on Broadway, the Lyrics of the American Musical Theatre from Hammerstein to Sondheim." All of these programs have been free, supported by funding from the Prudential Foundation, administered by the New Jersey Theatre Group. The New Jersey Council for the Humanities and Mercedes-Benz Tri-State Dealers also have been instrumental in the development of this series.

Director of Education Susan Speidel with Frank Donovan Tamez, Rising Star Winner.

S.T.A.R.— Student Training and Artistic Recognition

The goal of the S.T.A.R. program is to recognize and build excitement about student achievement in the arts—the same type of recognition and excitement that exists on a statewide level for excellence in sports and academic subjects. Simultaneously, the program seeks to provide affordable and accessible professional training of the highest caliber for New Jersey's emerging theatre artists. Although several statewide initiatives exist for high school actors, none focuses specifically on musical theatre performance. Fleet Bank made a major commitment to the S.T.A.R. program with a leadership gift that has led to increased opportunities for recognition, scholarships, and training opportunities for students statewide.

Rising Star Awards

The Rising Star Awards were created in 1996 to encourage and reward excellence in the production of high school musicals. Evaluators are sent to high school musical productions throughout the state to provide feedback on the productions and cast nominations for recognition in more than twenty categories. A ceremony modeled on the Tony Awards is held each spring. In addition to awards for technical and performance excellence, Educational Impact awards are given to schools where innovative activities connect the production of their musical to other areas of their school's curriculum. Scholarships are awarded to selected students who will continue their theatre studies in college.

> I'd like to thank the actress who played Mame, she helped me a lot memorizing my lines ... and my Mom and my Dad and my brothers and my dog and my two cats.
>
> DANIEL BARDER (age 10)
> *Recipient of the 1996 Rising Star Award*
> *for Outstanding Performance by a Child Actor*
> *in Piscataway High School's production of* Mame

New Jersey Secretary of State Lonna R. Hooks (center) with Nicole Martone and Christian Eastburn, recipients of the 1997 Rising Star Awards.

Rising Star Award winner Christopher Patterson of Perth Amboy, center, with Dana Lynn (left) and Andrea Szucs (right), both of *Call Me Madam.*

In 1996, at the First Rising Star Awards Ceremony, there was a tie for Outstanding Performance by a Leading Actress. The awards went to high school senior Debra Baumel, of Manalapan, for *Evita* and junior Laura Benanti, of Kinnelon, for *Hello, Dolly!* Deborah went on to college, pursuing a degree in theatre. Laura was invited to audition at Paper Mill productions and appeared in *Jane Eyre* and *Man of La Mancha.* She left New York University after one week of classes when she was cast in the Broadway revival of *The Sound of Music.* As a member of the ensemble, she also understudied the role of Maria and in March 1999 took over the starring role, appearing opposite Richard Chamberlin for the remainder of the Broadway run.

Paper Mill Playhouse is more than a theatre. It is a family. The two Paper Mill shows I was privileged to be a part of affect how I now behave in rehearsals, performances and backstage. I am forever grateful for the wonderful people I've met at Paper Mill, as well as for the opportunities that have been given to me since winning the 1996 Rising Star Award. Making my professional debut at Paper Mill Playhouse will always remain among my most cherished memories.

—Laura Benanti

1996 Rising Star recipient Laura Benanti returned to Paper Mill to present the 1997 award for Outstanding Performance by a Leading Actress to Nicole Martone.

The stage is among the richest resources in our educational system. Young men and women who chase their own dreams explore the universal language of music and song. They experiment with personal and social roles. They develop physical discipline with dance or expand their technical imagination with stage sets, costumes, and lighting. They become team players as they refine communication skills. Any of these students may become a brilliant rising star.

WILLIAM TANSEY
Paper Mill Trustee

Resident scenic designer Michael Anania teaches design basics to students.

Summer Musical Theatre Conservatory

The Summer Musical Theatre Conservatory is designed for gifted and talented young performers committed to developing their musical theatre performance skills in five weeks of intensive study. Most students enter the program through intensive auditions. Others, nominated for Rising Star Awards, are invited to attend on a scholarship basis. For four weeks, students take part in singing, acting, and dance classes and attend workshops and master classes conducted by actors, directors, designers, and casting agents. Each student also receives personalized instruction in a private voice lesson once each week. The fifth week of the Conservatory is devoted to rehearsals for an annual concert that showcases the talent of the students on the Paper Mill stage. All classes and rehearsals are under the supervision of Paper Mill's professional artistic and administrative staff. Graduates of the Summer Musical Theatre Conservatory have gone on to appear in Paper Mill mainstage productions, including *Children of Eden*, *Jane Eyre*, *Big River*, and *Gigi*. Many are continuing their training in theatre programs at the finest colleges and universities in the country.

Theatre School

Under the direction of Mickey McNany Damian, the Theatre School consists of classes designed to meet the needs of every age group.

Storybook Theatre focuses on students from age six to eight. It provides an introduction to theatre games and activities and works to build early reading skills. Students read stories as a group and then use creative drama and role-playing exercises to bring those stories to life.

The Junior Players, a program for children up to the age of twelve, has been so successful a lottery has been needed to select from a waiting list of over 350. Students are guided through productions involving hands-on projects in which they learn about scenery and music and work in an original production which they write and dramatize themselves. Some of the children travel with their productions, performing at schools, senior residences, and hospitals.

The Youth Theatre Ensemble, for ages thirteen to seventeen, selects students through auditions. The course includes two classes on musical theatre and one on acting. Students study improvisation and creative drama, and write and perform their own scripts.

The Youth Theatre Ensemble is a series of classes offered within the scope of the theatre school teenage students. They include classes in musical theatre performance, scene study, playwrighting, mime, dance, and acting for the camera. Students can also study improvisation and creative drama, and write and perform their own scripts. Theatre classes for adults are offered as well and include sessions in musical theatre performance, acting, and scene study.

The Musical Theatre Workshop, for accomplished singers seventeen and older, includes a study of musical theatre and two acting classes held at Paper Mill Playhouse. Students study with Paper Mill's professional theatre artists.

In addition to the regular classes noted, Paper Mill makes available private lessons in voice and technique.

The All-Stars, made up of the most outstanding students in the Junior Players classes, tour twice a year to nursing homes, hospital wards, community centers, and schools. Always a special occasion, these

Left: Mickey McNany Damian with Junior Players. Below: Students from Bishop Ahr High School in Edison performing "The Telephone Hour" from *Bye Bye Birdie* at Paper Mill at the 1997 Rising Star Awards.

performances are designed to give multiple performance experiences to the students and to help them learn to think on their feet and adapt quickly to new situations. The audiences are diverse and the students frequently prepare special material tailored for each audience. On one occasion, they took their performance of *The Little Princess* to a school for children ages four to twelve with hearing impairments. In the weeks prior to the performance, director Damian reviewed the script with the school's sign interpreter to make sure that even the youngest audience member would get the full impact of the story. As a special surprise for the young audience, she had the signer teach the All-Stars to sign their theme song, "We are the Paper Mill Players, performing for you, with spirit and style that will always shine through. Singing together and playing our parts. Sharing what's in our hearts." The performance at the school was a grand success and when Paper Mill's young actors launched into sign language, the children in the audience could barely contain themselves. Their

Teachers, staff members, and students all raved about *The Little Princess* for days afterwards....The students understood that you learned to sign the final song just for them, and it truly impressed them. I could feel the emotion in the air as you began to sign— and there were not many dry eyes among the adults!

MAUREEN BUTLER
Mountain Lakes Public Schools

faces lit up and they waved their hands joyfully in the air, applauding for all they were worth.

The Education Department works with the Marketing Department on student matinees of mainstage productions that relate to high school and middle school curricula. These matinees are scheduled to fit into the school day and feature discounted ticket prices, study guides, and post-show discussions with the cast.

In a tradition from the earliest days of the Playhouse's history, productions especially for children are presented each year, reflecting Paper Mill's view that live theatre is a unique experience in an age of video and computers. Acclaimed theatre companies from throughout North America present programs based on traditional storybook titles and classic literature in the Weekend Series and educationally based programming in the *On-School Time Series*.

Celebrations

Paper Mill Playhouse has hosted several gala evenings to acknowledge the varied talents of those who have worked at the theatre, recognize the accomplishments of the theatre itself, and salute the business and political leaders who have provided support and guidance. By far the most outstanding of these nights was Paper Mill's 60th Anniversary Gala. Under the leadership of Benefit Chairwoman Barbara Baldwin more than 750 guests gathered to share in a star-studded event. The evening featured an elaborate reception in Baldwin Court followed by performances highlighting sixty years of production, and tributes to actress Kitty Carlisle Hart and Paper Mill executive producer Angelo Del Rossi. Dinner and dancing concluded an evening that was a sparkling success and a perfect way to commemorate sixty years of excellence.

Students from the 1999 Summer Musical Theatre Conservatory perform in *New Voices of '99*.

60th Anniversary Gala

May 16, 1998

Robert Johanson and Angelo Del Rossi welcome Ann Miller to the stage of the Paper Mill gala.

Above: Former Governor Tom Kean and New Jersey Ballet's Carolyn Clark celebrate Paper Mill's 60th Anniversary. Below: On hand for the festivities (from left) Barbara Russo, Executive Director of the New Jersey State Council for the Arts, Tom Horan, Visual Arts Coordinator for the New Jersey State Council on the Arts and Delores Kirk, Secretary of the New Jersey State Senate.

Above: Lee Roy Reams and Leslie Uggams stop the show with Irving Berlin's "You're Just In Love." Left: Peter Filichia, theatre writer for the *Newark Star Ledger* and News 12 New Jersey, interviews *Children of Eden* composer Stephen Schwartz, and star Kelli Rabke.

Weddings

We're headin' for a weddin'! —Will Rogers' Follies

My One and Only

ORSON WELLES WAS ONCE ASKED IN AN interview: "If you could relive your life—would you choose the theatre?" He said: "No, there are too many little deaths."

This certainly is true. Every company comes together, bonds, puts their hearts and souls into this communal effort, sometimes to spectacular success—and then the show ends. The company go their separate ways, sometimes to reunite—it is a small world after all—but never to create the exact moment again. However, along with this loss there are also many, many happy memories, like those recounted in this book. They are moments to cherish. In a musical or a play the happiest moment usually occurs at a wedding, and there have been many of them on the Paper Mill stage. The Great Ziegfeld often ended his *Follies* with a wedding finale—so it is fitting to pay tribute to our happy brides and grooms.

Mack and Mabel

Great Expectations

Okalahoma

Jane Eyre

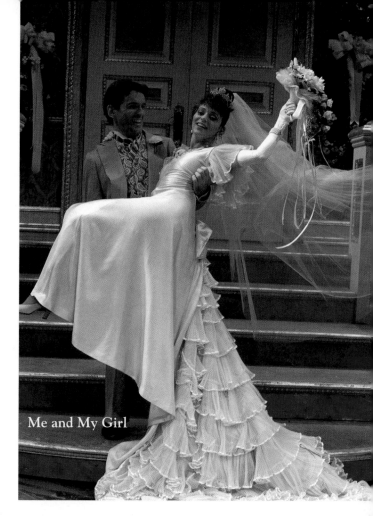

Me and My Girl

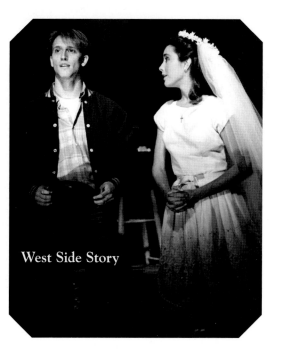

West Side Story

Of course, not all weddings were happy. The jilted bride in *Great Expectations*, Miss Havisham, never got over her aborted nuptials, and Jane Eyre faced similar problems when she learned on her wedding day that her fiancé was already married!

Camelot

Flower Drum Song

Brigadoon

Shenandoah

Will Rogers' Follies

The show's prologue, in which a parade of women dressed as butterflies materializes out of the darkness, is ravishing.

BEN BRANTLEY
The New York Times

Follies

The Paper Mill is as pretty as a Currier and Ives print, but don't let appearances deceive you.
This is a theater determined to give its best to its patrons. This is no small-scale, makeshift operation;
this is a powerhouse of talent, ambition, and efficiency.
—Simon Jones

THE SPECTACULAR PRODUCTION OF the monumental musical *Follies* was in many ways the Paper Mill's crowning achievement. The international reception was astounding, with glowing praise from the critics and patrons flying in from all over the globe to try to get a ticket to this sold-out event. The show had not had a major revival on the East Coast since its original Broadway run in 1971, but it had built up a great following due to Stephen Sondheim's brilliant score and James Goldman's provocative book. A challenging musical, the Paper Mill used all its resources, talent, manpower, and nerve to create its own legendary version.

The production coincided with the theatre's sixtieth anniversary, and could not have been more appropriate. As the haunting musical told the story of a reunion of old-time "Weissman Follies" girls who revisit their past, the Paper Mill itself revisited its glorious past. Almost all of the stars of the production had performed previously at Paper Mill: Eddie Bracken, Ann Miller, Kaye Ballard, Tony Roberts, Donna McKechnie, Phyllis Newman, Liliane Montevecchi, Donald Sadler, and Michael

Stephen Sondheim, Angelo Del Rossi and Robert Johanson.

Gruber were joined by Dee Hoty, Laurence Guittard, Natalie Mosco, and Carol Skarimbas. As the Paper Mill Playhouse had made its mark doing spectacular operettas and musicals, so too had the Weissman Follies. Luckily, Paper Mill was not in danger of being torn down to make way for a parking lot, like the Weissman Theatre in the show.

This was no re-creation of the original production, but a completely rethought version. I remember going to visit the Goldmans in their penthouse on Fifth Avenue with Robert, who began to outline his concepts for the new production and thoughts about rewrites on the book. James Goldman listened intently and after what seemed an interminable pause said, "Let's get to work." The rest is history.

ANGELO DEL ROSSI

Robert Johanson: *I had seen the original production of* Follies *in 1971 when I was still in college. I had been haunted by it for years, but I hadn't looked at the script until 1997 when we considered remounting it. When I first read it, I felt like I'd fallen into the Bermuda Triangle. I couldn't make any real sense out of it or get a strong picture in my head for the direction we should take. The layers are so complex: the present revisiting the past, the past locked firmly on itself and then sometimes insinuating itself into the present when not wanted—the addition of surreal dreams and nightmares that defy any reality. Finally, I asked Jim Goldman, "What were you on? This is totally wild and so depressing!" He replied, "We were all—Hal, Stephen, and myself—going through midlife crises that you wouldn't believe! And we wanted to put it all in the script." I said, "Well, it seems to me that a weakness in the script is the underdevelopment of the real old-timers who have great numbers, but very little else to do. Yet, to me they represent the light at the end of the tunnel. With songs like 'I'm Still Here' they've discovered how to survive and live each day to the max." Jim agreed, saying, "I see that now. I'm 71 and I don't feel the same way now as I felt then. There is a different message about moving on that I understand now and I think that's where the play ultimately wants to wind up." So Jim rethought the arc of the play and restructured it accordingly. The result was palpable and really transformed the evening. Of course, casting the right people, like Ann Miller, in the right parts had a lot to do with the success of the whole venture.*

The "Beautiful Girls" number.

When Ann arrived, she said, "You know, I'd like to do a few things a little differently with this song (I'm Still Here). You see, it just kinda sits there. Now the lyrics are o.k., but it needs a better ending—it needs some pizazz! For me, I mean. Do you think Mr. Sondheim would mind?" I thought "Oh, my lord!" but said, "Well, let's get to work on it and we'll show it to him." Now, I thought I might have to do some explaining to Ann about some of the lyrics— there are a lot of obscure references and I had researched them all to be ready—Charles W. Beebe's Bathysphere and Brenda Frazier, for example. Well, the first thing Ann says is, "I knew Brenda Frazier! She was very pretty, but not real bright! AND I was in George White's Scandals on Broadway when the Bathysphere was at the World's Fair AND my mother wouldn't let me go see it! Well, I was durn mad about that, I'll tell you!" And she did tell me a thing or two!

The day arrives for her to present the song to Sondheim. He's in a grumpy mood; he's not too amenable to people changing his idea of what his music should be, but he'll listen. Ann walks in and says, "Oh, Mr. Sondheim, I'm so nervous. I don't think I can sing this for you now—I'm just not ready!" A dark cloud descends over his face and steam is about to come out of his ears. I say,"Now, Ann, let's just give it a whirl—he needs to hear what you want to do with it—so we can see if it's gonna fly!" Suddenly, Sondheim barks "Ann, just get over to the

When I first called Ann Miller about playing Carlotta, who sings "I'm Still Here," she said, "Oh, Angelo, honey, I don't know. I've got my dogs and problems with my knees— I am 78 you know!" I said, "Oh, Annie get over it! You're sitting in your house in Arizona when you could be up on that stage doing what you do best! Now, come on!" "Oh, all right— you talked me into it!"

Angelo Del Rossi

piano and sing!" She does. Now here we are, just a few of us, in this room and this 78-year-old star starts the song: "Good times and bum times, I've seen them all and my dear, I'm still here." She gets to the lyric "danced in my scanties— three bucks a night was the pay." She really had danced for three bucks a night! The tempo starts to build and the list goes on—all the events she chronicles had actually happened to Ann Miller as well as her character, Carlotta. The line became very blurred. Suddenly, you see before you in this remarkable woman, the great tap-dancer who had filled the vast movie screens in forty films and she's singing "I'm still here!" over and over and then she takes a big pause (not a pause written by Mr. Sondheim) and belts out her final "I'm still here!" She's done. We all look to Mr. Sondheim. He has tears in his eyes, as we all do. He says, "Let her sing it any way she wants!" Well, every night on the stage of the Paper Mill, when she finished her number, the audience leapt up screaming. It was like a touchdown at the Super Bowl— they wouldn't stop clapping until she left the stage. It was one of the greatest theatrical moments I have ever witnessed. Every night the entire cast gathered in the wings to watch Ann perform. They all knew it was one of those rare moments when life and art totally become one.

Ben Brantley summed it up so beautifully in his New York Times review: "'I should have gone to acting school, that seems clear,' sings Ann Miller, without a flicker of apologetic cuteness, in the thrilling new

Carlotta (Ann Miller) comforts Benjamin Stone (Laurence Guittard).

revival of Stephen Sondheim's 1971 musical *Follies* at the Paper Mill Playhouse. 'Still someone said, "She's sincere," so I'm here.'

"The fact of the matter is, Ms. Miller is sincere—heartbreakingly, splendidly so—when she performs 'I'm Still Here,' the great anthem to survival in show business, and so is the production that features her to such revelatory advantage. She is the very essence of this emotionally rich, exquisite-looking produc-

tion, which has been lovingly and precisely directed by Robert Johanson, with matching choreography by Jerry Mitchell. Ms. Miller may get teary-eyed during her song (certainly, you will) but her vision isn't blurred by false sentiment.

"This fine, heartfelt production, which confirms *Follies* as a landmark musical and a work of art, finds the sad beauty as well as the folly in the urge to get lost in the past."

From left: Lawrence Guittard, Dee Hoty, Donna McKechnie, Tony Roberts.

Even better is the lead quartet given with almost definitive authority by an elegantly battered Laurence Guittard, a coolly sophisticated Dee Hoty, a desperately wistful Donna McKechnie, and an angry, baffled Tony Roberts. These four would warm the hearts of any marriage counselor they happened to encounter.

CLIVE BARNES
New York Post

Tony Roberts takes a comic spin.

The "Loveland" sequence.

Liliane Montevecchi
and Eddie Bracken.

Vaudevillian Solange, now a
perfume spokeswoman, tells us
about her travels in "Ah, Paris";
Liliane Montevecchi, star of
Broadway's *Nine* sells her song
with oomph and a red boa.

DONALD LYONS
Wall Street Journal

Phyllis Newman stops the show with
"Who's That Woman?"

REX REED

In the performance of her career, Donna McKechnie is beyond fault. The sweet, embattled overeagerness that has characterized her performances since her Tony-winning role in *A Chorus Line* has never been so appropriately or affectingly used. Nor has her voice, which marvelously plumbs the torchy despair of the ballad "Losing My Mind," ever seemed richer or more controlled.

BEN BRANTLEY
The New York Times

Personally, I am most grateful to Robert Johanson and Angelo Del Rossi for casting me in *Follies*. To return to performing after a long life of choreographing and directing was unexpected, to say the least, but just another example of the creativity of these two extraordinary gentlemen of the theatre.

DONALD SADLER

Donald Saddler and Natalie Mosco bring back memories of Fred and Adele Astaire dancing to "Listen to the Rain on the Roof..."

LARRY S. LEDORD, *At Your Leisure*

Dee Hoty in "Ah, But Underneath," an added number.

Kaye Ballard rips through "(I'm just a) Broadway Baby" with the exuberance that only a great Great White Way veteran such as she could deliver.

PETER FILICHIA
Newark Star-Ledger

Dimitri Weismann, the impresario of the Weismann Girls, is played by Eddie Bracken, the still nimble star of two great Preston Sturges comedies of the 1940s; Mr. Bracken gets no songs, but his mere presence is a tonic.

DONALD LYONS
Wall Street Journal

With all of the great press and terrific audience response, it seemed inevitable that *Follies* would move to Broadway. The financial backing was in place and the cast was thrilled at the possibility of continuing to perform together in this wonderful show. But for some reason that was never disclosed, James Goldman's wife, who handled his business affairs, withheld the rights for a Broadway transfer. It was a stunning decision. Shortly thereafter, James Goldman died suddenly of a heart attack. Paper Mill's *Follies* was the last production of one of his plays that he would ever see. Now more mystery and more ghosts surround this unique musical and once more it has receded into the past. Layers upon layers of nostalgia envelop this legend.

Howard Kissel made a final observation in the *New York Post*:

When it was reported that Paper Mill Playhouse's recent revival of Follies *would not be transferred to Broadway this fall, I breathed a sigh of relief. It's not that I didn't enjoy it. I was overwhelmed by it. But to bring to Broadway a production of* Follies *that was so emotionally powerful would have a very unhealthy effect. These days, no one expects emotional content in musicals. To give them a taste of such a thing would create unreasonable expectations.*

The grandes dames of *Follies*.

Top to bottom:
Ann Miller
Phyllis Newman
Billie Thrash
Liliane Montevecchi
Dee Hoty
Jo Ann Cunningham
Kaye Ballard
Natalie Mosco
Laura Kenyon
Donna McKechnie
Carol Skarimbas

FOLLIES

April 15 - May 31, 1998

PAPER MILL PLAYHOUSE

Follies *was the epitome of what it's like to work at* Paper Mill. *To think I actually got paid to come to work with such veterans as Stephen Sondheim, James Goldman, Ann Miller, Kaye Ballard, Dee Hoty, Donna McKechnie, and every member of the cast. My same feeling could be echoed with the* Jane Eyre *cast, the* Jesus Christ Superstar *cast, the cast of* Fanny, *and on and on. We are so privileged here to have such extraordinary talent on our stage. And all of them are supported by great designers, musicians, and behind-the-scenes technicians. All people who love doing theatre. The live experience. Meeting that opening night deadline—no "Oops! We're not ready yet!" Then maintaining the experience night after night for each audience. The show does go on and only the direst of circumstances keeps any of the company from performing at their peak. I've been proud to be associated with these wonderful people and this extraordinary institution. When you think that many Broadway producers will take two years or more to produce one show and Paper Mill has to present six Broadway level shows a year—you have to marvel at what goes on here. The memory of past glories here always informs the present. They set the standard by which each show at Paper Mill is measured. We strive each time to do the best show—everyone working to constantly come up to that standard. It is a challenge which will always be present and always welcome.*

—Robert Johanson

Director Robert Johanson, and choreographer Jerry Mitchell surrounded by the stars of Follies.

I was only a newborn when Frank Carrington and Antoinette Scudder conceived their dream of transforming an abandoned paper mill into a theatre. Their dream and my life have become inseparable in the Life of a Theatre. So many wonderful people have shared this experience with me and my life has been enriched by them.

This is not the last chapter of our journey rather it is the beginning of a new one, which holds all the dreams yet to be discovered. Who can predict the future of the American stage? I can only hope that we have built a foundation that will last far beyond this time and will allow for the creation and preservation of great theatre.

All whose names appear in this book have made a profound impact on our theatre and no one person deserves special praise. We have done all this together!

—Angelo Del Rossi

Paper Mill Playhouse Executive Producer Angelo Del Rossi and the ensemble of *Follies*.

Curtain Call

A final moment—The performers join hands in a closing bow; the curtain falls on yet another show; the sounds of words and music continue to resonate throughout the theatre as the exuberant applause begins to fade. The house lights brighten. The theatregoers hum and sing and chatter as they gather their programs and belongings. Lively conversation reflects upon the show and on some new and some old lessons in life which have been portrayed with the universal language of art. Images abound. The people meander alone and in groups, in the aisles, by a crackling fire in the lobby, and throughout the spacious courtyard. Some go on to their cars. The show has ended, but the exhilaration of mind and spirit will sustain all for a new day. In the time to come, the loyal audience—a "cast of thousands" themselves—will return to the Playhouse again and again as they have for over sixty years, through good times and bad, each time the stage comes alive. Their love the for theatre is returned in equal measure by the performers, by the producers, by the musicians, and by the entire artistic staff and crew. Together, they all are the Paper Mill Playhouse. Together they will usher this renowned theatre into the twenty-first century. They are, after all, the Life of the Theatre.

Frank Carrington and Agnes Morgan take an opening night bow, 1950.

Paper Mill Productions *1938 to 1999*

1938–1939–1940

The Kingdom of God
Directed by Frank Carrington

The Snow Queen

Anthony and Anna

March Hares

Rescue (one act)

Androcles and the Lion

Tonight at 8:30

Man in Possession

Flight into China
Starring: Jose Ferrer
Directed by Lee Strasburg

Men in White

Private Lives
Starring: Eva LeGallienne, Rex O'Malley
Directed by Frank Carrington

Pursuit of Happiness
Starring: Tonio Selwart, Uta Hagen
Directed by Rex O'Malley

Jeannie
Starring: Philip Tonge, Dorothy Sands, Ronda Keane
Directed by Frank Carrington and Agnes Morgan

Papa is All
Starring: Hunter Gardner, Emmett Rogers, Ronda Keane, Hathaway Kale
Directed by Frank Carrington and Agnes Morgan

I Killed the Count
Starring: Hunter Gardner, Emmett Rogers, Ronda Keane, Hathaway Kale
Directed by Frank Carrington and Agnes Morgan

Adventures of a Brownie
Starring: George Baehr
Directed by Frank Carrington

1941

Pinafore and **Trial by Jury**
Starring: Helen Gleason, Ralph Riggs, Nils Landin, Yolanda Lupachini
Produced by Joseph Tushinsky

The Mikado
Starring: Ralph Riggs, Helen Gleason
Produced by Joseph Tushinsky

The Chocolate Soldier
Starring: Dorothy Sandlin
Directed by Frank Carrington & Agnes Morgan

The Merry Widow
Starring: Walter Cassel, Helen Gleason
Directed by Frank Carrington & Agnes Morgan

Firefly
Starring: Donald Gage, Dorothy Sandlin
Staged by William H. Lynn

Bohemian Girl
Starring: Donald Gage, Annunciata Garrotto
Staged by Charles Sinclair

Blossom Time
Starring: Donald Gage, Paul Reed
Staged by John Pierce

Old English
Starring: C. Aubrey Smith
Directed by Frank Carrington and Agnes Morgan

Kind Lady
Starring: Grace George
Directed by Frank Carrington and Agnes Morgan

Western Union, Please
Starring: Charles Butterworth, June Walker
Directed by Frank Carrington and Agnes Morgan

U.S.90
Starring: Gloria Stuart, Warren Hull, Celeste Holm, E.J. Ballantine
Directed by Frank Carrington and Agnes Morgan

Dear Brutus
Starring: Henry Hull, Margaret Bannerman, A.G. Andrews
Directed by Frank Carrington and Agnes Morgan

The Shining Hour
Starring: Elissa Landi
Directed by Frank Carrington and Agnes Morgan

Seraphina
Starring: Leona Powers, Ann Andrews, Margaret Bannerman, Bert Lytell
Directed by Frank Carrington

1942

Naughty Marietta
Starring: Rosemarie Brancato, Donald Gage
Directed by Frank Carrington & Agnes Morgan

M'lle Modiste
Starring: Dorothy Sandlin, Donald Gage
Directed by Frank Carrington & Agnes Morgan

Sweethearts
Starring: Dorothy Sandlin, Donald Gage
Directed by Frank Carrington & Agnes Morgan

SHOW APPENDIX KEY
[WP] World Premiere
[AP] American Premiere
[OA] Original Adaptation by Robert Johanson
[PBS] Filmed and aired on PBS "Great Performances"

[LCL] Filmed and archived by Lincoln Center Library of the Performing Arts
[ST] Filmed and aired on Showtime network
[TTB Transferred to Broadway

Red Mill
Starring: Ralph Riggs, Ted Meza, Xenia Bank,
Robert Lyon
Directed by Frank Carrington & Agnes Morgan

The Pirates of Penzance

The Chocolate Soldier
Starring: Dorothy Sandlin, Donald Gage,
Yolanda Lupachini
Directed by Ralph Griggs

The Merry Widow
Starring: Dorothy Kirsten, Walter Cassel
Staged by Victor Morley

The Desert Song
Starring: Rosemarie Brancato, Donald Gage
Staged by Victor Morley

The New Moon
Starring: Dorothy Sandlin, Bob Lawrence,
Jane Hoffman
Staged by Victor Morley

The Vagabond King
Starring: Bob Lawrence, Dorothy Sandlin, Ralph Riggs
Staged by Frank Carrington & Agnes Morgan

Robin Hood
Starring: Donald Gage, Jean Dickenson, Ralph Riggs
Staged by Frank Carrington & Agnes Morgan

Babes in Toyland
Starring: Donald Gage, Stephanie Turash
Staged by Frank Carrington & Agnes Morgan

1943
Rosemarie
Starring: Rosemarie Brancato, Donald Gage
Staged by Frank Carrington & Agnes Morgan

Blossom Time
Starring: Donald Gage, Ruby Mercer, George Britton
Staged by Frank Carrington & Agnes Morgan

Desert Song
Starring: Lucille Manners, Donald Gage
Staged by Frank Carrington & Agnes Morgan

Rio Rita
Starring: Suzanne Sten, Donald Gage, Fred Hillebrand
Staged by Frank Carrington & Agnes Morgan

Countess Maritza
Starring: Helen Gleason, Donald Gage
Staged by Frank Carrington & Agnes Morgan

Sweethearts
Starring: Dorothy Sandlin, Donald Gage, Paul Reed
Staged by Frank Carrington & Agnes Morgan

Naughty Marietta
Starring: Andzia Kuzak James Montgomery
Staged by Frank Carrington & Agnes Morgan

The Vagabond King
Starring: Wilbur Evans, Dorothy Sandlin
Staged by Frank Carrington & Agnes Morgan

Katinka
Starring: Andzia Kuzak, Donald Gage
Staged by Frank Carrington & Agnes Morgan

Trial by Jury and **H.M.S. Pinafore**
Starring: Andzia Kuzak, Robert Shafer
Staged by Frank Carrington & Agnes Morgan

1944
The Red Mill
Starring: Billie Worth, Nils Landin
Staged by Frank Carrington & Agnes Morgan

The Fortune Teller
Starring: Rosemarie Brancato, Donald Gage
Staged by Frank Carrington & Agnes Morgan

The Prince of Pilsen
Starring: Elizabeth Houston, Donald Gage,
Clarence Nordstrom
Staged by Frank Carrington & Agnes Morgan

Blossom Time
Starring: Andzia Kuzak, Donald Gage, George Britton
Staged by Frank Carrington & Agnes Morgan

Sally
Starring: Donald Gage, Marjorie Belle,
Clarence Nordstrom
Staged by Frank Carrington & Agnes Morgan

Desert Song
Starring: Dorothy Sandlin, Donald Gage
Staged by Frank Carrington & Agnes Morgan

The Merry Widow
Starring: Dorothy Sandlin, Donald Gage, Eric Mattson
Staged by Frank Carrington & Agnes Morgan

Katinka
Starring: Donald Gage, Andzia Kuzak, Clarence
Nordstrom
Staged by Frank Carrington & Agnes Morgan

The Student Prince
Starring: Donald Gage, Andzia Kuzak, George Britton
Staged by Frank Carrington & Agnes Morgan

1945
Maytime
Starring: Dorothy Sandlin, Charles Yearsley,
Clarence Nordstrom
Staged by Frank Carrington & Agnes Morgan

The Cat and the Fiddle
Starring: Marguerite Piazza, Frank Nolton,
Olga Baclanova
Staged by Frank Carrington & Agnes Morgan

The Desert Song
Starring: Harold Patrick, Barbara Scully
Staged by Frank Carrington & Agnes Morgan

Naughty Marietta
Starring: Andzia Kuzak, Nils Landin, Nina Olivette,
Clarence Nordstrom
Staged by Frank Carrington & Agnes Morgan

The Count of Luxembourg
Starring: Rosemarie Brancato, Donald Gage
Staged by Frank Carrington & Agnes Morgan

The Student Prince
Starring: Gilbert Russell, Andzia Kuzak,
George Britton
Staged by Frank Carrington & Agnes Morgan

Roberta
Starring: Harold Patrick, Barbara Scully, Donald Gage
Staged by Frank Carrington & Agnes Morgan

Blossom Time
Starring: George Britton, Andzia Kuzak, Donald Gage

1946

Bitter Sweet
Starring: Dorothy Sandlin, Ralph Magelssen
Staged by Frank Carrington & Agnes Morgan

Rosalie
Starring: Andzia Kuzak, Donald Gage, Clarence
Nordstrom, Billie Worth, Albert Carroll
Staged by Frank Carrington & Agnes Morgan

The New Moon
Starring: Ruby Mercer, Charles Yearsley
Staged by Frank Carrington & Agnes Morgan

Sweethearts
Starring: Ralph Magelssen, Virginia Card
Staged by Frank Carrington & Agnes Morgan

Roberta
Starring: Harold Patrick, Helene Arthur
Staged by Frank Carrington & Agnes Morgan

Sally
Starring: Evelyn Wyckoff, Donald Gage, Clarence
Nordstrom
Staged by Frank Carrington & Agnes Morgan

The Mikado
Starring: Clarence Nordstrom, Rosemarie Brancato,
Donald Gage
Staged by Frank Carrington & Agnes Morgan

The Merry Widow
Starring: Ruby Mercer, Donald Gage, Clarence
Nordstrom
Staged by Frank Carrington & Agnes Morgan

1947

The Love Wagon
Starring: Dorothy Sandlin, Albert Carroll
Staged by Frank Carrington & Agnes Morgan

Naughty Marietta
Starring: Andzia Kuzak, Harold Patrick
Staged by Frank Carrington & Agnes Morgan

The Fortune Teller
Starring: Rosemarie Brancato, Harold Patrick,
Clarence Nordstrom
Staged by Frank Carrington & Agnes Morgan

The Desert Song
Starring: Donald Gage, Gail Manners,
Clarence Nordstrom
Staged by Frank Carrington & Agnes Morgan

Rito Rita
Starring: Donald Gage, Nita Carol,
Clarence Nordstrom, Billie Worth, Peter Birch
Staged by Frank Carrington & Agnes Morgan

Sunny
Starring: Andzia Kuzak, Jay Martin,
Clarence Nordstrom
Staged by Frank Carrington & Agnes Morgan

Contess Maritza
Starring: Helen Gleason, Donald Gage,
Clarence Nordstrom
Staged by Frank Carrington & Agnes Morgan

Girl Crazy
Starring: Gail Manners, Clarence Nordstrom
Staged by Frank Carrington & Agnes Morgan

The Student Prince
Starring: Frank Hornaday, Edith Fellows,
George Britton, Clarence Nordstrom
Staged by Frank Carrington & Agnes Morgan

1948

The Great Waltz
Starring: Gail Manners, Arthur Maxwell,
Ruth Altman
Staged by Frank Carrington & Agnes Morgan

Rosalie
Starring: Evelyn Wyckoff, Donald Gage,
Clarence Nordstrom
Staged by Frank Carrington & Agnes Morgan

The Vagabond King
Starring: Arthur Maxwell, Rose Inghram,
Clarence Nordstrom
Staged by Frank Carrington & Agnes Morgan

The Mikado
Starring: Andzia Kuzak, Donald Gage,
Clarence Nordstrom
Staged by Frank Carrington & Agnes Morgan

Blossom Time
Starring: Andzia Kuzak, Donald Gage, Paul Reed,
Roy Jacquemot
Staged by Frank Carrington & Agnes Morgan

The Chocolate Soldier
Starring: Dorothy Sandlin, Arthur Maxwell
Staged by Frank Carrington & Agnes Morgan

The Firefly
Starring: Rosemarie Brancato, Charles Yearsley
Staged by Frank Carrington & Agnes Morgan

Rosalinda
Starring: Wilbur Evans, Martha Errolle,
Clarence Nordstrom
Staged by Frank Carrington & Agnes Morgan

1949

Song of Norway
Starring: Rosemarie Brancato, John Elliot,
Virginia Oswald
Staged by Frank Carrington & Agnes Morgan

The Red Mill
Starring: Peter Birch, Clarence Nordstrom,
Diana Marsh, John Elliot, Davis Cunningham,
Leonne Hall
Staged by Frank Carrington & Agnes Morgan

The Great Waltz
Starring: Stephen Douglass, Gail Manners
Staged by Frank Carrington & Agnes Morgan

The Desert Song
Starring: Donald Gage, Gail Manners,
Clarence Nordstrom
Staged by Frank Carrington & Agnes Morgan

Bloomer Girl
Starring: Andzia Kuzak, Stephen Douglass,
Peggy Campbell
Staged by Frank Carrington & Agnes Morgan

Bitter Sweet
Starring: Dorothy Sandlin, Davis Cunningham,
Llse Marvenga, Alexander Clark
Staged by Frank Carrington & Agnes Morgan

The Merry Widow
Starring: Martha Errolle, Eric Mattson
Staged by Frank Carrington & Agnes Morgan

The Student Prince
Starring: Robert Shafer, Andzia Kuzak, George Britton
Staged by Frank Carrington & Agnes Morgan

1950

Show Boat
Starring: Andzia Kuzak, Robert Shafer,
Clarence Nordstrom
Staged by Frank Carrington & Agnes Morgan

Waltz for Three
Starring: Dorothy Sandlin, Robert Shafer,
George Britton
Staged by Frank Carrington & Agnes Morgan

Roberta
Starring: Harold Patrick, Sibyl Bowan,
Betty-Ann Busch, Clarence Nordstrom
Staged by Frank Carrington & Agnes Morgan

Naughty Marietta
Starring: Virginia MacWatters, Donald Gage
Staged by Frank Carrington & Agnes Morgan

Apple Blossoms
Starring: Virginia MacWatters, John Elliot
Staged by Frank Carrington & Agnes Morgan

Maytime
Starring: Betty-Ann Busch, Arthur Maxwell,
Clarence Nordstrom
Staged by Frank Carrington & Agnes Morgan

The New Moon
Starring: Rosemarie Brancato, Harry Stockwell
Staged by Frank Carrington & Agnes Morgan

Brigadoon
Starring: Andzia Kuzak, Arthur Maxwell,
Robert Smith
Staged by Frank Carrington & Agnes Morgan

1951

Annie Get Your Gun
Starring: Helena Seymour, Harold Patrick
Staged by Frank Carrington & Agnes Morgan

Music in the Air
Starring: Brenda Lewis, Ferdinand Hilt
Staged by Frank Carrington & Agnes Morgan

Up in Central Park
Starring: Andzia Kuzak, Ferdinand Hilt
Staged by Frank Carrington & Agnes Morgan

Sweethearts
Starring: Mary O'Fallon, David Atkinson,
Clarence Nordstrom
Staged by Frank Carrington & Agnes Morgan

Sally
Starring: Arthur Maxwell, Ronnie Cunningham,
Clarence Nordstrom
Staged by Frank Carrington & Agnes Morgan

Song of Norway
Starring: Rosemarie Brancato, David Atkinson,
Virginia Oswald
Staged by Frank Carrington & Agnes Morgan

Finian's Rainbow
Starring: Mary O'Fallon, Edward Chappel
Staged by Frank Carrington & Agnes Morgan

The Desert Song
Starring: David Atkinson, Gail Manners
Staged by Frank Carrington & Agnes Morgan

1952

Kiss Me Kate
Starring: Ted Scott, Virginia Oswald
Staged by Frank Carrington & Agnes Morgan

Where's Charley?
Starring: Peter Birch, Ronnie Cunningham
Staged by Frank Carrington & Agnes Morgan

Show Boat
Starring: Gail Manners, Wilton Clary,
Clarence Nordstrom
Staged by Frank Carrington & Agnes Morgan

The Student Prince
Starring: Gilbert Russell, Sylvia Karlton,
Harold Patrick
Staged by Frank Carrington & Agnes Morgan

Carousel
Starring: Stephen Douglass, Mary O'Fallon
Staged by Frank Carrington & Agnes Morgan

The Chocolate Soldier
Starring: Ted Scott, Virginia Oswald
Staged by Frank Carrington & Agnes Morgan

High Button Shoes
Starring: Robert Smith, Jacqueline James,
Walter Long, Leni Lynn
Staged by Frank Carrington & Agnes Morgan

1953

I Married an Angel
Starring: Eric Brotherson, Ruth Webb, Cynthia Scott
Staged by Frank Carrington & Agnes Morgan

Fledermaus
Starring: Gail Manners, Ted Scott
Staged by Frank Carrington & Agnes Morgan

On Your Toes
Starring: George Tapps, Patricia Bowman
Staged by Frank Carrington & Agnes Morgan

Blossom Time
Starring: Gail Manners, Andrew Gainey,
Jim Hawthorne, Clarence Nordstrom
Staged by Frank Carrington & Agnes Morgan

Mikado
Starring: Rosemarie Brancato, Jim Hawthorne,
George Tapps
Staged by Frank Carrington & Agnes Morgan

Merry Widow
Starring: Dorothy Sandlin, Ted Scott
Staged by Frank Carrington & Agnes Morgan

Brigadoon
Starring: Ted Scott, Mary O'Fallon, Peter Turgeon
Staged by Frank Carrington & Agnes Morgan

Call Me Madam
Starring: Jaqueline James, Dick Smart, Margot Moser
Staged by Frank Carrington & Agnes Morgan

1954

Paint Your Wagon
Starring: Edwin Steffe, Christine Mathews,
Andrew Gainey
Staged by Frank Carrington & Agnes Morgan

Oklahoma
Starring: Gail Manners, Ted Scott
Staged by Frank Carrington & Agnes Morgan

Carmen
Starring: Gloria Lane, Gene Hollmann,
Jim Hawthorne, Gail Manners
Staged by Frank Carrington & Agnes Morgan

The Great Waltz
Starring: Edith Gordon, John Scott Stamford
Staged by Frank Carrington & Agnes Morgan

Vagabond King
Starring: Dorothy Sandlin, Ted Scott,
Clarence Nordstrom
Staged by Frank Carrington & Agnes Morgan

Mr. Roberts
Starring: Jeffrey Lynn, Casey Walters,
Vincent Gardenia
Staged by Daniel F. Keyes

Sabrina Fair
Starring: Sara Anderson, William Roerick
Staged by Frank Carrington & Agnes Morgan

My Three Angels
Starring: Victor Jory
Staged by Frank Carrington & Agnes Morgan

Goodbye My Fancy
Starring: Conrad Nagel, Katherine Meskill,
Deidre Owens
Staged by Frank Carrington & Agnes Morgan

Stalag 17
Starring: Robert Lansing, Vincent Gardenia,
Richard Poston
Directed by Buford Armitage

Time Out for Ginger
Starring: Doris Dalton, John Graham, Deidre Owens
Staged by Frank Carrington & Agnes Morgan

1955

South Pacific
Starring: Kyle MacDonnell, James Norbert, Dort Clark
Staged by Frank Carrington & Agnes Morgan

Guys & Dolls
Starring: Sheila Arnold, Jerry Mann, Mary O'Fallon,
Warde Donovan
Staged by Frank Carrington & Agnes Morgan

Mother Was a Bachelor
Starring: Billie Burke, Susan Seaforth
Staged by Frank Carrington & Agnes Morgan

King of Hearts
Starring: Frankie Thomas, Ailsa Dawson
Staged by Frank Carrington & Agnes Morgan

The Caine Mutiny Court Martial
Starring: Chester Morris
Staged by William Cottrell

Happy Birthday
Starring: Joan Blondell, Stephen Elliot
Staged by Frank Carrington & Agnes Morgan

I Killed the Count
Starring: Ian Keith, Frances Helm
Staged by Frank Carrington & Agnes Morgan

The Music Master
Starring: Gene Lockhart, Patricia Peardon,
Joseph Macaulay
Staged by Frank Carrington & Agnes Morgan

Harvey
Starring: Joe E. Brown, Nydia Westman, Mary Chase
Staged by C.W. Christenberry, Jr.

1956
The King and I
Starring: Dorothy Sandlin, Ted Scott, Lee Venora
Staged by Frank Carrington & Agnes Morgan

Kismet
Starring: Ted Scott, Gail Manners
Staged by Frank Carrington & Agnes Morgan

The Solid Gold Cadillac
Starring: Frances Starr, John Boyd
Staged by Frank Carrington & Agnes Morgan

Chalk Garden
Starring: Lillian Gish, Dorothy Gish
Staged by Charles Bowden

The Spa
Starring: Turhan Bey, Gloria Vanderbilt,
Violet Heming
Directed by Edward Chodorey

The Heiress
Starring: Basil Rathbone, Dorothy Sands
Staged by Basil Rathbone

Plain and Fancy
Starring: Jacqueline James, Warde Donovan
Staged by Frank Carrington & Agnes Morgan

Kiss Me Kate
Starring: Ted Scott, Virginia Oswald, Lillian Hayman
Staged by Frank Carrington & Agnes Morgan

Teahouse of the August Moon
Starring: Gene Blakely, Robert Casper,
William La Massena
Directed by Frank Carrington & Agnes Morgan

1957
Can-Can
Starring: Evelyn Page, Ted Scott
Staged by Frank Carrington & Agnes Morgan

South Pacific
Starring: Jacqueline James, Henry Michel
Staged by Frank Carrington & Agnes Morgan

Pajama Game
Starring: Sara Dillon, Robert Busch
Staged by Jean Barrere

The Reluctant Debutante
Starring: Ruth Chatterton, Arthur Treacher
Directed by Walt Witcover

Witness for the Prosecution
Starring: Basil Rathbone, Anne Meacham,
Peter Brundon
Staged by Richard Bender

Oklahoma
Starring: Ted Scott, Gail Manners
Staged by Frank Carrington & Agnes Morgan

Silk Stockings
Starring: Dorothy Sandlin, Robert Busch
Staged by Frank Carrington & Agnes Morgan

The Matchmaker
Starring: Nina Olivette, Jack Harrold
Directed by Frank Carrington & Agnes Morgan

1958
No Time for Sergeants
Starring: Buck Henry, Wynn Pearce
Directed by Frank Carrington & Agnes Morgan

Most Happy Fella
Starring: Edwin Steffe, Arlyne Frank
Directed by Frank Carrington & Agnes Morgan

Damn Yankees
Starring: Richard Armbruster, Dorothy Love,
Wayne Sherwood
Directed by Frank Carrington & Agnes Morgan

Separate Tables
Starring: Geraldine Page, Basil Rathbone
Directed by John O'Shaughnessy

Student Prince
Starring: Glenn Burris, Monte Amundsen
Directed by Frank Carrington & Agnes Morgan

Wonderful Town
Starring: Jacqueline James, Ted Scott
Directed by Frank Carrington & Agnes Morgan

Desert Song
Starring: Ted Scott, Gail Manners
Staged by Frank Carrington & Agnes Morgan

1959
Fanny
Starring: Edwin Steffe, Jack Washburn, Henry Michel
Staged by Frank Carrington & Agnes Morgan

Bells are Ringing
Starring: Betty Jane Watson, Hal Hackett, Jeff Warren
Staged by Frank Carrington & Agnes Morgan

Brigadoon
Starring: Seth Riggs, Janet Pavek, Hal Hackett
Staged by Frank Carrington & Agnes Morgan

Visit to a Small Planet
Starring: Arthur Treacher, Irene Kane
Directed by Michael Howard

Time Remembered
Starring: Frances Starr, Donald Buka
Staged by Frank Carrington & Agnes Morgan

Once More, With Feeling
Starring: Joan Bennett, Donald Cook
Directed by Paul Leaf
Staged by Paul Stickles

Pal Joey
Starring: Helena Bliss, Richard Tone, Anita Gillette
Staged by Frank Carrington & Agnes Morgan

Annie Get Your Gun
Starring: Danny Scholl, Helena Seymour
Staged by Frank Carrington & Agnes Morgan

1960

Redhead
Starring: Patti Karr, Noland Van Way
Directed by Frank Carrington & Agnes Morgan

The Great Waltz
Starring: Dennis King, Christine Mathews
Directed by Frank Carrington & Agnes Morgan

Amphitryon 38
Starring: Arlene Francis, Kent Smith, George Grizzard
Directed by Martin Gabel

Two for the Seesaw
Starring: Shelley Winters, Kevin McCarthy
Directed by Frank Corsaro

Royal Enclosure
Starring: Celeste Holm, Cathleen Nesbitt, Sandor Szabo
Directed by Romney Brent

No Concern of Mine
Starring: Jane Fonda, Geoffrey Home, Ben Piazza
Directed by Andreas Voutsinas

Make a Million
Starring: Sam Levene, Norman Barasch, Carroll Moore
Directed by Sam Levene

Goodbye, Charlie
Starring: Eve Arden, Brooks West
Directed by Michael Egan

Susan and God
Starring: Joan Fontaine, Lauren Gilbert
Directed by John Larson

An Evening with Mike Nichols and Elaine May

The Marriage Go-Round
Starring: Constance Bennett, Edward Mulhare, Gene Blakely, Salome Jens
Directed by Warren Enters

West Side Story
Starring: Byrne Piven, Gerrianne Raphael
Directed by Byrne Piven

1961

Country Girl
Starring: Shelley Winters, Joseph Anthony, Joseph Campanella, Morgan Sterne
Directed by Milton Katselas

A View from the Bridge
Starring: Shelley Winters, David J. Stewart, Joseph Campanella
Directed by Milton Katselas

Destry Rides Again
Starring: Yvonne de Carlo, Ted Scott, John Frederick
Directed by Frank Carrington & Agnes Morgan

Once Upon a Mattress
Starring: Pat Carroll
Directed by Jack Sydow

The Pleasure of His Company
Starring: Cornelia Otis Skinner, Hans Conried
Directed by Charles Olsen

A Majority of One
Starring: Molly Picon, Martyn Green
Directed by Jacob Kalish

Between Seasons
Starring: Gloria Swanson
Directed by Bill Penn

Invitation to a March
Starring: Celeste Holm, Wesley Addy
Directed by Arthur Laurents

Period of Adjustment
Starring: Dane Clark, Rosemary Murphy
Directed by John Lehne

Under the Yum-Yum Tree
Starring: Margaret O'Brien, Hugh Marlow, James McArthur
Directed by James Monos

Three Penny Opera
Starring: Scott Merrill
Directed by Carmen Capolbo

Flower Drum Song
Starring: Yin Sun, Larry Leung
Directed by James Hammerstein

Music Man
Starring: Ted Scott, Barbara Williams
Directed by Robert Merriman

1962

Fiorello
Starring: Tom Bosley, Patrica Wilson
Directed by Howard da Silva

Maggie
Starring: Betsy Palmer, Stuart Damon
Directed by Word Baker

The Complacent Lover
Starring: Walter Pidgeon, Martha Scott
Directed by Del Hughes

Critic's Choice
Starring: Hans Conried, James Roos
Directed by Chas. Olsen

The Miracle Worker
Starring: Eileen Brennan, Donna Zimmerman
Directed by Porter Van Zandt

Old Acquaintance
Starring: Arlene Frances, Bill Berger, Linda Robinson
Directed by Martin Gabel

Sunday in New York
Starring: Margaret O'Brien, Tommy Sands
Directed by Russell McCaig & Joseph. Brownstone

Here Today
Starring: Tallulah Bankhead, Donald Symington, Bill Story
Directed by Jack Sydow

There Must be a Pony
Starring: Myrna Loy, Donald Woods, Peter Helm
Directed by John Stix

Bye Bye Birdie
Starring: Chita Rivera, Tom Poston, Selma Diamond
Directed by Duane Camp

Little Mary Sunshine
Starring: Eileen Brennan, G. Woods, Gary Oakes
Directed by Robert Moore

Gypsy
Starring: Julie Wilson, Jo Wilder, Alfred Sandos
Directed by Gerald Freedman

South Pacific
Starring: Betsy Palmer, Wm. Chapman, Gabriel Dell
Directed by James Hammerstein

1963

The Heroine
Starring: Kay Medford, Murray Hamilton, Joe Silver
Directed by Larry Arrick

A Gift Horse
Starring: Bert Wheeler, Glenda Farrell
Directed by David Pressman

The Mikado and H.M.S. Pinafore
Starring: Martyn Green and Company
Directed by Martyn Green

A Shot in the Dark
Starring: Eva Gabor, Donald Murphy, John Wetmore
Directed by David Hooks

Come Blow Your Horn
Starring: Menasha Skulnik, Mae Questel
Directed by James Hammerstein

Irma La Douce
Starring: Genevieve, Gabriel Dell, Igors Gavon
Staged by Don Driver

The King and I
Starring: Betsy Palmer, William Chapman
Directed by James Hammerstein

Tchin-Tchin
Starring: Dane Clark, Teresa Wright
Directed by Joseph Brownstone

Indoor Sport
Starring: Darren McGavin, Shari Lewis
Directed by Gerald Hiken

Take Her, She's Mine
Starring: Hans Conried, Irene Hervey, Tanya Everett
Directed by George Abbott

The Millionairess
Starring: Carol Channing, Gene Wilder, John McMartin
Directed by Gene Saks

The Irregular Verb to Love [TTB]
Starring: Claudette Colbert, Cyril Ritchard
Directed by Cyril Ritchard

Seidman and Son
Starring: Sam Levene, Janet Ward

Milk and Honey
Starring: Molly Picon, William Chapman
Directed by Burry Fredrik

The Unsinkable Molly Brown
Starring: Pat Carroll, Walter Farrell
Directed by Jean Barrere

The Tender Trap
Starring: Hal March, Taina Elg, Stan Watt
Directed by Gordon Davidson

1964

Kind Sir
Starring: Arlene Frances, Michael Allinson
Directed by William Francisco

Easy Does It
Starring: Tom Poston, Elizabeth Allen
Directed by Jerry Epstein

Carnival
Starring: Liza Minelli, David Daniels, Scott Merrill
Directed by Rudy Tronto

Not in the Book
Starring: Hans Conried
Directed by Charles Olsen

Calculated Risk
Starring: John Payne
Directed by Howard Erskine

1000 Clowns
Starring: Van Johnson, Richard Benjamin, Nancy Douglas, Doug Chapin
Directed by Malcolm Black

Dear Me, The Sky is Falling
Starring: Gertrude Berg, Joseph Buloff
Directed by Michael Thoma

My Fair Lady
Starring: Michael Evans, Margot Moser, John Michael King
Directed by Jerry Adler

Days of Dancing
Starring: Shelley Winters, Robert Walker
Directed by Timmy Everett

The White House
Starring: Helen Hayes, James Daly
Directed by Henry Kaplan

Oh, Dad, Poor Dad
Starring: Hermione Gingold
Directed by Chas. Forsythe

A Girl Could Get Lucky
Starring: Betty Garret, Pat Hingle
Directed by Don Appell

Who's Afraid of Virginia Woolf
Starring: Vicki Cummings, Kendall Clark
Directed by Alan Schneider

Heart's Delight
Starring: Michael Rennie, Nan Martin
Directed by Brian Shaw

The Sound of Music
Starring: Barbara Meister, Webb Tilton, Elizabeth Howell
Directed by Richard Via

Camelot
Starring: Margot Moser, John Cullum, Stuart Damon
Directed by Stone Widney

Enter Laughing
Starring: Alan Mobray, Lynn Bari, Dick Kallman
Directed by Iris O'Connor

1965

Janus
Starring: June Allyson, Scott McKay, Imogene Coca
Directed by Alfred deLiagre, Jr.

Affairs of State
Starring: Betsy Palmer, Walter Abel
Directed by Christopher Hewett

A Man for All Seasons
Starring: Dana Andrews, Albert Dekker
Directed by Albert Dekker

Bell, Book, and Candle
Starring: Allen Ludden, Betty White, James Coco
Directed by Christopher Hewett

Gigi
Starring: George Hamilton, Susan Watson,
Dorothy Sands
Staged by Christopher Hewett

The Glass Menagerie [TTB]
Starring: George Grizzard, Pat Hingle, Piper Laurie,
Maureen Stapleton
Directed by George Keathley

Most Happy Fella
Starring: Art Lund, Edwin Steffe, Margot Moser
Directed by Stone Widney

A Funny Thing Happened on the Way To the Forum
Starring: Jack Gifford, Dom DeLuise
Directed by Jack Gilford

High Spirits
Starring: Beatrice Lillie
Directed by Franklin Lacey

Never Too Late
Starring: Bert Lahr, Nancy Carroll
Directed by Wally Peterson

Absence of a Cello
Starring: Hans Conried, Ruth McDavitt
Directed by Charles Olsen

Come Back Little Sheba
Starring: Shirl Conway, Edward Binns
Directed by George Keathley

Everybody Loves Opal
Starring: Martha Raye
Directed by Vernon Schwartz

Minor Miracle
Starring: Lee Tracy, Dennis King, Pert Kelton
Directed by Howard Erskine

How to Succeed in Business without Really Trying
Starring: Len Gochman, Willard Waterman
Directed by Chars. Durand

Stop the World, I Want to Get Off
Starring: Kenneth Nelson, Joan Eastman
Directed by Kenneth Nelson

Guys and Dolls
Starring: Vivian Blaine, Sam Levene, Norwood Smith
Directed by Gus Schirmer

Mary, Mary
Starring: Betsy Palmer, Scott McKay
Directed by Barry Nelson

1966

A Case of Libel
Starring: Van Heflin, Paul McGrath
Directed by Leonard Patrick

Dial M for Murder
Starring: Joan Fontaine, Eric Berry
Directed by Eric Berry

Remains to be Seen
Starring: Gisele Mackenzie, Hal Linden,
Erik Rhodes
Directed by Leslie Cutler

The Boy Friend
Starring: Barbara Cook, Sandy Duncan, Isabell Farrell
Staged Entirely by Geoffrey Webb

The Women
Starring: Peggy Cass, Sheila Macrae, Phyllis Thaxter,
Bernice Massi
Directed by Stanley Prager

Oliver
Starring: Robin Ramsey, Maura K. Wedge,
Michael Kermoyan
Directed by Stone Widney

Peter Pan
Starring: Betsy Palmer, Sandy Duncan,
Constance Carpenter
Directed by Jacques d'Amboise

Do I Hear a Waltz
Starring: Dorothy Collins, Ron Holgate,
Dorothy Steinnette
Directed by Stone Widney

The Zula and the Zayda
Starring: Menasha Skulnik, Ed Hall, Ben Stone,
Albert Kirk, Ann Roman
Directed by Menasha Skulnik

The Boys from Syracuse
Starring: Emory Bass, Seth Riggs, Gino Conforti,
Hal Linden, Rudy Tronto
Directed by Murray Gitlin

The Roar of the Greasepaint, The Smell of the Crowd
Starring: Kenneth Nelson, Christopher Hewett,
Jill Choder
Staged by Buff Shurr

Fallen Angels
Starring: Nancy Walker, Margaret Phillips,
James Mitchell
Directed by Nancy Walker

Late Love
Starring: Virginia Graham, Mark O' Daniels,
Bert Thorn
Directed by Wayne Carson

The Subject Was Roses
Starring: Maureen O'Sullivan, Chester Morris,
Walter McGinn
Directed by Paul Leaf

Any Wednesday
Starring: George Gaynes, Monica Moran
Directed by Porter Van Zandt

Blossom Time
Starring: Allan Jones, Wm. Lewis, Barbara Meister
Directed by Stone Widney

Take Me Along
Starring: Tommy Sands, Tom Bosley, Lanny Ross,
   Louise Kirkland
Directed by Robert Ennis Turoff

John Loves Mary
Starring: Fabian, Zina Bethune, Roland Winters,
   Leo Gochman
Directed by Warren Enters

1967
The Owl and the Pussycat
Starring: Darryl Hickman, Rita Moreno
Directed by Philip Rose

Born Yesterday
Starring: Janis Page, Robert Strauss, Paul McGrath
Directed by David Pardoll

An Evening with Pearl Bailey

A Warm Body
Starring: Dina Merrill, Kevin McCarthy,
   Anne Meacham
Directed by Chas. Bowden

On a Clear Day You Can See Forever
Starring: Don Francks, Linda Lavin, Nolan Van Way
Directed by Stone Widney

Luv
Starring: Betsy Palmer, Ronny Graham,
   Robert Darnell
Directed by Harvey Medlinsky

Merry Widow
Starring: Dorothy Sandlin, Richard Fredericks,
   Edward Everett Horton
Directed by William Ross

Wait a Minum
Devised & Directed by Leon Gluckman

The Impossible Years
Starring: Sam Levene, Elizabeth Fleming
Directed by Arthur Storch

Killing of Sister George
Starring: Polly Rowles
Directed by Warren Crane

The Fantasticks
Starring: John Gavin, Bob Carroll, Doris Jamin
Directed by William Francisco

Half a Sixpence
Starring: Kenneth Nelson, Alice Cannon,
   Byron Webster
Directed by Christopher Hewett

Funny Girl
Starring: Barbara Minkus, James Mitchell,
   Danny Carroll, Irene Byatt
Directed by Larry Fuller

The Student Prince
Starring: Harry Danner, Barbara Meister,
   Adair McGowen
Directed by Frank Carrington

The Star-Spangled Girl
Starring: Anthony Perkins, Remak Ramsay,
   Lynn Benish
Directed by Anthony Perkins

1968
The Odd Couple
Starring: Harvey Stone, Avery Schreiber
Directed by Mike Kellin

Barefoot in the Park
Starring: Tab Hunter, Thelma Ritter
Directed by Harvey Medlinsky

Special Concert Week
Starring: Buffy Sainte-Marie, Maria Alba
Carlos Montoya, The Serendipity Singers

Oklahoma
Starring: Larry Roquemore, Marie Santell,
   Lois Holmes, Tom Noel
Directed by Gemze De Lappe

Black Comedy
Starring: Orson Bean, M'el Dowd, Robert Moore,
   Paula Trueman
Directed by Jerry Adler

Kiss Me Kate
Starring: Enzo Stuarti, Patricia Marand,
   Carleton Carpenter, Karen Arthur
Directed by Lawrence Kasha

The Midnite Ride of Alvin Blum
Starring: Harvey Stone, Dawn Wells, Jordan Chamey,
   Richard Niles, Anne Berger
Directed by William Hunt

Harvey
Starring: Paul Ford, Ruth McDevitt
Directed by Mark Gordon

Mister Roberts
Starring: John Gavin
Directed by Ray Parker

Don't Drink the Water
Starring: Sam Levene, Dody Goodman, Gary
   Krawford, Don Draper
Directed by Ross Bowman

Lil' Abner
Starring: Dagmar, Michael Beirne, Willi Burke
Directed by James Mitchell

I Do! I Do!
Starring: Stephen Douglass, Fran Hamilton
Directed by Wade Miller

The Little Angels
Starring: National Folk Ballet of Korea
Directed by Bo Hi Pak

1969
A Lamp at Midnight [WP]
Starring: Morris Carnovsky
Directed by Sir Tyrone Guthrie

Here Lies Jeremy Troy [TTB]
Starring: Will Hutchins, Murvyn Vye,
   Charles Braswell
Staged by Ronny Graham

Cactus Flower
Starring: Donald Barton, Betsy Palmer, Lionel Wilson
Directed by Amy Freeman

The King and I
Starring: Dorothy Sandlin, Michael Kermoyan, Terry Saunders
Directed by Stone Widney

You Know I Can't Hear You When The Water's Running
Starring: Eddie Bracken
Directed by Eddie Bracken

George M
Starring: Danny Meehan, Judith Hastings
Staged Entirely by Wakefield Poole

Red, White & Maddox
Starring: Jay Gardner
Assoc. Producers William Domnitz & Arthur Miller

The Show Off
Starring: George Grizzard, Jessie Royce Landis
Directed by George Grizzard

Pizazz on Ice
Conceived & Produced by Dennis W. Ritz

There's a Girl in My Soup
Starring: William Shatner, Jill Haworth
Directed by William Shatner

The Prime of Miss Jean Brodie
Starring: Betsy Palmer, Donald Watson
Directed by Porter Van Zandt

Cabaret
Starring: Martin Ross, Melissa Hart, John Cunningham
Directed by Fred Ebb

Your Own Thing
Staged (originally) by Donald Driver

1970
The Price
Starring: Douglass Watson, Betty Miller, Joseph Buloff, Carle Bensen
Directed by Joseph Anthony

My Daughter, Your Son
Starring: Vivian Vance, Dody Goodman, George S. Irving
Directed by Gordon Hunt

Mame
Starring: Janet Blair, Ann Mitchell, Isabell Farrell, Louise Kirkland
Directed by John Bowab

The Buttered Side
Starring: Art James, Milt Kamen, Jenny O'Hara, Conrad Bain
Directed by Clifford Ammon

The Tender Trap
Starring: William Shatner, Elizabeth Hubbard, Dennis Patrick
Directed by Michael Simone

Charley's Aunt
Starring: Louis Nye, Maureen O'Sullivan, Martyn Green, Melville Cooper
Directed by Harold Stone

The Sound of Music
Starring: Barbara Meister, Erik Silju
Directed by Christopher Hewett

Private Lives
Starring: Tammy Grimes, Brian Bedford
Directed by Stephen Porter

Zorba
Starring: Titos Vandis, Dolores Wilson
Directed by William Francisco

Plaza Suite
Starring: Eddie Bracken, Barbara Baxley
Directed by Harvey Medlinsky

1971
The Vinegar Tree
Starring: Shirley Booth, Staats Cotsworth
Directed by Christopher Hewett

The Secretary Bird
Starring: Edward Mulhare, Angela Thornton, William Mooney
Directed by Porter Van Zandt

Period of Adjustment
Starring: William Shatner, William Mooney, Gloria Maddox
Directed by William Shatner

A Thousand Clowns
Starring: Hugh O'Brian, Bonnie Franklin
Directed by Harvey Medlinsky

Hello, Dolly!
Starring: Betsy Palmer, Max Showalter
Directed by Jack Timmers

Man of La Mancha
Starring: Jerome Hines, Jana Robbins, Louis Criscuolo

You're a Good Man, Charlie Brown
Starring: Peter Platten, Trip Plymale, George Ryland, Don Potter, Carol Ann Ziske, Merry Flershem
Directed by Joseph Hardy

Nutcracker Suite
New Jersey Ballet
Starring: Edward Villella
Directed by Carolyn Clark

Last of the Red Hot Lovers
Starring: Shelley Berman, Constance Ford
Directed by Harvey Medlinsky

1972
The Pleasure of His Company
Starring: Douglas Fairbanks, Jr., Jen Nelson
Directed by Neal Kenyon

Forty Carats
Starring: Barbara Rush, Audrey Christie, Joel Crothers
Staged by Gene Blakely

Fiddler on the Roof
Starring: Jerry Jarrett, Dolores Wilson
Directed by Stanley Soble

1776
Starring: Robert Horton, Jay Gardner
Directed by Larry Forde

Man of La Mancha
Starring: Jerome Hines, Marion Marlowe, Louis Criscuolo
Directed by Rudy Tronto

Nutcracker Suite
New Jersey Ballet
Starring: Edward Villella
Produced by Carolyn Clark

Butterflies Are Free
    Starring: Gloria Swanson, Richard Backus,
        Erin Connor
    Directed by Arthur Whitelaw

1973
Dames at Sea
    Starring: Bernadette Peters, Kathryn Hays,
        David Christmas
    Directed by Voight Kempson

Mary, Mary
    Starring: Betsy Palmer, Robert Moore
    Directed by Porter Van Zandt

**The Effect of Gamma Rays on Man-in-the-Moon
Marigolds**
    Starring: Shelley Winters, Anne Ives
    Directed by Robert H. Livingston

Ballet
    Starring: Edward Villella, Giorgio Tozzi, Allegra Kent
    Produced by Carolyn Clark

Promises, Promises
    Starring: Bill Hinnant, Jill Corey, Joe Silver,
        Jerry Lanning
    Directed by Larry Forde

Twigs
    Starring: Sada Thompson
    Staged by Bud Coffey

No, No, Nanette
    Starring: Dennis Day, Barbara Britton,
        Helen Gallagher, Lillian Hayman, Jerry Andes,
        Cynthia Parva
    Directed by John Lowe III

A Midsummer Night's Dream
    Starring: Mickey Rooney, Sheldon Epps
    Directed by Frank Carrington

Nutcracker Suite
    New Jersey Ballet
    Produced by Carolyn Clark

Sleuth
    Starring: Patrick MacNee, Jordan Christopher
    Directed by Warren Crane

1974
Play it Again, Sam
    Starring: Tony Roberts, Marcia Rodd, Mark Shapiro
    Directed by Jeremiah Morris

Prisoner of Second Ave.
    Starring: Jerry Stiller, Anne Meara
    Directed by Jeremiah Morris

Anything Goes
    Starring: Ann Miller, Coley Worth, Leonard Drum,
        Isabelle Farrell, Louise Kirkland, Ronald Young
    Directed by Lawrence Kasha

South Pacific
    Starring: Jerome Hines, Betsy Palmer, Sylvia Syms,
        John Stewart, Barney Martin
    Directed by Larry Forde

The Sunshine Boys
    Starring: Jack Gilford, Lou Jacobi, Lee Meredith,
        Jeremy Stevens
    Directed by James Bernardi

The Music Man
    Starring: Susan Watson, Ken Berry, Louise Kirkland,
        Gary Gage
    Directed by Larry Forde

Camelot
    Starring: Michael Allinson, Leigh Beery, Don Stewart,
        Noel Craig, Michael Lewis
    Directed by Stone Widney

Nutcracker
    New Jersey Ballet
    Produced by Carolyn Clark

Godspell
    Starring: Walter Gaber
    Directed by Clint Spencer

1975
Light Up the Sky
    Starring: Sam Levene, Kay Medford, Celeste Holm,
        Vivian Blaine, Wesley Addy
    Directed by Harold J. Kennedy

The Fantasticks
    Starring: John Gavin
    Directed by Jay Hampton

The Marriage Go-Round
    Starring: Arlene Dahl, Scott McKay, Julie Newmar,
        Peter Turgeon
    Directed by Bill Ross

Irene
    Starring: Nancy Dussault, Bibi Osterwald, Elliott Reid,
        Paul Dumont, Marijane Maricle, Ted Pritchard
    Directed by Larry Forde

Life With Father
    Starring: Betsy Palmer, Laurence Hugo
    Directed by Barry Nelson

God's Favorite
    Starring: Godfrey Cambridge
    Directed by Tom Porter

Something's Afoot
    Starring: Pat Carroll
    Directed by Tony Tanner

Annie Get Your Gun
    Starring: Phyllis Newman, Don Stewart
    Directed by Bill Guske

Nutcracker
    New Jersey Ballet
    Produced by: Carolyn Clark

The Myron Cohen Show
    Starring: Myron Cohen, Lyn Kellogg
    Directed by Myron Cohen

1976
You Never Know
    Starring: Kitty Carlisle, Bob Wright, Joe Masiell,
        Bernice Massi
    Directed by Bruce Blaine

6 RMS. RIV VU
    Starring: Tab Hunter, Monica Moran
    Directed by Harvey Medlinsky

Luv
    Starring: Ann Meara, Jerry Stiller
    Directed by Harvey Medlinsky

Jesus Christ Superstar
    Starring: Robert Corff, Larry Marshall,
        Kathleen Dezina
    Directed by Charles Gray

A Funny Thing Happened on the Way to the Forum
Starring: Eddie Bracken, Coley Worth,
Lizabeth Pritchett
Directed by Sue Lawless

Panama Hattie
Starring: Ann Miller, Terence Monk, Jill Choder
Directed by Leslie B. Cutler

Grease
Starring: Adrian Zmed, Andrea Walters,
Cynthia Darlow
Directed by Tom Moore

Gypsy
Starring: Dolores Gray
Directed by Bill Guske

Oliver
Starring: John Carradine, Michael Kermoyan,
Barbara Marineau
Directed by Charles Gray

Nutcracker
New Jersey Ballet
Directed by Carolyn Clark

New Year's Eve Special
Starring: George Kirby, Marilyn Michaels

1977
The Belle of Amherst
Starring: Julie Harris
Directed by Charles Nelson Reilly

The Mousetrap
Starring: David McCallum
Directed by David McCallum

The Fatal Weakness
Starring: Eva Marie Saint
Directed by Jeffrey Hayden

Jesus Christ Superstar
Starring: Robert Corff, Kurt Kahjian, Judy Kaye
Directed by Charles Gray

My Fair Lady
Starring: Michael Evans, Leigh Beery,
Christopher Hewett, Roderick Cook
Directed by Jerry Adler

The Ginger Rogers Show
Starring: Ginger Rogers, Rick Podell, Michael Cody,
Jeff Parker, Ron Steinbeck, Jim Taylor,
Christie Westmoreland
Directed by Oona White

Good News
Starring: Virginia Mayo, Bert Parks, Tom Batten,
Jill Choder
Directed by Bill Guske

Grease
Starring: Gail Edwards, Peter Gallagher
Directed by Tom Moore

Shenandoah
Starring: Ed Ames, Christine Ebersole,
Deborah Combs
Directed by Philip Rose

Nutcracker
New Jersey Ballet
Directed by Joseph Carow, George Tomal

New Year's Eve Special
Starring: Victor Borge

1978
Fallen Angels
Starring: Sandy Dennis, Jean Marsh
Directed by Philip Minor

The Little Foxes
Starring: Sandy Dennis, Geraldine Page, Rip Torn
Directed by Philip Minor

Bubbling Brown Sugar
Starring: Cab Callaway
Directed by Robert M. Cooper

Pippin
Starring: Northern Callaway
Directed by Gene Foote

Count Dracula
Starring: Farley Granger
Directed by Joel Friedman

Same Time, Next Year
Starring: Besty Palmer, Nicholas Hormann
Directed by Warren Crane

Jolson
Starring: Clive Baldwin, Sherry Rooney
Directed by Bill Guske

1979
No Sex Please, We're British
Starring: Rachel Gumey, Francis Bethencourt,
Alexander Reed, Susan Sharkey, David Snell
Directed by Vivian Matalon

The Miracle Worker
Starring: Christine Kathy, Rose Bernard
Directed by Ted Weiant

Shenandoah
Starring: John Raitt
Directed and choreographed by Robert Johanson

The Sound of Music
Starring: Barbara Meister, Jean-Pierre Aumont
Directed and choreographed by Robert Johanson

The Student Prince
Starring: Allan Jones, Harry Danner, Judith McCauley
Directed and choreographed by Robert Johanson

The Magic Show
Starring: Joseph Abaldo
Directed by Jay Fox

Fiorello!
Starring: William Linton, Paige O'Hara,
Laura McDuffie
Directed and choreographed by Bill Guske

Nutcracker
New Jersey Ballet
Directed by Carolyn Clark

Shows in the new theatre

1982–83

Robert & Elizabeth
Starring: Leigh Beery, Mark Jacoby, Ron Randell
Directed and Choreographed by Robert Johanson
Musical Director Jim Coleman
Scenic Design by Paul Wonsek
Lighting Design by Nananne Porcher
Costumes by Guy Geoly

You Can't Take it With You [TTB] [ST]
Starring: Jason Robards, Colleen Dewhurst,
    Bill McCutcheon, George Rose, Elizabeth Wilson
Directed by Ellis Rabb
Scenic and Lighting Design by James Tilton
Costumes by Neil Spisak

Mass Appeal
Starring: Milo O'Shea, Shaun Cassidy
Directed by Geraldine Fitzgerald
Scenic Design by David Gropman
Lighting Design by F. Mitchell Dana
Costumes by William Ivey Long

Suite in Two Keys
Starring: Barry Nelson, Betsy Palmer, Elaine Stritch
Directed by Richard Barr
Scenic Design by Helen Pond & Herbert Senn
Lighting Design by Deirdre A. Taylor
Costumes by Guy Geoly

The New Moon
Starring: Judith McCauley, Richard White,
    Norman A. Large, Christopher Hewett,
Directed and Choreographed by Robert Johanson
Musical Director Kay Cameron
Musical Supervisor Jim Coleman
Scenic Design by James Morgan and Daniel Ettinger
Lighting Design by Steve Cochrane
Costumes by Guy Geoly

Man of La Mancha
Starring Jerome Hines, Bernice Massi
Directed and Choreographed by Rudy Tronto
Musical Direction by Rudolph Bennett,
Scenic and Lighting Design by Howard Bay
Costume Coordinator Vida Thomas

1983–84

Annie
Starring: Gary Holcombe, Tara Kennedy, Marcia Lewis
Directed by Jerry Adler
Choreography by Mimi B. Wallace
Musical Direction by Glen Clugston
Scenic Design by Associated Theatrical Designs
Lighting Design by David Kissel
Costumes by Gail Cooper-Hecht

Fiddler on the Roof
Starring Joe Cusanelli, Dolores Wilson
Directed and Choreographed by Frank Coppola
Musical Direction by Michael Dansicker
Scenic Design by Philip Rodzen
Lighting Design by Patricia Donovan
Costumes by Guy Geoly

The Guardsman
Starring Lucie Arnaz, Laurence Luckinbill,
    Jane Connell, Michael Lipton
Directed by David Rothkopf
Scenic Design by Robert Barnes
Lighting Design by Frances Aronson
Costumes by Julie Weiss

The Show Off
Starring: Jean Stapleton, Orson Bean, Sally Dunn,
    Pamela Burrell
Directed by William H. Putch
Scenic Design by James M. Fouchard
Lighting Design by David Kissel
Costumes by Arnold S. Levine

Joseph and the Amazing Technicolor Dream Coat
Starring: Davis Gaines, Liz Larsen, Tom Carder
Directed and Choreographed by Tony Tanner
Musical Direction by Michael Tornick
Scenic Design by Karl Eigsti
Lighting Design by Barry Arnold
Costumes by Guy Geoly

Desert Song
Starring: Judith McCauley, Richard White,
    Philip Wm. McKinley, Roy Alan Wilson,
    Lillian Graff, Keith Ryan, Ira Hawkins,
    Ruth Gottschall
Directed and Choreographed by Robert Johanson
Musical Direction by Phil Hall
Scenic Design by Michael Anania
Lighting Design by David Kissel
Costumes by Guy Geoly

1984–85

Amadeus
Starring: Bob Gunton, John Thomas Waite,
    Sally Ann Flynn, Melody Meitrott, Jack Harrold
Directed by Robert Johanson
Scenic Design by John Bury
Lighting Design by Frances Aronson
Costumes by Guy Geoly

Guys and Dolls
Starring: Jack Carter, Larry Kert, Susan Powell,
    Lenora Nemetz, Philip Wm. McKinley, Jack Harrold
Directed by Robert Johanson
Choreography by Michael Shawn
Musical Direction by Jim Coleman
Scenic Design by Michael Anania
Lighting Design by Frances Aronson
Costumes by Guy Geoly

Side by Side by Sondheim
Starring: Helen Gallagher, Judy Kaye, Larry Kert,
    George Rose
Directed by Robert Johanson
Musical Direction by Jim Coleman
Scenic & Lighting Design by David Kissel
Costumes by Alice S. Hughes

Inherit the Wind [LCL]
Starring: E.G. Marshall, Robert Vaughn
Directed by John Going
Scenic Design by Michael Anania
Lighting Design by Mimi Jordan Sherin
Costumes by Guy Geoly

Show Boat
Starring: Leigh Beery, Eddie Bracken, Judith
McCauley, Richard White
Directed by Robert Johanson
Choreography by Sharon Halley
Musical Direction by Jim Coleman
Scenic Supervision by Michael Anania
Lighting Design by Brian MacDevitt
Costumes by Guy Geoly

Evita
Starring: Lori Ackerman, David Brummel, John
Herrera
Directed by Frank Marino
Choreographed by Sam Viverito
Musical Direction by Pam Drews
Scenic Design by Jim O'Brian
Lighting Design by Jackie Manassee
Costumes by Guy Geoly

1985–86

Windy City
Starring: Gary Sandy, Ronald Holgate, Judy Kaye,
Alan Sues
Directed and Choreographed by David H. Bell
Musical Direction by Jim Coleman
Scenic Design by Michael Anania
Lighting Design by Jeff Davis
Costumes by Guy Geoly

Carousel
Starring: Marsha Bagwell, Maureen Brennan,
Tom Ligon, Judith McCauley, Richard White
Directed by Robert Johanson
Choreography by Sharon Halley
Musical Direction by Jim Coleman
Scenic Design by Michael Anania
Lighting Design by Brian MacDevitt
Costumes by Guy Geoly

Run For Your Wife [AP]
Starring: David McCallum
Directed by Chris Johnson
Scenic Design by Michael Anania
Lighting Design by David Kissel
Costumes by Alice S. Hughes

The Foreigner
Starring: Bob Denver, Jane Connell
Directed by David Saint
Scenic Design by Michael Anania
Lighting Design by David Kissel
Costumes by Alice S. Hughes

The 1940's Radio Hour
Starring: Robert Cenedella, David Chaney,
Larry Grey, Donna Kane, Melody Savage,
Susan Elizabeth Scott, John Scherer,
Dorothy Stanley, Bob Walton, Lenny Wolpe
Directed and Choreographed by Robert Johanson
Musical Direction by Jim Coleman
Scenic Design by Michael Anania
Lighting Design by David Kissel
Costume Design by Guy Geoly and Alice S. Hughes

Candide
Starring: Patti Allison, Marsha Bagwell, Maureen
Brennan, Jack Harrold, Robert Johanson, Kenneth
Kantor, Sal Mistretta, Patrick Quinn,
Directed and Choreographed by Robert Johanson and
Phillip Wm. McKinley
Musical Direction by Jim Coleman
Scenic Design by Michael Anania
Lighting Design by Brian MacDevitt
Costumes by Guy Geoly

1986–87

Damn Yankees
Starring: Orson Bean, Davis Gaines, Alyson Reed
Directed by George Abbott
Musical Staging by Michael Shawn
Scenic Design by Michael Anania
Lighting Design by Mimi Jordan Sherin
Costumes by Guy Geoly & Alice S. Hughes

Barnum
Starring: P.J. Benjamin, Meg Bussert, Judith McCauley
Directed by Neal Kenyon
Choreography by Dick Lumbard
Scenic Design by David Mitchell
Lighting Design by Brian MacDevitt
Costumes by Guy Geoly & Alice S. Hughes

Brighton Beach Memoirs
Starring: Barbara Andres, Barbara Caruso,
Rudy Goldschmidt, Alan Mixon, Marc Riffon
Directed by John Going
Scenic Design by David Mitchell
Lighting Design by David Kissel
Costumes by Alice S. Hughes

Sunrise at Campobello
Starring: Ron Parady and Kathleen Chalfant
Directed by John Going
Scenic Design by Michael Anania
Lighting Design by David Kissel
Costumes by Guy Geoly

Naughty Marietta
Starring: Maryanne Telese, Stephen Lehew,
Allan Jones
Directed by Robert Johanson
Choreography by Sharon Halley
Scenic Design by Michael Anania
Lighting Design by Brian MacDevitt
Costumes by Alice S. Hughes

Annie Get Your Gun
Starring: Judy Kaye, Richard White
Directed by Robert Johanson
Choreography by D. J. Giagni
Scenic Design by Robert O'Hearn
Lighting Design by David Kissel
Costumes by Guy Geoly

1987–88

Sayonara [WP] [LCL]
Starring: Richard White, June Angela, Kevin
Sweeney, Miho, Ako
Directed by Robert Johanson
Choreography by Susan Stroman
Musical Direction by Ted Kociolek
Scenic Design by Michael Anania
Lighting Design by Brian MacDevitt
Costumes by David Toser & Eiko Yamaguchi

My One and Only
Starring: George Dvorsky, Donna Kane
Directed by Richard Casper
Choreography by Patti D'Beck
Musical Direction by Mark Goodman
Scenic Design by Adrianne Lobel & Tony Walton
Lighting Design by Marc B. Weiss
Costumes by Guy Geoly

Biloxi Blues
Starring: Marc Riffon, Barry Cullinson
Directed by John Going
Scenic Design by David Mitchell
Lighting Design by Phil Monat
Costumes by Alice S. Hughes.

Two Into One [AP]
Starring: Tony Randall, Millicent Martin,
    Paxton Whitehead, Davis Gaines, Karen Shallo
Directed by Ray Cooney
Scenic Design by Michael Anania
Lighting Design by Jeff Davis
Costumes by Alice S. Hughes

Jesus Christ Superstar
Starring: Robert Johanson, James Rocco, Kim Criswell,
    Robert Cuccioli, George Dvorsky, Judith McCauley,
    John Sloman
Directed by Robert Johanson
Choreography by Susan Stroman
Musical Direction by Andrew Carl Wilk
Scenic Design by Michael Anania
Lighting Design by Jeff Davis
Costumes by Cecilia A. Friederichs

Mack and Mabel
Starring: Lee Horsley, Janet Metz, Scott Ellis,
    Ed Evanko, Dorothy Stanley, Ruth Williamson
Directed by Robert Johanson
Choreography by Scott Salmon
Musical Direction by Larry Blank
Scenic Design by Michael Anania
Lighting Design by Jeff Davis
Costumes by Guy Geoly

1988–89

La Cage Aux Folles
Starring: Lee Roy Reams, Walter Charles,
    Darrel Carey, Sheila Smith
Directed by James Pentecost
Choreography by Linda Haberman
Musical Direction by Kay Cameron
Scenic Design by David Mitchell
Lighting Design by Jules Fisher & Natasha Katz
Costumes by Theoni V. Aldredge

1776
Starring: William Linton, Sam Kressen, Brent Barrett,
    Robert Cuccioli, George Dvorsky, Judith McCauley,
    Ron Parody, Susan Powell, Patrick Quinn,
    John Scherer,
Directed & Choreographed by Robert Johanson
Musical Direction by Andrew Carl Wilk
Scenic Design by Kevin Rupnik
Lighting Design by Jeff Davis
Costumes by Guy Geoly

Broadway Bound
Starring: Barbara Caruso, Rudy Goldschmidt,
    Salem Ludwig, Bernice Massi, Alan Mixon,
    Marc Riffon
Directed by Philip Minor
Scenic Design by David Mitchell
Lighting Design by David Kissel
Costumes by Alice S. Hughes

Beyond A Reasonable Doubt [WP]
Starring: Karen Valentine, David Groh
Directed by Thomas Gruenewald
Scenic Design by Michael Anania
Lighting Design by Marilyn Rennagel
Costumes by Alice. S. Hughes

Shenandoah
Starring: Walter Charles, Brent Barrett,
    George Dvorsky, Malcolm Gets, Ron Gibbs,
    Patricia Ben Peterson, Michael Piontek
Directed by Robert Johanson
Choreography by Susan Stroman
Musical Direction by Kay Cameron
Scenic Design by Michael Anania
Lighting Design by Mark Stanley
Costumes by Guy Geoly

Show Boat [PBS] [LCL]
Starring: Marshal Bagwell, Rebecca Baxter,
    Eddie Bracken, P.L. Brown, Shelly Burch,
    Elia English, Lenora Nemetz, Lee Roy Reams,
    Richard White
Directed by Robert Johanson
Choreography by Sharon Halley
Musical Direction by Peter Howard
Scenic Design by Michael Anania
Lighting Design by Ken Billington
Costumes by Gregory A. Poplyk & Bradford Wood

1989–90

42nd Street
Starring: Joy Franz, John Scherer, Tom Urich,
    Cathy Wydner
Directed and Choreographed by Lee Roy Reams
Musical Direction by Phil Hall
Scenic Design by Robin Wagner
Lighting Design by Kirk Bookman
Costumes by Guy Geoly

Rhythm Ranch [WP]
Starring: Robert Cuccioli, Christopher Durham,
    Liz Larsen, Nora Mae Lyng
Directed by Philip Wm. McKinley
Choreography by Susan Stroman
Scenic Design by Michael Anania
Lighting Design by Jeff Davis
Costumes by Lindsay W. Davis

The Cocktail Hour
Starring: Ivar Brogger, Burt Edwards,
    Monica Merryman, Phyllis Thaxter
Directed by John Going
Scenic Design by Michael Anania
Lighting Design by Tim Saternow
Costumes by José M. Rivera

Steel Magnolias
Starring: Barbara Andres, Veanne Cox, Mary Fogarty,
    Barbara Gulan, Pamela Lewis, Billie Lou Watt
Directed by Jane Dentinger
Scenic Design by Michael Anania
Lighting Design by Rick Butler
Costume Design by Alice S. Hughes

Fanny [LCL]
    Starring: Jose Ferrer, George S. Irving, Terri Bibb,
        John Leone, Karen Shallo
    Directed by Robert Johanson
    Choreography by Sharon Halley
    Scenic Design by Michael Anania
    Lighting Design by Mark Stanley
    Costumes by Gregg Barnes

Mikado Inc. [WP]
    Starring: Marsha Bagwell, Phillip Wm. McKinley,
        James Rocco, Christine Toy
    Directed & Choreographed by Robert Johanson
    Scenic Design by Michael Anania
    Lighting Design by Phil Monat
    Costumes by Lindsay W. Davis

1990–91
Me and My Girl
    Starring: James Brennan, Judy Blazer, Jane Connell,
        George S. Irving
    Directed and choreographed by Tony Parise
    Scenic Design by Michael Anania
    Lighting Design by Phil Monat
    Costumes by Guy Geoly

The Roar of the Greasepaint, The Smell of the Crowd
    Starring: George S. Irving, Robert Johanson, Mia
        Malm, Denise Nolan, Ron Richardson
    Directed by Robert Johanson & Larry Grey
    Musical direction by Tom Helm
    Choreography by Susan Stroman
    Scenic Design by Michael Anania
    Lighting Design by Mark Stanley
    Costumes by Gregg Barnes

Lend Me a Tenor
    Starring: Judy Blazer, Robert Cuccioli, Patrick Quinn,
        David Sabin
    Directed by Steven Beckler
    Scenic Design by Tony Walton & Ron Kadri
    Lighting Design by Michael Lincoln
    Costumes by Jennifer Arnold

To Kill a Mockingbird
    Starring: George Grizzard, Katharine Houghton
    Directed by Robert Johanson
    Scenic Design by Michael Anania
    Lighting Design by Mark Stanley
    Costumes by Gregg Barnes

Merry Widow
    Starring: Judy Kaye and Richard White
    Directed by Robert Johanson
    Choreography by Sharon Halley
    Musical Direction by Jim Coleman
    Scenic Design by Michael Anania
    Lighting Design by Mark Stanley
    Costumes by Gregg Barnes

A Chorus Line
    Starring: Jan Leigh Herndon, Jane Lanier,
        Robert Longbottom, Michelle Mallardi,
        Eric Paeper, Matt Zarley
    Michael Bennett's Original Direction and
        Choreography Restaged by Baayork Lee
    Original Scenic Design by Robin Wagner Adapted by
        Michael Anania
    Original Lighting Design by Tharon Musser Recreated
        by Marilyn Rennagel
    Original Costume Design by Theoni V. Aldredge
        Recreated by Jose M. Rivera

1991–92
West Side Story
    Starring: Scott Carollo, Lauri Landry, Renee Stork,
        Angelo Fraboni, Rick Manning
    Jerome Robbins' Original Direction and Choreography
        Reproduced by Alan Johnson
    Musical Direction by Richard Parrinello
    Scenic Design by Campell Baird
    Lighting Design by Ken Billington
    Costumes by Gail Cooper-Hecht

Camelot
    Starring: James Brennan, Mari Nelson, Joseph
        Mahowald, Robert Johanson, Larry Grey
    Directed and Choreographed by Robert Johanson
    Musical Direction by Jim Coleman
    Scenic Design by Michael Anania
    Lighting Design by Mark Stanely
    Costumes by Gregg Barnes

Rumors
    Starring: Stephen Berger, Linda Cameron,
        Catherine Campbell, Suzanne Dawson,
        Ken Kliban, Heather MacRae, Michael Minor,
        Wiley Moore, Reno Roop
    Directed by John Brigleb
    Scenic Design by Tony Straiges
    Lighting Design by Tim Hunter
    Costumes by Joseph G. Aulisi

Great Expectations [OA] [LCL]
    Starring: Michael James Reed, Elizabeth Franz,
        Nancy Bell
    Directed by Robert Johanson
    Scenic Design by Michael Anania
    Lighting Design by Tim Hunter
    Costumes by Gregg Barnes

Oklahoma
    Starring: Susan Powell, Richard White,
        Robert Cuccioli
    Directed by James Rocco
    Choreography by Sharon Halley
    Musical Direction by Tom Helm
    Scenic Design by John Lee Beatty
    Lighting Design by Jeff Davis
    Costumes by Gregg Barnes

Chess
    Starring: P.J. Benjamin, Steve Blanchard, Susan Dawn
        Carson, David Cryer, John DeLuca, Judy McLane,
        Keith Rice
    Directed and Choreographed by Rob Marshall
    Musical Direction by Jeff Rizzo
    Scenic Design by Michael Anania
    Lighting Design by Tim Hunter
    Costumes by Gregg Barnes

1992–93

The Wizard of Oz
Starring: Evan Bell, Eddie Bracken, Mark Chimel, Elizabeth Franz, Michael Hayward-Jones, Judith McCauley, Michael O'Gorman, Kelli Rabke
Directed and Choreographed by Robert Johanson and James Rocco
Scenic Design by Michael Anania
Musical Direction by Jeff Rizzo
Lighting Design by Tim Hunter
Costumes by Gregg Barnes

Sweeney Todd
Starring: Rebecca Baxter, Stephen Hanan, Steven Harrison, George Hearn, Robert Johanson, Judy Kaye, Jay Montgomery, Mary Beth Peil, Nick Wyman
Directed by Michael Montel
Choregraphed by Sharon Halley
Musical Direction by Jeffrey Saver
Scenic Design by Eugene Lee
Lighting Design by Ken Billington
Costumes by Gregg Barnes

Don't Dress for Dinner [AP]
Starring: Patricia Conolly, Simon Jones, Caroline Lagerfelt, Alexandra O'Karma, Reno Roop, Timothy Wheeler
Directed by Pamela Hunt
Scenic Design by Michael Anania
Lighting Design by F. Mitchell Dana
Costumes by Gregg Barnes

Lost in Yonkers
Starring: John Anson, Irene Daily Carol Harris, Tim Jerome, Eric Michael, Justin Walker, Marsha Waterbury
Directed by Philip Cusak
Set and Costume Design by Santo Loquasto
Lighting Design by Tharon Musser, Recreated by Fred Hancock

My Fair Lady
Starring: Judy Blazer, Michael DeVries, Pauline Flanagan, George S. Irving, Simon Jones, Patricia Kilgarriff, Russell Leib, Tom Toner
Directed by Larry Carpenter
Choreography by Daniel Pelzig
Scenic Design by Michael Anania
Lighting Design by Tim Hunter
Costumes by Gregg Barnes

Phantom
Starring: Richard White, Marie-Laurence Danvers, Patti Allison, Jack Dabdoub, Paul Schoeffler
Directed by Robert Johanson
Choreography by Sharon Halley
Scenic Design by Michael Anania
Lighting Design by F. Mitchell Dana
Costumes by Gregg Barnes

1993–94

Paper Moon [WP]
Starring: Natalie DeLucia, John Dossett, Christine Ebersole, Gregory Harrison, Linda Hart, Chandra Wilson
Directed by Matt Casella
Musical Direction by Steve Marzullo
Choreography by Alan Johnson
Scenic Design by Michael Anania
Lighting Design by Pat Collins
Costumes by Jeffrey Kurland

Animal Crackers
Starring: Robert Michael Baker, Kristin Chenoweth, Frank Ferrante, Les Marsden, Jan Neuberger, Michael O'Steen, Hal Robinson, John Scherer, Carol Swarbrick
Directed by Charles Repole
Choregraphy by Michael Lichtefeld
Musical Direction by Keith Thompson
Scenic Design by Michael Anania
Lighting Design by F. Mitchell Dana
Costumes by David Toser

It Runs in the Family [AP]
Starring: Eddie Bracken, Ray Cooney, Barbara Rosenblat, Anne Rogers Robert Mandan, Kay Walbye
Directed by Ray Cooney
Scenic Design by Michael Anania
Lighting Design by F. Mitchell Dana
Costumes by Gregg Barnes

A Tale of Two Cities [OA] [LCL]
Starring: Nancy Bell, Kevin Chamberlin, Margaret Hall, Christopher Innvar, Kathleen Mahoney-Bennett, Ron Parody, James Pritchett, Michael James Reed, Judith Roberts
Directed by Robert Johanson
Scenic Design by Michael Anania
Lighting Design by Ken Billington
Costumes by Gregg Barnes

South Pacific
Starring: Tina Fabrigue, Marguerite MacIntyre, Gary Marachek, J. Mark McVey , Ron Raines
Directed by Robert Johanson
Choreography by Sharon Halley
Musical Direction by Don Jones
Scenic Design by Michael Anania
Lighting Design by F. Mitchell Dana
Costumes by Gregg Barnes

Peter Pan
Starring: Robert Creighton, Christopher Innvar, Ken Jennings, Robert Johanson, Melody Meitrott, Elizabeth Walsh, Becky Watson
Directed by Robert Johanson
Choreography by Daniel Pelzig
Musical Direction by Fred Lassen
Scenic Design by Michael Anania
Lighting Design by F. Mitchell Dana
Costumes by Gregg Barnes

1994–95

Singin' in the Rain
Starring: Charles Goff, Michael Gruber, Deborah Jolly,
Randy Rogel, Christina Saffran
Directed by James Rocco
Choreography by Linda Goodrich and James Rocco
Musical Direction by Steve Tyler
Scenic Design by Michael Anania
Lighting Design by Tim Hunter
Costumes by Gregg Barnes

Oliver!
Starring: Robert Creighton, Christopher Innvar,
George S. Irving, Judy McLane,
David Lloyd Watson, Eileen Quinn
Directed by Robert Johanson
Choreography by Daniel Stewart
Musical Direction by Jim Coleman
Scenic Design by Michael Anania
Lighting Design by F. Mitchell Dana
Costumes by Gregg Barnes

Forever Plaid
Starring: Jonathan Brody, Roy Chicas, David Engel,
Robert Lambert
Directed and Choreographed by Stuart Ross
Musical Direction by David Gursky
Scenic Design by Neil Peter Jampolis
Lighting Design by Jane Reisman
Costumes by Debra Stein

The Prisoner of Zenda [WP]
Starring: Steve Boles, Nancy Bell, Robert Carin,
Michael James Reed, Jonathan Wade, John Wylie
Directed by Robert Johanson
Scenic Design by Michael Anania
Lighting Design by Ken Billington
Costumes by Gregg Barnes
Fight Direction by Rick Sordelet

Brigadoon
Starring: P.J. Benjamin, John Clonts, Leah Hocking,
Joseph Mahowald, Lee Merrill, Alex Sanchez
Directed by David Holdgrive
Musical Direction by Jim Coleman
Choreography by Greg Ganakas
Set & Costume Design by Desmond Heeley
Lighting Design by Mark Stanley

The Secret Garden
Starring Cherie Bebout, Glory Crampton,
Stephanie Douglas, Chad Hudson, Robert
Johanson, Keith Rice, David Lloyd Watson
Directed and Choreographed by David Holdgrive and
Robert Johanson
Musical Direction by Wendy Bobbitt
Scenic Design by Michael Anania
Lighting Design by F. Mitchell Dana
Costumes by Gregg Barnes

1995–96

Nine
Starring: Paul Schoeffler, Glory Crampton,
Lauren Kennedy, Judith McCauley, Judy McLane,
Stephanie Pope
Directed by Robert Johanson
Choreography by D. J. Salisbury
Musical Direction by Jim Coleman
Scenic Design by Michael Anania
Lighting Design by Tim Hunter
Costumes by Gregg Barnes

Dreamgirls
Starring: Curtis l' Cook, Herb Downer,
LaTonya Holmes, Deidre Lang, Angela Robinson,
Marshall Titus, Alton Fitzgerald White,
Sharon Wilkins
Directed by Mark S. Hoebee
Choreography by Kenny Ingram
Musical Direction by Wendy Bobbitt
Scenic Design by Michael Annania
Lighting Design by Tim Hunter
Costumes by Gregg Barnes

You Never Know
Starring: Stephanie Douglas, Nancy Hess, Tom Ligon,
Michael O'Steen, John Scherer, KT Sullivan
Directed by Charles Repole
Choreography by Michael Lichtefeld
Musical Direction by John Mulcahy
Scenic Design by Michael Anania
Lighting Design by Tom Sturge
Costumes by Gregg Barnes

Comfortable Shoes [WP]
Starring: Clint Holmes, Scott Irby-Ranniar, LaChanze,
Nancy Ringham, Adam Wade
Directed by Robert Johanson
Choreography by John Carrafa
Musical Direction by Nelson Kole
Scenic Design by Michael Anania
Lighting Design by Tim Hunter
Costumes by Gregg Barnes

Call Me Madam
Starring: Leslie Uggams, Mark Baker, Neal Benari,
Vanessa Dorman Jonathan Hadley, Nancy Johnston
Directed by Charles Repole
Choreography by Daniel Stewart
Musical Direction by Jim Coleman
Scenic Design by Michael Anania
Lighting Design by Mark Stanley
Costumes by Gregg Barnes

Evita
Starring: Judy McLane, Daniel M. Cooney,
Raymond McLeod
Directed and Choreographed by Larry Fuller
Musical Direction by Tim Stella
Set provided by San Bernardino Civic Light Opera
Lighting Design by Richard Winkler
Costumes by Eaves-Brooks Costumes

1996–97

Applause
Starring: Stephanie Powers, John Dossett,
   Kate Jennings Grant
Directed by Gene Saks
Choreography by Ann Reinking
Musical Supervision by John McDaniel
Scenic Design by Michael Anania
Lighting Design by Howell Binkley
Costumes by Robert Mackintosh & Tomasz Starzewski

Gigi
Starring: Glory Crampton, Gavin MacLeod,
   Liliane Montevecchi, Anne Rogers, Richard White
Directed by Robert Johanson
Choreography by Sharon Halley
Musical Direction by Wendy Bobbitt
Scenic Design by Michael Anania
Lighting Design by Tim Hunter
Costumes by Gregg Barnes

Out of Order [AP]
Starring: Paxton Whitehead, Delphi Harrington,
   Reno Roop, Kay Walbye
Directed by David Warwick
Scenic Design by Douglas Heap
Lighting Design by Martin Aronstein
Costumes by Ellis Tillman

Jane Eyre [OA]
Starring: Glory Crampton, Tom Hewitt,
   Mikel Sarah Lambert, John Littlefield,
   Elizabeth Roby
Directed by Robert Johanson
Scenic Design by Michael Anania
Lighting Design by Tim Hunter
Costumes by Gregg Barnes

No, No, Nanette [LCL]
Starring: Kaye Ballard, Eddie Bracken,
   Helen Gallagher, Daniel Herron, Lee Roy Reams,
   Virginia Sandifur, Debra Wiseman
Directed and Choreographed by Donald Saddler
Musical Direction by Jim Coleman
Set by by San Bernardino Civic Light Opera
Lighting Design by Mark Stanley
Costumes by Gregg Barnes

Man of La Mancha
Starring: Philip Hernandez, Judy McLane,
   Michael J. Farina, Tom Hewitt
Directed and Choreographed by Dorothy Danner &
   Robert Johanson
Musical Direction by Jim Coleman
Scenic Design by James Noone
Lighting Design by F. Mitchell Dana
Costumes by Gregg Barnes
Fight Direction by Rick Sordelet

1997–98

Big River
Starring: Lawrence Clayton, David Gunderman,
   Steve Boles, John Hillner, Shannon Stoeke,
   Jessica Wright
Directed and Choreographed by James Rocco
Musical Direction by Vicki Carter
Scenic Design by Michael Anania
Lighting Design by Jack Mehler
Costumes by Michele Wynne

Children of Eden [OCR]
Starring: Stephanie Mills, Darius De Haas,
   Hunter Foster, Kelli Rabke, William Solo,
   Adrian Zmed
Directed by Robert Johanson
Choreographed by Dawn DiPasquale
Musical Direction by Danny Kosarin
Scenic Design by Michael Anania
Lighting Design by Jack Mehler
Costumes by Gregg Barnes

Mask of Moriarity
Starring: Paxton Whitehead, Susan Knight, Tom Lacy,
   Jon Patrick Walker
Directed by Nicholas Martin
Scenic Design by James Joy
Lighting Design by Jeff Davis
Costumes by Michael Krass

Death of a Salesman
Starring: Ralph Waite, Lisa Richards, Rob Sedjwick,
   Sean Runnette
Directed by David Wheeler
Scenic Design by Michael Anania
Lighting Design by Dennis Parichy
Costumes by Gregg Barnes

Follies [OCR]
Starring: Kaye Ballard, Eddie Bracken,
   Michael Gruber, Laurence Guittard, Billy Hartung,
   Dee Hoty, Vahan Khanzadian, Ingrid Ladendorf,
   Donna McKechnie, Ann Miller,
   Liliane Montevecchi, Natalie Mosco,
   Phyllis Newman, Meredith Patterson,
   Tony Roberts, Donald Saddler,
Directed by Robert Johanson
Choreography by Jerry Mitchell
Musical Direction by Jim Coleman and Tom Helm
Scenic Design by Michael Anania
Lighting Design by Mark Stanley
Costumes by Gregg Barnes

Will Rogers Follies
Starring: Ann Crumb, John Davidson, Robert E. Fitch,
   Pamela Jordan
Directed by Mark S. Hoebee
Choreography by D.J. Salisbury
Musical Direction by Michael Biagi
Scenic Design by Tony Walton
Lighting Design by Marcia Madeira
Costumes by Willa Kim

1998–99

Gypsy
    Starring: Betty Buckley, Deborah Gibson,
      Lenny Wolpe, Laura Bell Bundy,
      Alexandra Kiesman, Anna McNeely,
      Joe Machota, Jana Robbins, Dorothy Stanley
    Directed by Mark Waldrop
    Choreography by Liza Gennaro
    Musical Direction by Edward Strauss
    Scenic Design by Michael Anania
    Lighting Design by Mark Stanley
    Costumes by Michael Bottari & Ron Case

Dr. Jekyll and Mr. Hyde
    Starring: Glory Crampton, Bob Dorian, Marc Kudisch,
      Judy McLane, Richard White
    Directed & Choreographed by Philip Wm. McKinley
    Musical Direction by Jim Coleman
    Scenic Design by Michael Anania
    Lighting Design by Kirk Bookman
    Costumes by Scott A. Lane

Up, Up and Away—The Songs of Jimmy Webb [WP]
    Starring: Darius deHaas, Robert Johanson,
      Judy McLane, Kelli Rabke
    Directed by Robert Johanson
    Choreography by Rob Ashford
    Musical Direction by Lon Hoyt
    Scenic Design by Michael Anania
    Lighting Design by Jack Mehler
    Costumes by Angelina Avallone

Wuthering Heights [OA]
    Starring: Libby Christophersen, Mark H. Dold,
      David Ledingham, Jodie Lynne McClintock,
      Elizabeth Roby
    Directed by Robert Johanson
    Scenic Design by Michael Anania
    Lighting Design by Jack Mehler
    Costumes by Gregg Barnes

Crazy for You [PBS]
    Starring: Bruce Adler, Jeb Brown, Jane Connell,
      Sandy Edgerton, Larry Linville, Stacey Logan,
      Jim Walton
    Directed by James Brennan
    Original Choreography by Susan Stroman, recreated
      by Angelique Ilo
    Musical Direction by Tom Helm
    Scenic Design by Robin Wagner
    Lighting Design by Michael Lincoln
    Costumes by William Ivey Long

Joseph and the Amazing Technicolor Dreamcoat
    Starring: Patrick Cassidy, Deborah Gibson
    Directed by Dallett Norris
    Choreography by Richard Stafford
    Musical Direction by Helen Gregory
    Scenic Design by James Fouchard
    Lighting Design by Rick Belzer
    Costumes by Bruce Harrow

APPENDIX II:
Musical Theatre Project

The Musical Theatre Project was created to develop new scripts for the American Musical Theatre. Original works were solicited by Paper Mill to be developed in a series of staged readings and workshop or lab productions. Several of these scripts went on to receive World Premiere productions as part of a Paper Mill mainstage season. When funding from the New Jersey State Council on the Arts was cut in the late 1980s, funding for the Musical Theatre Project was eliminated and the project was disbanded.

STAGED READINGS

Sleeping Beauty
April 10, 1984
Book by Robert Johanson
Directed by Robert Johanson
Musical Direction by Phil Hall and Brad Garside

One More Song
April 20 & 21, 1987
Music/Lyrics by Stephen Citron
Book by Anne Edwards & Mike Evans
Directed by Philip Wm. McKinley
Musical Direction by Luther Henderson and
Leonard Oakly

Grand Duchy
November, 1985
Music by John Bayless
Book/Lyrics by Robert L. Freedman
Directed by Philip Wm. McKinley
Musical Direction by Jim Coleman

Winter In Paradise
November, 1985
Book/Lyrics/Music by Stephen Hanan

Lost Illusions
November, 1985
Music/Lyrics by Daniel Troob
Book by David Morgan
Conceived by Arthur Masella with Daniel Troob and
David Morgan
Directed by Arthur Masella

Going Hollywood
November 1985
Music by Jonathan Sheffer
Lyrics by David Zippel
Book by Joe Leonardo & David Zippel
Directed by Joe Leonardo
Musical Direction by Phil Hall

Play It by Heart
April 21 & 22, 1986
Music by David Spangler
Lyrics by Jerry Taylor
Directed by Robert Johanson
Musical Direction by Phil Hall

Mother Eddy
June 9 & 10, 1986
Music and Lyrics by David Spangler and Jerry Taylor
Book by Mark St. Germain
Conceived by Hugh Key and Robert Pesola
Directed by Robert Pesola and Robert Johanson
Musical Direction by Ted Kociolek and
David Spangler

All Girl Band
June 23 & 29, 1986
Music/Lyrics/Book by Bradford Craig
Directed by Larry Fuller
Musical Direction by Susan Kingwell

Kingfish, The Huey Long Musical
November 17 & 18, 1986
Music by John Franceschina
Book/Lyrics by Jeff Eric Frankel
Directed by Tom Greunenwald
Musical Direction by Donald Chan

Sayonara
December 8 & 9, 1986
Music by George Fischoff
Lyrics: Hy Gilbert
Book by William Luce
Directed by Robert Johanson
Musical Direction by Jim Coleman

Strides
October 5 & 6, 1987
Music by Bob Bejan & Godfrey Nelson
Book/Lyrics by Bob Bejan
Directed by Michael Hotopp
Musical Direction by Glen Kelly

Juba
November 9 & 10, 1987
Book/Lyrics by Wendy Lamb
Directed by: Sheldon Epps
Choreographer: Mercedes Ellington
Music by Russel Walden

Beyond a Reasonable Doubt
January 26, 1988
    Written by Nathan Mayer
    Directed by Janet Herzenberg

Worlds
March 7 & 8, 1988
    Book/Music/Lyrics: Michael Levine
    Directed by Susan Stroman
    Musical Directed by: Glen Kelly

Mrs. Skeffington
March 7 & 8, 1988
    Book/Music/Lyrics by Anthony Zaleski
    Directed by Susan Stroman
    Musical Directed by Glen Kelly

Rhythm Ranch
October 4 & 5, 1988
    Directed by Susan Stroman
    Music by Fred Stark
    Lyrics by Hal Hackady
    Musical Direction by Doug Reed

Love Life
November 7, 1988
    Music by Kurt Weill
    Book/Lyrics by Alan Jay Lerner
    Directed and Choreographed by Graciela Daniele

The Land of Little Horses
March 6 & 7, 1989
    Written by Rebecca Gilman
    Directed by Jane Dentinger

Ties That Bind
January 30 & 31, 1989
    Written by Rob Melnyk
    Directed by Jane Dentinger

Arthur, The Musical
April 17 & 18, 1989
    Book/Lyrics by David Crane, Marta Kauffman
    Music by Michael Skloff
    Directed by Richard Maltby Jr.

Back Home, The War Brides Musical
October 2 & 3, 1989
    Music by Christopher Berg
    Book by Ron Sproat
    Lyrics by Frank Evans
    Directed by J. Barry Lewis

Mikado, Inc.
December 4 & 5, 1989
    Music by Arthur Sullivan
    Lyrics adapted by Albert Evans
      (based on William S. Gilbert)
    Book by Jane Waterhouse
    Conceived/Directed by Robert Johanson

Malice Aforethought
January 29 & 30, 1990
    Written by Eric C. Jenderson
    Directed by Fredrick Rolf

A Wonderful Life
June 4 & 5, 1990
    Music by Joe Raposo
    Book/Lyrics by Sheldon Harnick
    Directed by Dorothy Danner

Lambarene
June 10 & 11, 1991
    Music by John Purifoy
    Book/Lyrics by Linda Parsons
    Directed by Robert Johanson

LAB PRODUCTIONS

Sayonara
June, 1987
    Music by George Fischoff
    Book by William Luce
    Lyrics by Hy Gilbert
    Directed by Robert Johanson
    Musical Direction by Jim Coleman
    Choreographed by Susan Stroman

Beyond a Reasonable Doubt
June 6, 7, 8 & 10, 1988
    Written by Nathan Mayer
    Directed by Janet Herzenberg

Rhythm Ranch
February 27–March 4, 1989
    Music by Fred Stark
    Book/Lyrics by Hal Hackady
    Directed and choreographed by Pamela Hunt
    Musical Direction by Ted Kociolek

Mikado, Inc.
February 26–March 3, 1990
    Music by Arthur Sullivan
    Lyrics by Albert Evans (based on William S. Gilbert)
    Directed and Conceived by Robert Johanson
    Book by Jane Waterhouse
    Musical Direction by Glen Kelly

MAINSTAGE WORLD PREMIERES

1987	*Sayonara*
1989	*Beyond a Reasonable Doubt*
1989	*Rhythm Ranch*
1990	*Mikado, Inc.*
1992	*Great Expectations*
1993	*Paper Moon*
1994	*A Tale of Two Cities*
1995	*The Prisoner of Zenda*
1996	*Comfortable Shoes*
1997	*Jane Eyre*
1999	*Up, Up & Away*
1999	*Wuthering Heights*

MAINSTAGE AMERICAN PREMIERES

1986	*Run For Your Wife*
1993	*Don't Dress For Dinner*
1997	*Out of Order*

People of Paper Mill *1982 to 1999*

With appreciation to all those who spent a great part of their careers making the Paper Mill Playhouse the wonderful theatre it is today. With apologies to part-time staff members, interns, volunteers, and various professionals jobbed in on a per-show basis—all too numerous to mention.

Ted Agress Associate General Manager
Michael Anania Scenic Designer
Colleen Atwood Costume Designer
Don Aurnhammer Properties Master
Rebecca A. R. Baker Director of Patron Services
Greg Barnes Resident Costume Designer
Jill Barrie Development Associate
Heather Bennett Casting Director
Dirk Benson Box Office Sales
Anita Bentz Box Office Sales
Elaine Bergeron Prop Stylist
Denise Biel Box Office Sales
David Blankenship Assistant Scenic Designer
Marthea Blewitt Office Manager
Lisa Bonifacio Box Office Sales
Jennifer Bornstein Assistant to the Producers
Jeanine Botta Properties Shopper
Alica Boucher Groups Sales & Special Promotions
Joelle Bouchner Production Finance Director
Elizabeth Brantley-Holmes joined the Paper Mill family in 1985 part-time in the Subscription Department and then became full-time in October 1985, while attending Jersey City State University majoring in Business Administration. In February 1989 she became Assistant Subscription Manager and in August 1995 she was transferred to Assistant Patron Services/Box Office Manager. The following year she became Office Manager. "While trying to continue my education, I became Director of Volunteer Services here at the Paper Mill. I'm also an active member of many Newark community volunteer services."
Thomas Brennan has been at the Playhouse since 1974. He was then a stagehand, but in 1976 became Master Flyman and in 1978 Master Carpenter. His most difficult show was *Wizard of Oz*, which had many special effects. He also set up the show when it went to the Theatre at Madison Square Garden in New York City. Although sets for Paper Mill productions are built at the theatre's facility in Edison, New Jersey, Brennan and other members of the stage crew are responsible for seeing that each works and is maintained during production.

Mary Brenycz started at the Paper Mill in 1988 as a part-time box office employee while she finished her degree at Seton Hall University. She was the Assistant Box Office Manager for five years, until she became Subscription Manager in 1996. Besides overseeing the subscription campaign, Mary is also the liaison with Advantix, Paper Mill's ticketing system, preparing performances for the computer system. She also works closely with the Development Department during the Tele-Fundraising Campaign.
David E. Briggs Production Manager
Raymond Burns Hairdresser
Jane Byrnes Subscription Manager
Shannon Campbell Box Office Sales
Daniel Cannizzo Box Office Sales
Hariette Carpozi Development Assistant
Gene Carrington Gallery Director
Brian Carroll Benefits Administrator. A lifelong resident of Millburn Township, Brian's earliest memory of Paper Mill dates back to 1977 when he attended the production of *Shenandoah*. Fifteen years later, he joined the staff as a member of the subscription department, and then moved to the finance department where he currently holds the position of Benefits Administrator. Brian's involvement with Paper Mill productions has heightened his interest and appreciation for live theatre.
Andrea Caskey Box Office Sales
Rita C. Chanley Wardrobe Mistress
Andrew Chipok Managing Director
Nancy Cleary Box Office Sales
Geoffrey Merrill Cohen was General Manager of Paper Mill Playhouse for nine years. He came to Paper Mill in 1988 after having managed the George Street Playhouse in New Brunswick, New Jersey. He is now general manager of the Theatre at Madison Square Garden in New York City.
Jim Coleman, Resident Conductor—On Broadway, Mr. Coleman conducted the Lincoln Center revival of *Anything Goes*, the revival of *Mame*, and *Sweeney Todd*. National Tours include *42nd Street*, *South Pacific*, *Sweeney Todd*, *A Little Night Music*, *The Sound of Music* and *The Best Little Whorehouse In Texas*. He has guest-conducted at regional opera companies and at New York City Opera At Paper Mill, he has conducted 23 productions. His favorites include *The Merry Widow*, *Nine*, *Brigadoon*, *Follies* and *No, No, Nanette*. He conducted the PBS broadcast of Paper Mill's *Show Boat* on Great Performances.
Lisa E. Cooney Education Associate

Lonnie E. J. Cooper Assistant to the General Manager
Anthony Coppola House Physician
Merrilyn Crane has been Director of the Art Gallery since its reopening in 1982. With Paper Mill's status as the State Theatre of New Jersey, the gallery has become a prestigious venue for the showing of the work of New Jersey artists. In addition to the various exhibitions held throughout the year, the gallery holds the annual International Miniature Art Exposition, which Ms. Crane and her assistant, Ray Lenhart, have built over the years into a very special event with festivities that attract hundreds of artists and art patrons.
Peter Croken came to the Paper Mill Playhouse in 1997 after thirteen years as Vice President of Production at Radio City Music Hall and at Carabiner, an industrial entertainment company. As General Manager of the Playhouse, he is responsible for securing Paper Mill's financial footing.
Joe D'Addario Orchestra Contractor
James D'Asaro Production Manager
Quashon Davis Box Office Sales
Angelo Del Rossi Executive Producer
Anna DeSilver Education Assistant
Robert Devone Systems Technician
Rita Donald Children's Theatre Representative
Jessica Donovan has been resident Casting Director at Paper Mill since 1997. Her favorite Paper Mill credits include *Follies*, *Children of Eden*, and *Crazy for You*. Previously Casting Associate at Ortlip and Filderman Casting, New York City, her projects included the Broadway production of *Master Class*, with Zoe Caldwell, Patti LuPone, and Dixie Carter, and the national tour company of the show, with Faye Dunaway. She has worked with Theatre Virginia, Pioneer Theatre, Berkshire Theatre Festival and the Oregon Shakespeare Festival, and with independent feature films such as *As Things Fell Out* and *Broadway Damage*, shown at the Cannes, Seattle, and Chicago film festivals. Jessica is a graduate of St. Michael's College, Vermont, with a BA in Drama. She resides in Manhattan.
Marc A. Dorfman Director of Development
Dennis C. Dougherty Publicity Coordinator
Susan L. Duncalf Office Manager
Michael Dundon, Group Sales Coordinator—Prior to working at Paper Mill, Michael was Box Office Manager for the New Jersey Shakespeare Festival. After pursuing a career as a performer, he found himself, in 1993, as Paper Mill's Group Sales Coordinator not only selling to school

groups, senior groups and corporate groups, but also marketing the theater within the travel and tourism industry. The trick to being a good salesman is loving the product that you sell; a theory that is reinforced with each phone call or letter Michael receives from a group leader, teacher or student, delighted by an incredible evening of theater.

Martin Duus Development Associate

Dennette Dyton Assistant Subscriptions Manager

James Eisner Properties Master

Gregory J. Ellmer Patron Services Manager

Donna Emeric Marketing Assistant

Albert Evans, Resident Composer—Evans began his long association with Paper Mill providing original and updated lyrics for *Mikado, Inc.* and *The Merry Widow.* He has also written the music for the theatre's classic adaptations: *Great Expectations, A Tale of Two Cities, Jane Eyre,* and *Wuthering Heights.* Off-Broadway, his work has been heard in *Pageant, Nite-Club Confidential* and *The Texas Chainsaw Musical* and his holiday musical, *A Country Christmas Carol,* gives Dickens an unusual twist. As a dedicated collector of theatre music and lore, he is a frequent participant in Paper Mill's Symposium Series and also teaches Musical Theatre for the Paper Mill Theatre School.

Ralph Fandetta, as a young schoolboy, first worked for the Playhouse in 1937 doing small jobs for Frank Carrington, including selling candy in the lobby and being an usher in the old theatre. He grew up and left, but returned again thirty years ago working as a dresser and a dozen other jobs. Eventually he became Wardrobe Master, a job he loves.

Monica Fantauzzi Assistant House Manager

Kurt Faunce Production Assistant

David N. Feight Production Manager

Terri-Ann Feindt-Stoeckle Systems Technician

Joe Feola Special Effects

William S. Fergus, House Manager, grew up across the brook from the Playhouse. As a college student he worked for the concession at the theatre, and in 1984 he was hired as House Manager. His memories include watching the gentlemanly Frank Carrington tipping his fedora to all the ladies as he crossed the lobby or passing through in his riding clothes, seeing the theatre consumed by the great fire, and appeasing the members of the mezzanine audience who wore scarves and hats to ward off the chill of the air conditioning in the new theatre. His one regret is never getting autographs of the many stars who came to the theatre—except for Leonard Bernstein, who came to visit one of Paper Mill's stars.

Heidi R. Fielding Group Sales & Special Promotions Manager

Jeffrey E. Fleming Systems Administrator

Karen Ford Properties Shopper

Millie Foti Box Office Sales

Anne Foti-Pollack Finance Assistant

Roger Franklin Production Supervisor

Brett Garan Box Office Sales

Jeffry George Resident Stage Manager

Paul Germano Hair Designer

Terence A. Gili played a dual role at the Paper Mill Playhouse. Hired by Frank Carrington as House Manager, he went on to be Paper Mill's in-house photographer, creating a voluminous portfolio that records every star and every show presented there during his tenure. Many of the photographs used in this book are his. He was devoted to the Playhouse, carrying through in any emergency and even housing performers at his own home when necessary. After his retirement, he continued his warm relationship with Paper Mill. He died in 1996 at the age of eighty-four.

Jonathan Glass-Riley Properties Manager

Gerry Goodstein Production Photographer

K.D. Gorman Head Craftsperson

Dan Grace Properties Shopper

Larry Grey Assistant to the Artistic Director

Stan Gutowski Purchasing

Anne Hamilton Development Assistant

Nikki Hansen Head Craftsperson

Robin Harris Development Assistant

Marina Harrison Office Manager

David Harwell Head Craftsperson

Ann Marie Heckmann, Director of Information Systems—Ann Marie joined the theatre's staff full-time in 1996, after being employed by Beneficial Management Corporation for twelve years. Following in the footsteps of her mother, Millie Heckmann, she had worked at the Playhouse as an usher while in school. As Director of Information Systems, she is responsible for planning and implementing Paper Mill's computer and communications systems. She loves working in a place where co-workers come up with a show tune for every spoken word and her greatest challenge is naming the musical it came from! She also loves "Music Day"—when, on the Friday prior to every opening night, the orchestra rehearses down the hall from her office.

Mildred E. Heckmann—Millie began at Paper Mill as a matinee usher in 1967 and loved every minute of it. After a ten-year hiatus, she returned to work in the Subscription Department and was soon promoted to Subscription Manager, a post she filled for fifteen years. For the last three years, she has been the VIP Patron Services Manager, making ticket arrangements for special members of the Paper Mill family, as well as representatives of other regional and Broadway theatres. Growing up in Millburn, Millie would often throw a penny in the Paper Mill wishing well in the hope of someday appearing on the Paper Mill stage. That wish came true when she appeared as an extra in *Shenandoah* and *To Kill a Mockingbird.*

Allen G. Hegarty Staff Consultant

Donna Hely Box Office Sales

Patricia Hetherington Group Sales Coordinator

Marjorie Hiene Assistant House Manager

Susan Hill France Assistant to the Producer

Keith A. Hoovier Production Manager

Janet Howe Hairdresser

Alice S. Hughes Costume Coordinator

Wendy Hutton Marketing Associate

Jennie L. Hyer Box Office Sales

Colleen Janich Casting Assistant

Carla Jeffers has been Accounts Payable Manager of Paper Mill Playhouse since June 1998. Prior to that she held leading positions in accounts payable and accounts receivable at Saybolt in Parsippany and Just Us Books in East Orange, New Jersey. She received her certification in accounting at Bergen County Community College. She is a long-time resident of Newark, New Jersey.

Gary Jennings Scenic Charge Painter

Robert Johanson Artistic Director

Greg Jupa Box Office Sales

Ron Kadri Assistant Scenic Designer

Rik Kaye Production Manager

Cheri Kechely Scene Shop Administrator

Gary Kechley Production Manager

Paul King Production Manager

Tom Kinnebrew Accounts Payable

David Kissel Production Manager

Michele Klinsky Assistant House Manager

Ted Kociolek Music Director

Marvin Krauss New York Representative

Charles J. Kronengold, M.D. House Physician

Barbara Kurceski Marketing Assistant

Donna Marie Larson Costume Coordinator

Susanne Lauber Assistant Director of Marketing

John C. Lawler—Started at Paper Mill in 1982 as Controller, after working for Warner-Lambert for the first half of his career. He became Director of Finance in 1998 and is responsible for all accounting, banking, insurance and payroll functions. He is an avid collector of musical theatre recordings and books and as such, enjoys following a Paper Mill production from conception through performance. He also enjoys the opportunity of meeting and talking with many of the performers who work at the theatre.

Robin Leeds Assistant Box Office Treasurer

Ray Lenhart, Assistant Gallery Curator—Ray first came to Paper Mill in 1963, to assist Frank and Gene Carrington with the art exhibit on display during the production of *Milk and Honey.* Since then, he has been involved in hanging almost every gallery exhibit in both the old and new theatres. A retired fire fighter from the adjacent community of Springfield, New Jersey, Ray was on duty the day that the old theatre burned and was one of the first to reach the burning building once assistance was called in from other towns. After the collapse of the roof, he worked to save the lobby of the old building, which, thanks to his efforts and those of his fellow fire fighters, continues to welcome patrons to the theatre today.

Howard Leonard Hair Designer

Loree Levine Box Office Sales

Elli Lewis Assistant to the Producer

Carol Ann Liano Office Manager

Tom Loftis Properties Manager

Peggy Lovett Payroll/ Benefits

Joan Lynch Hair Dresser

Bill Lynch, who began at the Playhouse as an extra stage-hand in 1976, became Head Flyman in 1982, and Master Electrician in 1983. Among the many shows he has worked on in the course of twenty-three years, several stand out in his memory for different reasons. His personal favorites to watch have been *Chess* and *Amadeus*. The most challenging was *Mikado, Inc.*, because of the short time available to put it into production. And of the many stars who have been at the Playhouse, Jason Robards and E.G. Marshall have impressed him most with their performances and offstage personalities.

Carol Maczko Staff Benefits Administrator

Christine Agriesti Malley began her twenty-one years at Paper Mill in 1964 as Box Office Treasurer. In 1981 she became Business Manager and a year later, Director of Business Operations. Her responsibilities covered group sales, subscriptions, tickets, benefits, and dozens of extra jobs such as driving stars to the airport and helping in the gallery. For the past eleven years, she has been with AT&T.

Debbie Maneri Box Office Sales

Nancy Marino, Program Editor joined Paper Mill's Marketing Department in January 1994. Every day, she would return home and fill her mother in on her day-to-day experiences in "show business" and on the exploits of her warm, wonderful, and always entertaining co-workers. When, in February 1994, her mother passed away and Nancy recalls that it was her co-workers, two in particular who have remained close friends, who helped her get through that very difficult time. She will never forget the love and support of the dedicated, hard-working, extraordinary individuals that make up the Paper Mill family. She serves as Paper Mill's Program Editor.

John Maris Box Office Treasurer

Stephanie Marletta Hair Supervisor

Jennifer Martone Box Office Sales

Andrew Masini Assistant House Manager

David Mayhew, Director of Marketing joined Paper Mill as Director of Marketing in 1999, with responsibility for sales, promotions, advertising, and publicity. Prior to that he was Deputy Director of The Newark Museum (1997–99), Director of Marketing for McCarter Theatre (1991–97), and Director of Communications for Long Wharf Theatre (1986–91). He has also served as Marketing Director or Publicist for the Berkshire Theatre Festival, Off-Broadway's WPA Theatre and the Ridiculous Theatrical Company, and the original productions of Harvey Fierstein's *Torch Song Trilogy*, *The Miss Firecracker Contest*,

The Foreigner and many other Broadway and Off-Broadway plays. He is a graduate of New York University.

Judith P. Mayo Assistant Director of Marketing

Joseph McConnell arrived at Paper MIll in 1984 as Assistant Director of Development and assistant to then Administrative Director, Jim Thesing. His years at the Playhouse coincided with the arts-minded administration of Governor Thomas Kean and the fundraising of that time included substantial grants from the State of New Jersey and the National Endowment for the Arts, including funds that allowed the establishment of Paper Mill's Musical Theatre Project. He also had hands-on involvement with Paper Mill's outreach program for the disabled, leading him to become a national advocate for such projects. In 1987, he became Assistant to the Producer and Secretary to the Board of Trustees. In 1990 he left the Playhouse to become Executive Director and Producer of the Cohoes Music Hall in upstate New York, and from 1992 through 1997 he worked again with Jim Thesing in New York City with the National Alliance for Musical Theatre. He is now a casting director.

Madeleine McDonough Public Relations Assistant

John McEwen, Director of Development—John was Assistant to the General Manager at New York's Ensemble Studio Theatre, prior to joining Paper Mill's staff in 1986. At Paper Mill, he served as Assistant Box Office Treasurer, Administrative Coordinator of the Musical Theatre Project, and Development Associate prior to becoming the Director of Development in 1988. As such, he supervises all fund-raising activities and plays an instrumental role in community outreach programs, especially the access programs for people with disabilities. One of many favorite Paper Mill memories came after the theatre's first Audio Description performance. A patron, who had not been to the theatre for more than 15 years after losing her sight, explained through tears of joy how Paper Mill's service had enriched her life and enabled her to attend the theatre once again.

Philip Wm. McKinley, Casting Director/Musical Theatre Project—Prior to Paper Mill, Philip worked as a actor and director in New York and at the Meadows Playhouse (which he founded with Maryan Stephens) in Las Vegas. His first performance at Paper Mill was in the 1983 production of *Desert Song* where he stole the show in the comic role of Bennie. He soon joined the company as Casting Director and Artistic Coordinator of the Musical Theater Project. In speaking of the staff at Paper Mill, he recalled, "Together we created quality productions and programs and we did it with a great deal of joy, enthusiasm and fun." Since leaving Paper Mill in 1985, he has directed all over the world, and received a Drama Desk nomination for his work on the Off-Broadway hit *Thwack*. He is the director/choreographer of The Ringling Brothers/Barnum & Bailey Circus and returned to Paper Mill in 1998 to direct *Dr. Jekyll and Mr. Hyde*.

David McMurtrie Assistant Scene Shop Forman

Mickey McNany-Damian, Theatre School Director, has been

with the Playhouse since 1984, first working in the box office and as Group Sales Coordinator. In 1989, she started the theatre school, a job she delights in: "To watch students discover how theatre can be a key that opens them up to a whole new world of possibilities, self-confidence, and discovery, to leave them with a real energy and enthusiasm to continue to learn more about the theatre and themselves, to watch each one shine—that's the magic that I love to share with my students."

Heather Meisner Receptionist

Michael Miller, Production Manager, has worked in all aspects of the theatre. Now in his second season at Paper Mill Playhouse, Michael is responsible for coordinating all technical and financial requirements of the mainstage. Before coming to Paper Mill, Michael was Production Manager at the American Musical Theatre of San Jose, California. With his wife Melinda, he produced shows for Holland America Cruise Line and both produced and co-created industrial shows nationally and internationally. He has toured extensively with musicals, revues, and concert performances.

Michelle Miller Box Office Sales

Wade Miller came to Paper Mill in 1955 as a dancer in *Guys and Dolls* and followed that with roles in several other shows. In the 1960s, Frank Carrington offered him the job of stage manager, and in that capacity he took Paper Mill's production of *The Glass Menagerie* to Broadway, where he remained to do several other major shows. He returned to Paper Mill as General Manager in 1971. When he retired from the Paper Mill Playhouse in 1990, after a thirty-five-year association, he had served there as performer, stage manager, general manager, and company manager. He continues working as a director for New Jersey amateur theatre.

Roy Miller, Associate Producer, joined Paper Mill in 1991. A graduate of the Commercial Theatre Institute's "Producing for the Commercial Theatre" program, he has produced, written, and directed both films and television programs. A panelist for the ASCAP Foundation Musical Theatre Workshop, he strongly supports and encourages the development of new musicals and plays. He says of his present position, "Paper Mill's use of the industry's most talented individuals while also cultivating the stars and artisans of tomorrow, combined with award-winning outreach and education programs, and with an outstanding Board of Trustees and staff, makes this a unique organization. I am thrilled to be part of it." Among Roy's most notable experiences since joining Paper Mill are *Children of Eden* and the subsequent RCA Victor cast recording, which was the first album in the theatre's history, *Follies* and the cast recording for TVT Records, *Comfortable Shoes*, *Gypsy*, and the taping of *Crazy for You* for the PBS Great Performances series.

Paula Minniti Box Office Sales

Michael T. Mooney, Manager of Donor Relations, came to Paper Mill in 1994 as a part-time Development Assistant. In addition to acting as liaison to our donors, Michael also edits the Paper Mill Calendar, serves as Access Services Coordinator, Audio-Describer, Rising Star Award Evaluator, and volunteers at ArtPride and New Jersey Arts Access Task Force events. Michael was seen onstage in *Life on Earth* (1996), *New Year's Eve* (1997), and *Floyd Flood Follies* (1999). He wrote a short play four our 1998 Mystery Writers symposium and regularly contributes to the annual Angelo Awards.

Anna L. Morone Publicist

Kathleen Morris Box Office Sales

Anna Morrome Publicist

James P. Murphy Production Manager

Bob Murphy Scene Shop Foreman

Steven Myers Company Manager

Meara Nigro Assistant Public Relations Director

Lisa Marie Nolan Box Office Sales

Paul Novembre Box Office Sales

Rob Nunez, Company Manager—Hailing from Dubuque Iowa, Robert Nunez joined the Paper Mill staff in 1991 as Company Manager. Initially trained in voice and piano, he began his career in arts administration with Michigan Opera Theater in Detroit and later relocated to Denver where he was the Festival Administrator for the Central City Opera House. He has been on the adjunct voice faculty of Eastern New Mexico University, continuing a private studio while in Detroit. He holds an A.B. in Music and an M.M. in Vocal Performance and Vocal Pedagogy. He received the "Angelo Award for Best Featured Performer" (voted by the Paper Mill staff) for his portrayal as Mr. Goldstone in *Gypsy,* opposite Betty Buckley.

Helen Nuse, Receptionist—A native of Brooklyn, Helen worked for Lord & Taylor's department store in Millburn before joining the Paper Mill staff as a receptionist in 1987. The thing she enjoys most about her job is the greeting she gets everyday from the actors and crew members as they pass her desk by the stage door entrance. A special favorite was George Hearn, who would stop and chat with her each morning as he picked up his newspaper while appearing in Paper Mill's production of *Sweeney Todd.*

Mark O'Brien, Scene Shop Manager—Before arriving at Paper Mill, Mark earned a BFA from Rutgers University and worked at various regional theaters and commercial scene shops in as a Scenic Carpenter, Welder, Draftsman, Assistant Production Manager, and Assistant General Manager. In 1993 Mark came to the Paper Mill as a Scenic Carpenter/Welder. In 1994 he left to manage a new scene shop, followed by a position as a Project Coordinator in the Custom Exhibit Industry. In November 1995 he returned to Paper Mill in his current position. Managing the shop and maintaining Paper Mill's high production standards requires constant ingenuity and really keeps Mark hopping. He looks forward to many future seasons at Paper Mill.

Kathleen O'Donnell Marketing Associate

Annette O'Toole Box Office Sales

Beth O'Toole Box office Sales

Peter Ortner Publicist

Patrick Parker, Assistant to the Artistic Director, gave up performing and choreography after knee surgery and spent the next five years with an entertainment law firm before coming to Paper Mill in 1995. His multifaceted background has served him well in the many aspects of his job at the Playhouse, where he has been involved with administrative work as well as the creative details of each production.

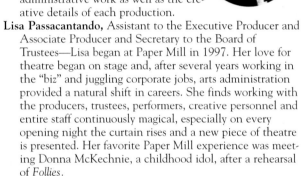

Lisa Passacantando, Assistant to the Executive Producer and Associate Producer and Secretary to the Board of Trustees—Lisa began at Paper Mill in 1997. Her love for theatre began on stage and, after several years working in the "biz" and juggling corporate jobs, arts administration provided a natural shift in careers. She finds working with the producers, trustees, performers, creative personnel and entire staff continuously magical, especially on every opening night when the curtain rises and a new piece of theatre is presented. Her favorite Paper Mill experience was meeting Donna McKechnie, a childhood idol, after a rehearsal of *Follies.*

David R. Paterson, Sound Engineer, first worked in the old theatre in 1973, and although it was charming, he prefers the efficiency and ease of the facilities in the present theatre. He is in charge of setting up the sound for each production—stage microphones, individual microphones, sound levels that accommodate the audience, the orchestra, and the performers—and, working from a control booth at the back of the house, maintaining it all for each performance.

Bob Pearson, Child Wrangler

Connie (Cornelia) Pearson, Head Usher for many years, started as a Thursday matinee usher in the early 1970s. Prior to the Paper Mill fire, she was a dresser for two shows and worked in the box office when "we sold tickets racked on the wall" (pre-computer days). For the *Wizard of Oz,* she made the lifesize Munchkin puppets that peered from the second story windows. She also appeared in several productions, with the role of Queen of Transylvania in *My Fair Lady* being one of her favorite times at Paper Mill. An Audio-Describer for many years, she continues in this capacity even after retiring in 1998 to study in New York City at the Art Students' League. With husband Bob, Child Wrangler for all Paper Mill productions, and Guild duties, she will be here for many more years.

Janet Pepsin Assistant to the General Manager

Alan Perry Box Office Treasurer

Randi Peter was Box Office Sales

Raven Petretti Box Office Sales

Charles Pierson Box Office Sales

Susan Pietruski Box Office Sales

Mark Pinheiro Scenic Warehouse Rental Manager

Eileen Pirez Box Office Sales

Gary Plowman Box Office Sales

Loretta Politano Group Sales Coordinator

Bruce Pollack Properties Master

Joan Pope Box Office Sales

Maryann Post Group Sales Coordinator

Eo Poulos Ticketing Systems Manager

Lora K. Powell, Resident Stage Manager—Lora first came to Paper Mill in the spring of 1992 as the stage manager for *Oklahoma.* She was named resident stage manager the following fall and was responsible for taking Paper Mill 's *Wizard of Oz* to Madison Square Garden and eventually served as the Assistant Stage Manager of the Broadway revival of *Annie Get Your Gun.* She credits her experiences at Paper Mill with making her a better stage manager and says her favorite memories include working with George Hearn on *Sweeney Todd* and working with the entire cast of *Dreamgirls.*

Tricia Quidor Marketing Associate/Program Editor

Stephanie Rakovic Hairdresser

Richard C. Rauscher Resident Stage Manager

Tracey Redling, Marketing Associate—Shortly after relocating back to her native New Jersey in 1997, Tracey joined the staff of Paper Mill as Marketing Associate. She is responsible for and oversees all advertising for the theatre's six mainstage productions, children's theatre, concerts and special events. In addition to its being challenging and fun, she says the most rewarding aspect of the job is working alongside a group of bright, dynamic, and creative individuals who truly make Paper Mill Playhouse a wonderful place.

Virginia Reed Public Relations Assistant

Debra Reed Costume Warehouse Rental Manager

Albertina Reilly first worked at Paper Mill as a volunteer and a member of the Guild. Aware of her energetic efforts, Angelo Del Rossi asked her to become a staff member, first as a receptionist, then as assistant to the head of public relations. She subsequently became Director of Public Relations, a position she held for seventeen years until September 1992. Among her many responsibilities and the one she most enjoyed was interviewing the many stars who came to Paper Mill. She continues to attend all opening nights at the Playhouse.

Jacky Riotto came to Paper Mill as a dresser. Her first show was the colorful *Wizard of Oz* in 1992, and later that season she became Wardrobe Mistress. Before a show, she  discusses the costume plans and requirements with the costume designer, and while most costumes present no problems for the wardrobe department, there have been moments of difficulty. When Paper Mill presented *Dreamgirls*, the character of Effie was performed by a young woman who wore size 24. Her understudy was size 12. With little advance warning, it was necessary for the understudy to take the part and the wardrobe department had to pin, tape, and devise many tucks to refit the costumes. It was a great success and the audience was none the wiser.

José M. Rivera Costume Coordinator

Sharon Rork Properties Manager

Virginia Rose, Research Assistant—For many years, Virginia Rose worked as the research assistant for Resident Designer Michael Anania, providing him with volumes of visual references and historical information as he prepared each set-design. A visual artist in her own-right, she also worked as a part-time receptionist for the theatre and delighted in mixing with the actors, artists and audiences during receptions and opening night parties.

David Rosenberg Box Office Sales

David Rosenfeld Box Office Sales

Claire Russo Box Office Sales

Joanne Russo Box Office Sales

Anthony Salerno Properties Master

Pete Saubers Box Office Sales

Walter Schweikardt, Orchestra Contractor, has been a member of the Paper Mill Orchestra for 32 years and has served as the Orchestra Contractor for the past 12 seasons. As such, he works closely with each musical director to gather the perfect assembly of professional musicians for each show. He enjoys the fact that Paper Mill is a professional organization unique in regional theatre—run like a business, but with a family feeling.

John Shimrock Properties Shopper

Charlie Siedenburg, Publicity and Public Relations Manager, joined the Paper Mill in June 1999. He has attended many Paper Mill productions, dating back *My One and Only* in 1987. Charlie has worked as a publicist for college theatre, summer stock, Off-Broadway, and the Broadway productions of *The Heiress, Racing Demon, The Gin Game, The Sunshine Boys, Night Must Fall,* and *Side Man.* He hails from Staten Island, and is a graduate of Wagner College.

Edith Sikorski was Subscription Manager at Paper Mil for twenty-eight years and was on hand the day of the fire, repeatedly running back into the offices to save cash boxes and subscription lists. She was known for her per-

sonal touch with subscribers, writing individual notes to them expressing her concern for their health and families. In return, she credits the personal interest of Frank Carrington and Angelo Del Rossi with her everyday pleasure in her work at the Playhouse for those many years.

Janet Smith Receptionist

Erin Mary Snow Office Manager

Jeffrey Solis Box Office Treasurer

Deborah Solomine Box Office Sales

Fred Solomine is an independent contractor with his own company, which employs six or seven people who maintain the Playhouse buildings and grounds, but he is very much a part of the Paper Mill family. He came to the Playhouse during the rebuilding after the great fire, and watching the new theatre rise was one of his most exciting times. He well remembers the last-minute construction details going on right to the night of the reopening gala.

Susan E. Speidel came to Paper MIll in 1988 as an associate in the development department. At that time, no separate education department existed, but combining the theatre's work with schools and the existing children's theatre, a new entity was formed and, in 1993, Ms. Speidel became Director of Education, a department that is now one of the very important extensions of the Playhouse. Her great pleasure and pride is in the Rising Star awards, working with young people who are gifted, recognizing their talents, having the opportunity to introduce them to high-quality theatre, and offering them a chance to appear in Paper Mill productions.

Eric Sprosty, Resident Stage Manager— Eric served as Paper Mill's resident stage manager for both the 1998/99 and 1999/2000 seasons. He has worked for numerous regional theatres, including the Pittsburgh Civic Light Opera (resident stage manager for eight seasons) the Santa Barbara Civic Light Opera and Center Stage.

Susanna Stanek Development Secretary

Mike Stas has been Head Flyman at Paper Mill for twenty years. He handles all the rigging for every set in every production.

Suzanne Steiner Box Office Sales

Michelle Steir Coordinator of Donor Relations

Maryann Stephens, Literary Advisor/Casting Assistant— Prior to coming to Paper Mill in 1983 as the theatre's Literary Advisor, Maryann worked as a performer and was a founding member of the Meadows Theatre in Las Vegas. She was also an assistant in David Merrick's office during the producer's heyday. At Paper Mill she worked closely with Philip McKinley in the casting department and the Musical Theatre Project, and was responsible for bringing the scripts of *Sayonara* and *Rhythm Ranch*, along with many other new plays and musicals, to the theatre's attention.

Debby Stewart Box Office Sales

Sheri Stroud Theatre Parties/Volunteer Coordinator

J. Thomas Stuart Director of Marketing

Kent Sweeney Assistant Scene Shop Forman

Glenn Taglieri, Director of Patron Services, has been at Paper Mill Playhouse since February 1999, responsible for the Box Office, Subscriptions, and Telemarketing. He works closely with the Marketing Department to develop strategies for ticket sales and handles customer service problems. Glenn has spent most of his adult life working in the ticketing business starting at Ticketron in 1981. He joined the Shubert Organization Inc. in 1985 as a member of the MIS department, and became an account representative responsible for fifty clients. Glenn received a BA from William Paterson College in 1981.

Jim Thesing came to Paper Mill in 1979 only a year before the great fire that destroyed the old theatre. He took charge of fund raising and when the theatre reopened in 1982 he was given the new title of Administrative Director, a position he held until he left the Playhouse in 1987 to become the first director of the National Alliance for Musical Theatre, an association of United States musical theatres. He counts his involvement with the rebuilding of the Playhouse and his work with the members of the Board of Directors as among the most satisfying activities during his years at Paper Mill. For the past two years, he has been a management consultant for several arts organizations.

Marc Thibodeau National Press Rep

Vida Thomas Costume Supervisor

Jana Thompson became Assistant Scenic Designer in 1993 after a year of working on Paper Mill productions as a free-lance; she continues to work on a number of outside productions each year. Being located at the Paper Mill's vast Edison, N.J. workshop, where she can see designs evolve, gives her the advantage of being able to respond directly and immediately to design and construction problems. She drafts the Scenic Designer's ideas and assists in planning the numerous staging aspects of each production. Among her favorite productions at the Playhouse have been *Follies*, with its grand staircase and beautiful proscenium, and *Oliver*, with its revolving multiple sets.

Johanna Timmerman Concession Manager

Lisa Trapani Assistant Box Office Manager

Barbara Trapani Box Office Sales

Jim Van Anda Box Office Sales

Barbara Villani Marketing Assistant

Frank Viner Scenic Charge Painter

Mary Vining-Lambert Administrator of Donor Services

Mary Ellen Waggoner, Associate Director of Development, has been with the development department of Paper Mill Playhouse since 1993. Her career in the arts and fund-raising spans more than seventeen years. Her fundraising responsibilities include the design and implementation of the theatre's annual fund and endowment fund campaigns. She received a BA from Montclair State University and is currently pursuing a Master's Degree in

Corporate and Public Communications/MBA Track at Seton Hall University. She is a 1999 Leadership New Jersey fellow, a program sponsored by The Partnership for New Jersey, and for the past fifteen years has been a professional classical musician active in many cultural groups throughout New Jersey. Her favorite memories of Paper Mill are from 1985 to 1987 when she was principal oboist in the Paper Mill Orchestra under the musical direction of Jim Coleman.

Debra A. Waxman was Director of Marketing for thirteen years, commencing in January 1983, and then Director of Press and Marketing for three more years. During her tenure the Paper Mill Playhouse subscriber base increased to 43,000. She was one of the original audio describers for the program to assist hearing-impaired audience members, and worked for many years with the Arts Council of New Jersey. Her daughter, Jessica, has appeared in numerous productions at the Playhouse. Debra left the Paper Mill in January 1999 to become Director of Marketing for the Manhattan Theatre Club.

Marci K. Weinstein Assistant to the Artistic Director
Deborah Whittaker Receptionist & Subscriptions
Karen Wiktorowicz Assistant Patron Services Manager
Anna M. Wild Groups Sales Coordinator
Patrick Wiley Resident Assistant Costume Designer

Randy Wyble Box Office Sales
Steven P. Yagozinski, Controller, is a graduate of Seton Hall University. Since joining the Paper Mill staff in 1991, Steven has become very familiar with the financial aspect of the theatre. Currently he coordinates the annual budget process and supplies all the financial details needed for grant applications. Steven believes that Paper Mill has been successful because each employee understands that the work done at Paper Mill makes a difference to the community.

Brigette Yerich Assistant Subscriptions Manager
Marion Yerich-Tyms Box Office Treasurer
Steven Yuhasz, Production Coordinator—An actor, director and producer, Steven's chief job as Paper Mill's Production Coordinator was to work out the details of scenery shifts and costume changes with the crew during technical rehearsals. He recalled how at the dress rehearsal for *Singin' in the Rain,* he got caught onstage in the midst of a "big showgirl number" after trying to help a dresser and an actor make a fast change. He left Paper Mill to join Capital Repertory as Producing Director and is currently an independent producer. He looks back at his time at Paper Mill as a wonderful opportunity to be part of an incredible team who worked relentlessly back-stage to make the audience's dreams come to life on stage.

An extraordinary number of dedicated actors, dancers, directors, choreographers, conductors, musicians, playwrights, composers, lyricists, technicians, designers and administrators were integral to Paper Mill's history. We regret that this book may not include the names of everyone who deserves to be acknowledged. If your name has not been included, please know that we are extremely grateful to you for your contribution to Paper Mill Playhouse.

Acknowledgments

There are a great many valuable contributors to a project of this scope. The author is very grateful to the entire staff of the Paper Mill Playhouse, and especially to Susan Speidel, Patrick Parker, Ralph Fandetta, Mildred Heckmann, Fred Solomine, Merrilyn Crane, Ray Lenhart, Mickey McNany-Damian, Michael T. Mooney, and Lisa Passacantando, all of whom gave often and generously of their time, knowledge, and patience. She also thanks the many others who, through interviews and correspondence, contributed to the making of this book. They include: Michael Anania, David M. Baldwin, Gregg Barnes, Ashok Bhavnani, Eddie Bracken, Dawn DiPasquale, Becky Garrett, the family of Terence Gili, Allen Hagerty, Sharon Hazard, Robert B. Heintz, William Linton, Jack Mehler, Wade Miller, Maureen Ogden, Kelli Rabke, Albertina, Reilly, Elmore R. Reese Jr., Stephen Schwartz, Edward W. Scudder, Jr., William Solo, Mark Stanley, William A. Tansey III, and Leslie Uggams.

Photography credits

Photographs and illustrations not otherwise credited are from the Paper Mill Playhouse (PMP) archives.

Friedman-Abeles—34.

Bert Andrews—27 (bottom right), 31 (top left inset), 33 (bottom right).

George S. Bolster—32 (bottom left).

Frank F. Brown—20 (bottom right), 21 (right).

Devon Cass—163 (top right).

Jerry Dahlia—front cover (bottom), 10 (top), 11 (top), 59 (top right), 82 (bottom), 83 (top), 86 (top right), 86 (middle), 86 (bottom left), 86 (bottom right), 87 (top left), 88 (right), 92 (left), 92 (middle). 92 (right), 93 (top left), 93 (top right), 93 (bottom right), 94, 99 (top left), 99 (bottom right), 104, 105, 106, 107, 114 (top right), 120 (top), 121 (right), 125, 126 (top right), 126 (bottom left), 130 (top left), 132 (top left), 133 (top right), 135 (bottom left), 139 (bottom left), 140 (left), 140 (top right), 142 (bottom left), 143 (top left), 143 (bottom), 148, 150 (bottom), 152 (lower right), 154 (middle), 155, 156, 157, 159 (middle), 160, 168, 169, 171, 172 (left), 177, 179, 180 (bottom right), 181, 182 (top right), 182 (bottom), 183 (left), 184 (bottom), 185, 190, 195, 204 (top left), 206, 210 (top), 212, 221 (top), 225, 230, 231, 232 (top), 232 (bottom), 233, 234 (top), 234 (bottom), 235 (top left), 235 (top right), 236 (top right), 237 (right inset), 245 (top right), 245 (bottom), 246 (top), 249 (top right inset), 253 (bottom), 256 (bottom), 258 (bottom), 260 (bottom), 261 (top left), 264 (left), 265, 266, 267, (bottom), 268, 271 (top right), 273, 274, 276, 281 (left), 285, 286.

Drew B. Peters Studios—25 (left), 37 (left).

Peter Aaron/Esto—62,63, 255 (bottom).

Fred Fehl—30 (bottom left), 41 (top left), back cover (bottom).

Ray Fisher—44 (top right).

George French—10 (bottom).

Terence A. Gili—6 (bottom right), 13 (bottom right), 21 (right), 25 (top right), 26 (bottom), 27 (top right), 28 (top left), 28 (top right), 31 (right), 33 (top right), 37

(right), 41 (top right), 41 (bottom left), 42 (top left), 44 (bottom right), 46, 47 (bottom left), 48 (top right), 48 (bottom right), 49, 55, 56, 57, (bottom right), 59 (left), 60, 61, 66 (bottom left), 67 (top left), 67 (top right), 68 (bottom right), 72 (bottom), 81 (bottom left), 81 (bottom right inset), 91 (bottom right), 115 (right), 122 (bottom right), 123 (left), 162 (middle), 162 (top), 164 (bottom left). 252 (top left),272 (top right).

Gerry Goodstein—front cover (top), 91 (top left), 91 (bottom left), 97 (bottom right), 100 (botom right) 102 (top right inset), 102 (bottom left), 103, 109 (top), 110, 111 (top), 111 (bottom right), 112, (bottom left), 112 (bottom right), 114 (bottom left), 115 (left), 118 (bottom inset), 119, 127 (top left), 127 (bottom left), 130 (top right inset), 130 (bottom), 131, 132 (top right), 132 (bottom right), 134 (middle), 134 (bottom right),144 (top right), 144 (bottom left), 145 (left), 146, 147 (top middle), 147 (right), 147 (bottom middle), 149 (right), 152 (top left), 173 (top left). 173 (top right), 174 (top right), 174 bottom left), 186 (top right), 186 (bottom left). 188 (top right), 188 (bottom left), 189 (top left),192 (top right), 192 (bottom), 193, 196 (left), 197, 198 (left), 200 (right), 202 (top), 203, 205 (top), 205 (bottom left), 206 (right), 207, 213, 214 (right), 217, 218, 219, 220, 221 (bottom right), 222, 223, 224, 225, 226, 227, 240 (bottom left), 241 (bottom left), 242 (top left), 243 (bottom left), 246 (left middle), 246 (right middle), 247 (top right), 250 (left). 250 (top), 272 (bottom left), 277, 278, 279, 280, 281 (right), 282, 283 (right), back cover (center, right).

Greg Gorman—166 (top right).

Russ Harrington—167 (bottom left).

E. C. Heinzinger—290.

Ken Howard—123 (right).

Image Works—5 (top left).

Murray Korman—12 (top left).

Werner J. Kuhn—31 (bottom left).

Linda Bohm Studio—237 (top middle inset).

Joan Marcus—154 (top right), 154 (botom left)158 (bottom right), 159 (left), 159 (right), 161 (top), 166 (left), 176, 251 (top left), 251 (top right), back cover (center left).

Millburn/Short Hills Historical Society—3 (top right, bottom right), 4 (inset).

Millburn Item—51, 53, 54.

Modernage—133 (bottom right).

New Jersey Newsphotos—228 (bottom).

New York Public Library for the Performing Arts—12 (left). *

Lynda Pawelak/Gerry Goodstein—front cover (center left and right), 95, 98 (botom right), 100 (top left), 136 (bottom left), 175, 198 (bottom right), 205 (bottom right), 250 (bottom right).

Phyllis Reison/Gerry Goodstein—90.

Josephine Rossi—26 (left).

Joseph Schembri—74, 75 (top left), 75 (bottom).

Thos. O. Sheckell—14 (bottom)

Shubert Archive—12 (top left).

Martha Swope/Paper Mill Archive—125, 236 (bottom left), 236 (bottom right).

Shonna Valeska—163 (bottom right).

George Van Photos—248 (left).

Vandamm Studio—13 (top, right), 13 (bottom, left)*

White Studio—12 (top, right and bottom)*

*Billy Rose Theatre Collection
The New York Public Library for the Performing Arts
Astor, Lenox and Tilden Foundations

APPENDIX IV:

Patrons, Sponsors, and Benefactors

LEADERS

Paper Mill Playhouse thanks the following individuals, corporations, foundations, and government agencies for playing an ongoing leadership role in the theatre's growth and development.

Shirley Aidekman-Kaye
American Airlines
Arizona Iced Tea
Barbara & David Baldwin
Bell Atlantic
Joan & Allen Bildner
Bristol Myers-Squibb Company
The Geraldine R. Dodge Foundation
The Howard Gilman Foundation
E.J. Grassman Trust
The Hyde and Watson Foundation
The F.M. Kirby Foundation
The Blanche and Irving Laurie Foundation
Mercedes-Benz Tri-State Dealers
The Merck Company Foundation
The Selma Morris Charitable Trust
National Endowment for the Arts
New Jersey State Council on the Arts/
    Department of State
Novartis
The Paper Mill Playhouse Guild
PNC Bank
The Prudential Foundation
Schering-Plough Foundation
The Shubert Foundation
The Smart Family Foundation
The John Ben Snow Memorial Trust
The Star-Ledger

FOUNDER'S CLUB

Paper Mill Playhouse thanks the following individuals, corporations and foundations for making rebuilding of the theatre a reality. (Compiled from "The Curtain Rises," October, 1982.)

Allied Foundation
American Telephone and Telegraph
    Company
Exxon Corporation
First National State Bank
Henry W. & Patricia P. Gadsden
Lillia Babbitt Hyde Foundation
The Merck Company Foundation
Mildred & Mark Model
Prospect Hill Foundation
The Prudential Foundation
National Endowment for the Arts
New Jersey Bell Telephone Company
New Jersey State Council on the Arts
Mr. & Mrs. William C. Ridgway
Shering-Plough Foundation
Florence & John Schumann Foundation
John Jay & Eliza Jane Watson Foundation

With deep appreciation to:
The Honorable Thomas H. Kean
The Honorable Brendan T. Byrne
The Honorable Jane Burgio
The Honorable Walter Cavanaugh
The New Jersey Senate and Assembly

PRODUCER'S CLUB

American Cyanamid Company
Becton Dickinson & Company
Bell Telephone Laboratories
Helen & Floyd H. Bragg
The Chubb Corporation
Pharmaceuticals Division/Ciba-Geigy
    Corporation
Crum & Forster Foundation
Charles Engelhard Foundation
Mrs. Alfred H. Hauser
Consuelo & Allen Hegarty
Mrs. John L. Kemmerer
Kings Super Markets, Inc.
Midlantic National Bank
Mobil Foundation, Inc.
Jay R. Monroe Memorial Foundation
Nabisco Brands, Inc.
Harriet, Frank, Genesia & David
    Perlmutter
Charles E. & Joy C. Pettinos Foundation
Public Service Electric & Gas Company
Robert S. & Margery N. Puder
Shirley & Paul Sarpi
Mr. Edward W. Scudder, Jr.
Mr. & Mrs. Richard B. Scudder
Thomas & Betts Corporation
Touche Ross & Co.
Triangle Industries, Inc.
Vincent Visceglia
Western Electric Fund
Westinghouse Electric Corporation
Mr. & Mrs. John W. White, Jr.

BENEFACTORS

Mr. & Mrs. Vincent Apruzzese
Automatic Data Processing, Inc.
Mr. & Mrs. David M. Baldwin
Mr. & Mrs. S.A. Barnhard
Mr. & Mrs. Edward G. Beimfohr
Mr. & Mrs. William H. Borden
Dr. & Mrs. Clifford Botwin
Mr. & Mrs. Coleman Burke
Campbell Soup Fund
Gene Carrington
Mr. & Mrs. S. Barclay Colt
Deloitte, Haskins & Sells
Angelo Del Rossi
Engelhard Industries
The Gannett Foundation
Grace Foundation, Inc.
Jane & Harold E. Grotta
A.G. Hegarty & Co., Inc.
Mrs. Frank T. Kennedy
M.F. Kent & Co. Ltd. (Tipperary, Ireland)
F.M. Kirby Foundation, Inc.
Kucklinsky Foundation
Lasky Company
Mr. & Mrs. Ulyesse J. Le Grange
Mr. & Mrs. Albert Livermore
Mr. & Mrs. Irving Marsh
Millburn Short Hills Arts Center
Anna M. & Thomas L. Nolan
Mrs. Hobart C. Ramsey
The Romano Family - Ronetco, Inc.
Sarasohn & Company, Inc.
Mr. & Mrs. Richard J. Schlenger
Mr. & Mrs. Joseph A. Sullivan
Warner-Lambert Company
Tamar & Emil Weiss

PATRONS

Mr. Michael Belmont
Bevill, Bressler & Schulman, Inc.
Mr. & Mrs. Henry J. Brucker
Ralph N. Del Deo, Esq.
Robert P. & Margaret M. Denise
C.H. & Judie Draper
Mr. & Mrs. Allan Feldman
Mr. & Mrs. Arthur M. Goldberg
Mr. John Hanemann
J.M. Huber Corporation
Mr. & Mrs. Gene Lear
Lessner Electric Co.
Mintz-Jaffe-Gold & Co.
Mr. & Mrs. Robert C. Moore
Mr. John Morace
NL Industries Foundation
Dr. & Mrs. Leo Sicat
The Jack Silberberg Foundation
Mr. & Mrs. J. Henry Smith
The Sperry & Hutchison Company, Inc.
Mr. & Mrs. John C. Walcott
Mr. Alfred Willette
Mr. & Mrs. Henry F. Wood, Jr.

SPONSORS

Actors Equity Foundation
AGH Company
Anheuser Busch, Inc.
Mr. & Mrs. Frank Armour
Avery International
Bally's Park Place Casino Hotel, Atlantic
    City, NJ
Mr. & Mrs. Frederick W. Baur
Mrs. Florence Bentivegna
Marc E. Berson, Esq.
Helene & Richard Billera
Mr. Arthur Borinsky
Mr. & Mrs. Paul Bosland
Bernard & Teresa Bressler
Mr. & Mrs. E. Freeman Bunn
Mr. Tom & Arthurlyn Burleigh
Carter Wallace, Inc.
Junia M. Chapin
Marguerite & Frank Cleminshaw
Mr. & Mrs. John T. Connor
Mr. & Mrs. Eugene Conroy
Dr. & Mrs. Donald L. Davidson
Day Family Fund
Mrs. Livingston T. Dickason
Flora Dombrow

Mrs. Marjorie Engle
Mr. & Mrs. James Fellowes
Mr. & Mrs. Maurice J. Ferris, Jr.
Mr. & Mrs. Bernard Fingerhut
Mr. & Mrs. Eric S. Francis
Mr. & Mrs. Michael D. Francis
Mr. Harold Gabe
Mrs. Joan R. Gadek
Mr. & Mrs. Hunter B. Grant, Jr.
Corinne P. & Robert H. Harvey
Mrs. Alfred H. Hauser
Mr. & Mrs. Edward L. Hennessey, Jr.
Mr. Louis V. Henston
Clement Holgate
Mr. & Mrs. Frederick C. Horan
The Hudson Foundation
Mr. Loren Hulber
Katherine L. Hulse
E.F. Hutton & Company, Inc.
International Flavors & Fragrances, Inc.
International Ticket Co.
Fred Jablons
Jaydor Corp.
Mr. Martin Jelin
Mr. & Mrs. Albion U. Jenkins, Jr.
Michael & Mary Johnston
Mr. Richard C. Kaempfer
Philip D. Kaltenbacher
Mr. & Mrs. Howard C. Kauffmann
Kellogg Family
Mr. & Mrs. Robert A. Krantz, Jr.
C.J. Kreitler Foundation
William B. Leavens, Jr.
Mrs. Mayer Lederer
Myron Lehman, Esq.
Mr. & Mrs. Robert Z. Lehrer
Myron Levey
Mr. & Mrs. Ralph Libonati
Mr. & Mrs. William B. Licklider
Lindberg Foundation
LSI Avionics Systems Corporation
Mr. & Mrs. Harold J. Malley
Mr. Walter Mannheimer
Margaretten & Co., Inc.
Mr. & Mrs. Charles Menagh
Mr. & Mrs. John Merritt, Jr.
John & Geri Mielach
Wade & Pat Miller
Mr. Jack Mintzer
Mr. & Mrs. Kenneth C. Nichols
Mr. Richard D. Nelson
Mr. & Mrs. R.M. Ogden

Milos & Renie Ondrejcek
Julius W. Phoenix, Jr.
Admiral & Mrs. Robert Price, USCG
Prospect Foundation
Mr. Joseph R. Purcell
Dr. & Mrs. John Qualter
Mr. & Mrs. John Reilly
Rolodex Corporation
Mr. & Mrs. Ralph J. Russo
Irene Saftlas
St. Rose of Lima Church
Saks Fifth Avenue
Sawtelle Foundation
Mr. & Mrs. E.J. Schaffer
Mrs. Jerome Scherzer
Victor Scudiery
Mr. & Mrs. Thomas J. Sharp
Dr. & Mrs. A. Gary Shilling
Mr. & Mrs. Edmund S. Sikorski
Dr. & Mrs. George Staehle
John & Naomi Stevens
Mr. & Mrs. Henry G. Stifel
Suburban Propane Gas Corp.
Mrs. O.W. Switz
Mr. & Mrs. Morris Tanenbaum
Mr. Hyman Temkin
Jim Thesing
Mr. & Mrs. William I. Thompson
Nancy Dale Trone
Lynn, John, Scott, Stephen, Sandy, Sef
    Vergano
Mr. & Mrs. J. Vogel
Mr. & Mrs. Alan Weill
Roger H. & Josephine Banky Welt
Walter A. Whitnack
Wilf Family Foundation
Mr. C.E. Williams
Mr. & Mrs. Samuel C. Williams, Jr.
Doug & Rhonda Willies
Woman's Club of Millburn

1999–2000 ANNUAL FUND CAMPAIGN

The Board of Trustees wishes to express its appreciation to the individuals, corporations, foundations, and government agencies who support the ongoing activities of the theatre.
(listing as of August 20, 1999)

THE PREMIERE CIRCLE

Barbara & David Baldwin *
The F.M. Kirby Foundation *
The Blanche & Irving Laurie Foundation
The Selma Morris Charitable Trust **
New Jersey State Council on the
    Arts/Department of State,
a partner agency of the National
Endowment for the Arts

THE STAR CIRCLE

Shirley Aidekman-Kaye
Anonymous
The Howard Gilman Foundation
Mercedes-Benz Tri-State Dealers
Betty & Bob Moore +
Paper Mill Playhouse Guild

THE DIRECTOR'S CIRCLE

Ms. Elizabeth H. Allan +
ALMAR Party & Tent Rental
American Airlines®
Bell Atlantic
The Geraldine R. Dodge Foundation
Fleet Bank
The Hyde & Watson Foundation *
Mr. & Mrs. John L. Kemmerer
F.M. Kirby Foundation
Novartis Corporation
The Prudential Foundation
The Shubert Foundation
John Ben Snow Memorial Trust
The Star-Ledger

THE COMPOSER'S CIRCLE

C.R. Bard, Inc.
Allen & Joan Bildner & The Bildner Family Foundation
Helen & Floyd H. Bragg
Bristol-Myers Squibb Foundation
The Chase Manhattan Bank
The CIT Group
Croda Inc.
Givaudan-Roure
E.J. Grassmann Trust
Household International
Peter R. Kellogg
The Leavens Foundation
The Merck Company Foundation
Charles Pascarella +
Rhodia Inc.
Mrs. William C. Ridgway, Jr.
The Schering-Plough Foundation
The Smart Family Foundation, Inc.
Inez & Robert W. Smith +
Szerlip & Company
Warner-Lambert Company

THE AUTHOR'S CIRCLE

Automatic Data Processing, Inc.
Robert & Eileen Berkowitz
The Carter Wallace Foundation
The Thomas & Agnes Carvel Foundation
The Citigroup Foundation/Solomon Smith Barney
Donaldson Lufkin & Jenrette, Inc.
David Dougherty
The Dun & Bradstreet Corporation Foundation
Judy & Al Garland
Robert Johanson
Mr. Harold Klein +
Lucent Technologies
Noke & Heard
PNC Bank
Dominick V. Romano Family/Ronetco Supermarkets
Sharon F. Sandbach
Mr. & Mrs. Richard B. Scudder
Mr. & Mrs. Rick Sherlund

THE CHAIRMAN'S CIRCLE

2 Anonymous Donors
Lorraine & Jerome Aresty
Rob & Sandi Arthur +
Mr. & Mrs. Timothy M. Barrett
Doris & Felix Beck
Mr. & Mrs. Steven H. Berg
Marguerite & Frank Cleminshaw
Sondra Harris & Bud Cohen
Carol Deem
Ronald J. Del Mauro
Rachel & Michael Emposimato
Frank & Jo Farinella
Glebar Company, Inc.
GMP Systems
Mr. & Mrs. William E. Gusmer
Mr. & Mrs. Robert B. Heintz
Investors Savings Bank
Johnson & Johnson
Pamela & James Landry
Longo Industries
Macy's East
Anthony Marchand, M.D.
Marjorie & Edward Marlowe
The MCJ Foundation
Mildred & Mark Model
Jay R. Monroe Memorial Foundation
Betty & Bob Moore
New Jersey Commission for the Blind
Mr. & Mrs. William B. Nicholson
Nordstrom
Jonathan & Lisa Ostroff
Mr. & Mrs. Werner C. Schon
Daniel & Kristina Shak
Stern's
Mr. & Mrs. Henry F. Wood, Jr.

PRODUCER'S CIRCLE

Sylvia & Jerry Baron
Mr. & Mrs. Martin Bartner
Mr. & Mrs. W.W. Betteridge
Amanda & Francesco Borghese
Mrs. Edward J. Cafruny
Mary & Dominick Caruso
Mr. & Mrs. Carman J. Cedola
John & Joan Chrysikopoulos
Ryan & C.J. Conlon
Suzanne M. Crossley & James T. Shelby
Larry & Dawne Drake
The Ferriday Fund

Mr. & Mrs. Maurice J. Ferris, Jr.
Mr. & Mrs. Brian Gagnon
Mr. & Mrs. T. Carter Hagaman
Anita & Franklin Hannoch, Jr.
The Deborah L. Hansen Memorial Fund
Mr. & Mrs. Keith A. Hightower
Jean Kellogg
Mrs. Corinne M. Kennedy
Mrs. John R. Kukucka
Louise & Arthur Schwartz
George & Irene Lionikis
Mr. & Mrs. John P. Mullen
Nabisco, Inc.
Edwin & Catherine Olsen
The Parker Foundation
Mrs. Harriet Perlmutter-Pilchik
Pat & Tom Sayles
Inez & Robert W. Smith
Mrs. Freda Renz Spagnola
Harold & Anita Staenberg
Barbara & David Stoller
William Tremont
Dr. & Mrs. Ronald Uszenski
Westfield Oral Surgery Associates
Mr. & Mrs. John Zervas

BENEFACTORS

Anheuser-Busch, Inc.
Anonymous
Rob & Sandi Arthur
Mr. & Mrs. Herbert Bachelor
Mr. & Mrs. Harrison Ball, Jr.
Jean & Frank Batula
Ruth & Stanley Bedford
Mr. & Mrs. John P. Bent, Jr.
Mr. & Mrs. R.H. Beresford
Rita & Bernard S. Berkowitz
Mark & Karen Bigos
Mr. & Mrs. W. Theodore Bourke
Warren & Virginia Braunwarth
Constance & Ferd Brewer
Marion Brozowski
Mike Bruno Plumbing & Heating
Mr. & Mrs. E. Freeman Bunn
Mr. & Mrs. Joseph C. Cornwall
Joanne & Al Daloisio
David A. Dersh, D.M.D.
Mr. & Mrs. Eric DeVos
Mr. & Mrs. James Dietze
Fund for the New Jersey Blind, Inc.

Mr. & Mrs. Michael Geering
Gianni Family Fund
Gibraltar Title Agency, Inc.
Dr. William Goldberg
Lois & Gary Goldring
Clifford & Linda Gordon
The Goss Foundation, Inc.
Eva Gottscho
Bonnie Guyre
Richard Haenssler
Nancy Hamilton
Barbara & Louis Henston
Barbara Hunter & Associates
International Specialty Products
Arlene D. Jonach
Mr. & Mrs. Victor H. Kasner
Kobo Products, Inc.
Mr. & Mrs. Paul E. Krystow
Mr. & Mrs. Michael Kudryk
Karen & Simon Lack
Mr. & Mrs. Robert Lien
Mr. & Mrs. Dean B. Livingston
Valerie Davia & Warren Luce
The Martin Family Fund, Inc.
Diana & Lester Max
McCarter & English
Monsen Engineering
Helena & Jillian Moseman
Clarke & Martha Neal
Mr. & Mrs. Denis Newman
Mr. & Mrs. John G. O'Leary
Maureen & Robert Ogden
Mr. & Mrs. Carter E. Porter
The Charles L. Read Foundation
John & Albertina Reilly
Martha & E.J. Schaffer
Arlene Schicker
Mr. & Mrs. Alexander Sirotkin
John Howell Smith
Harold & Anita Staenberg
The Standish Foundation
Ann & Mike Suchomel
Robert Sweeney
Barbara & Steven Tasher
Rosemary H. Teeple
TKL Research, Inc.
Union Camp Corporation
Donna & Jack Walcott
Dian & Jeffrey Weisman
Roger & Josephine Welt
Michael Wolfson
Sylvia Zucker

* capital project support
** artistic initiative support
+ Oration Society Members in support of Paper Mill's Endowment Fund

APPENDIX V:
Board of Trustees

Index of Names

See also Appendix III, People of Paper Mill; IV Patrons, Sponsors, and Benefactors; V Board of Trustees.

Force, Jeffrey 239
Ford, Paul 42
Ford, Timothy 132
Foster, Hunter 212, 213
Francis, Arlene 27
Frankel, Mary Jane 120
Franklin, Bonnie 43
Franz, Elizabeth 181, 236
Fredericks, Richard 21
Friml, Rudolph 20
Fuller, Loie 107

G

Gabel, Martin 27
Gadsden, Henry 59, 61
Gage, Donald 20, 21
Gaines, David 154
Gallagher, Helen 139
Garrett, Becky 226
Garrick, Beulah 126
Gavin, John 42, 46, 61
Genevieve 28
Geoly, Danny 92
Geoly, Guy 70, 92
George III 3
George, Peter 57, 61
Germann, Greg 122
Gero, Ralph 49
Gershwin, George 12, 20
Gets, Malcolm 132
Geva, Tamara 12
Gibbs, Ron 132
Gibson, Deborah 154, 158, 159, 160, 251
Gilbert and Sullivan 20, 172
Gilbert, W. S. 173
Gilbert, Hy 169
Gilford, Jack 38
Gillespie, Dizzy 162
Gilman, Howard 88, 93, 260
Gish, Dorothy 24, 25
Gish, Lillian 24, 25, 67
Glover, Savion 263
Golden Dragon Acrobats and Magicians 162
Goldman, James 275, 276, 283, 284
Goldman, Milton 40
Goldsmith, Merwyn 91
Goodman, Dody 43
Gottfried, Martin 129

Graff, Lillian 252
Graham, Martha 40
Gray, Dolores 44, 161
Green, Mitzi 13
Grey, Larry 81, 99, 132, 209
Grimes, Tammy 43
Grizzard, George 39, 67, 179
Groh, David 172
Grossman, Larry 175
Gruber, Michael 195, 196, 275
Guittard, Laurence 275, 278, 279
Gunderman, David 133
Gunton, Bob 120
Guthrie, Tyrone 42

H

Hack, Harold W. 9
Hale, David 239
Hall, Carol 175
Halley, Sharon 88, 97, 100, 107, 109, 204
Hamilton, George 38
Hammerstein, III, Oscar 95, 100, 103, 109
Hampton, Lionel 162
Hansen, Everett and Bernice 259
Harding, Ann 16
Harrold, Jack 86
Haroldson, Marjan 122
Harriman, Fawne 44
Harris, Julie 42
Harris, Rosemary 70
Harrison, Gregory 175
Harrold, Jack 120
Hasada, Ann 173
Hart, Kitty Carlisle. *See* Carlisle, Kitty.
Hart, Lorenz 12, 13
Hayes, Helen 12, 13, 39, 66, 70
Hazard, Sharon 218
Hearn, George 145
Heatherton, Ray 13
Heckman, Millie 165
Heeley, Desmond 106
Heflin, Van 38
Hegarty, Allen G. 59, 61
Heintz, Robert B. 58, 59, 61, 256
Helm, Tom 155, 204
Herbert, Victor 84
Herman, Jerry 76, 77, 191, 192
Hernandez, Philip 144

Herring, Joseph 50
Herroeth, Tiffany 189
Hewett, Christopher 81
Hewitt, Tom 187
Hicks, Bessie V. 40
Higgins, Daren Edward 181
Hill, Dulé 132
Hines, Jerome 43, 44, 61, 63, 66, 72, 144
Hingle, Pat 39
Hoebee, Mark S. 146
Holgate, Ron 42
Holm, Celeste 24, 26, 44, 61, 261
Holmes, Clint 176
Holmes, Tanya 147
Hooks, Lonna R. 264, 265
Hope, Anthony 184
Hope, Bob 13
Horan, Tom 269
Horsley, Lee 142
Horst, Louis 40
Horton, Edward Everett 21
Horton, Robert 67
Hoshko, John 207
Hoty, Dee 275, 279, 282, 283, 284
Houghton, Katherine 179
Housley, John 264
Houston, Walter 12, 13
Howard, Eugene 13
Howard, Willie 13
Howe, Gwyda Don 72
Hughes, Tresa 33
Hunter, Tab 42, 44, 47
Hunter, Tim 21

I

Iacono, Paul 221, 253
Ilo, Angelique 155
Images in Illuminations 243
Innvar, Christopher 183, 238, 243
Irby-Ranniar, Scott 176, 251
Irving, George S. 95, 193, 194, 208
Irving, Herman 189

J

Jacoby, Mark 13, 68
James, Duke of York 3
James, Jacqueline 30
Janicello, Mark 91

Telese, Marianne 84
Thaxter, Phyllis 124
Tennant, Mary 49
Thesing, Jim 60
Thomas, Richard 61
Thompson, Jana 256
Thompson, Sada 43
Thrash, Billie 283
Tilley, Vesta 9
Torn, Rip 42, 43
Toner, Tom 95
Toto 233, 253
Toy, Christine 173, 174
Tune, Tommy 76, 82, 136

U

Uggams, Leslie 206, 269
Ullendorf, Jacqueline 37
Ulvaeus, Bjorn 198

V

Valentine, Karen 172
Vallee, Rudy 13
Vance, Vivian 43
Van Kleef, Natalie 186
Vaughan, Robert 117
Vaughn, Sarah 165
Venza, Jac 109
Victoria, Queen of England 5
Villamar, Marilyn 102
Villella, Edward 74, 75
Viola, Tom 259
Visceglia, Vincent and Anna 255
Voutsinas, Andreas 34

W

Wade, Jonathan 184
Waggoner, Mary Ellen 260
Waite, John Thomas 120
Waite, Ralph 119
Walbye, Kay 127
Walker, June 14
Walker, Monique 214
Walker, Nancy 42
Walsh, Elizabeth 238
Walton, Bob 209
Walton, Jim 155, 156
Waterhouse, Jane 172

Waters, Ethel 13
Watson, Becky 239
Watson, David 246
Waxman, Debra 224
Webb, Clifton 12, 16
Webb, Jimmy 176, 177
Webber, Andrew Lloyd 76, 149, 154, 204
Webster, Margaret 16
Weill, Kurt 13
Weinstein, Henry 27-28
Weisler, Fran and Barry 209
Welles, Orson 12, 270
Wetmore, Joan 41
White, George 12, 13, 269
White, John 49
White, Richard 78, 80, 81, 91, 97, 100, 105, 106, 109,
    110, 132, 170, 204, 250
White, Ruth 40
Whitehead, Paxton 123, 126
Whitman, Christine Todd 168, 175
Wilder, Gene 35, 36
Wilder, Thornton 13
Williams, Robert Neff 40
Wilson, Chandra 175
Wilson, Elizabeth 70
Wilson, Ransom 162
Winters, Shelley 25, 42, 43
Winwood, Estelle 29
Witham, Tricia 132
Wolpe, Leonard 158
Wonsek, Paul 70
Wood, Bradford 109
Woods, Richard 180
Wright, Teresa 33

Y

Yeston, Maury 202, 204
Yurka, Blanche 14

Z

Ziegfeld, Florenz 12
Zmed, Adrian 211, 213

Index of Titles

See also Appendix I, Paper Mill Productions 1938–1999; II, Musical Theatre Project.